Springer Series on Social Work

Albert R. Roberts, D.S.W., Series Editor

School of Social Work, Indiana University, Indianapolis

Advisory Board: Joseph D. Anderson, D.S.W., Barbara Berkman, D.S.W., Paul H. Ephross, Ph.D., Sheldon R. Gelman, Ph.D., Nancy A. Humphreys, D.S.W., Sheldon Siegel, Ph.D., and Julia Watkins, Ph.D.

Raymond Albert, M.S.W., J.D. is an Assistant Professor at Bryn Mawr College Graduate School of Social Work and Social Research, where he teaches in the Master's of Law and Social Policy and Master's of Social Service program. He is a graduate of the dual-degree program of the University of Connecticut, where he received the M.S.W. and J.D. degrees.

Mr. Albert's longstanding interest in the social work and law connection is reflected in other writings, including articles that address social work advocacy in the regulatory process and socio-legal problems in social work practice. He has also published on the topic of alternative dispute resolution, particularly mediation and its implications for social work professionals.

LAW AND SOCIAL WORK PRACTICE

Raymond Albert, M.S.W., J.D.

Springer Publishing Company
New York

Springer Publishing Company, Inc.
536 Broadway
New York, NY 10012

86 87 88 89 90 / 5 4 3 2 1

Library of Congress Cataloging-in-Publication Data

Albert, Raymond.
  Law and social work practice.

  (Springer series on social work; v. 9)
  Bibliography: p.
  Includes index.
  1. Law—United States.   2. Public welfare—
Law and legislation—United States.   3. Social
workers—Legal status, laws, etc.—United States.
4. Social workers—United States—Handbooks, manuals,
etc.   I. Title.   II. Series.
KF390.S6A4   1986   344.73'03   86-13948
ISBN 0-8261-4890-5   347.3043

Printed in the United States of America

To Susan Gadiel and Richard Goldstein

Contents

Preface

ORGANIZATION OF THE TEXT

The text's thirteen chapters are grouped in three parts. Part I is a preliminary perspective on law and the social environment and an introduction to legal processes. Part II includes selected skill prerequisites for working with problems where law and social work overlap. Part III explores the practical implications of the social work and law connection.

OBJECTIVES OF THE TEXT

The text seeks to accomplish four objectives.

The first is to offer an introduction to legal processes and their interdependence. Chapters 2 through 6 describe key features of the methods and processes by which courts, legislatures, and administrative agencies resolve problems. Specifically, Chapter 2 describes the judicial process (e.g. case analysis, case law development and synthesis, and the civil process). Chapters 3, 4, and 5 deal with the legislative process (e.g. legislative analysis, judicial interpretation of legislation, and the implementation of legislation). Chapter 6 describes the administrative process (e.g. key features of administrative authority and the stages in the rule making process). The content is necessarily selective, but the essential institutional characteristics and decision-making mechanisms are described. These chapters give the reader a comprehensive look at the legal system, and should supply sufficient incentive for further investigation.

The second objective is to provoke reflection about the law's relation to the social environment generally; and to social work specifically. Chapter 1 introduces the idea that law and legal processes are best understood as part of a larger social environment. The key point is the interplay between the two and the implications for our view of law and legal institutions. Chapters 11 through 13 address the social work and law connection. Chapter 11 presents a perspective for practice with socio-legal problems. Chapter 12 explores the prospects and problems of social worker–lawyer partnerships. Chapter 13 explores five areas (child welfare, education, developmental disabilities, corrections and criminal justice, and liability for nonprofit agencies) where the overlap between law and social work pose significant practical challenges. Chapter 13's focus is less on an exhaustive review of the law and more on selected legal issues that surface in social work practice.

The third objective is to present some of the skills and techniques necessary for working with systems and problems where social work and law converge. Chapters 8 through 10 deal with prominent examples, although other chapters present related techniques. Chapter 8 describes selected legal research resources; the focus is on how to find the law. The reader is also given some guidelines that should help him or her maximize the search for legal documents. Chapter 9 deals with the prerequisites for presenting testimony in court. The chapter describes selected concepts from evidence law and provides guidelines on how to testify in court. Chapter 10 explores the privileged communications principle and its impact on social worker–client relationships.

Additional skills and techniques are presented in Chapters 2 through 6 in conjunction with the description of institutional processes. Chapter 2 illustrates the skill involved in case analysis—how to read a judicial opinion; how to understand an opinion in relation to cases that precede or follow it. The case analysis technique is an extremely important tool in legal analysis. Chapters 3, 4, and 5 demonstrate techniques for analyzing the formulation, implementaion, and modification of legislation. Chapter 3 explains how to read a statute or a bill and analyze its text. Chapter 4 describes the intricacies of statutory interpretation and the role of legislative history.

Chapter 5 focuses on legislative implementation and concomitant techniques for legislative advocacy. Chapter 6 depicts techniques for social work advocacy in the administrative process—how to analyze regulations and participate in administrative hearings.

The fourth objective is to underscore the relation between law, legal skills, and social work advocacy. The skills and techniques are cast not only as tactics for change but also as intervention strategies that reflect the social worker-as-advocate ethic.

A NOTE ON THE MATERIALS AND THEIR EDITING

The text relies on original legal documents, such as judicial opinions and the content of legislative debates, to demonstrate a point or to illustrate the substance of legal development (e.g. through debates or case law), to provide an opportunity for additional skill development (e.g. analyzing judicial opinions and consolidating legislative history with statutory goals and regulatory objectives), and to underscore the constant interplay of institutional conduct.

In editing the cases and other materials, many of the citations and footnotes have been omitted. This was done to maintain manageable portions of text, particularly for the cases and materials that were extremely lengthy. Economy aside, however, the portions thought to be most instructive have been retained.

SCOPE AND USE OF TEXT

There is much to be said about the relationship between social work and law. The text, however, offers a selective treatment of the content that professionals need to know to make sense of this relationship. There is, therefore, a major focus on understanding legal processes, their interdependence and their relation to social work practice, and on the knowledge and skill base connected with this focus.

Specific substantive topics are given relatively little attention because the evolutionary nature of legal development would undermine such an effort. The law would be "old" before the text got to print, and the reader would thus be left to expand a lot of energy updating information. The time would be better spent focusing on the key legal principles and processes that really expose the constant interplay between law and social work. Chapter 13 presents five substantive topics and exemplifies the approach just described. The legal issues and their practical implications are highlighted, but this is done by reference to selected cases. It is then anticipated that the discussion will spur the reader to use his or her newly acquired understanding of legal resources to keep informed about evolving developments. This approach is built around the recognition that "keeping up" with the law is critical for social workers. It also reflects the nonstatic nature of legal rules in any substantive area.

The text can be used in several ways:

- In conjunction with the various one-semester, social-work-and-law-type courses that exist in most undergraduate and graduate programs.

Such a course might unfold in four stages. The first stage could stress understanding legal processes and analyzing judicial opinions, legislation and regulations. This stage could easily use the first six weeks of this semester-long course and would rely on the materials in the text's first seven chapters. The second stage could emphasize skill development in legal research (a topic that might be introduced at this point reinforcing it throughout subsequent discussions and assignments) and familiarity with techniques for testifying in court and for establishing legally sound worker–client relationships. This part of the course could take place during weeks seven to nine. The third stage could supply a foundation for conceptual integration. Thus, weeks ten and eleven might examine the conditions under which socio-legal issues are addressed. The final stage, which would cover the final three or four weeks of the course, could give students an opportunity to apply their knowledge and skills to various substantive areas, such as those covered in the text's final chapter. This portion of the course would not only allow exploration of specific socio-legal topics but provide additional opportunities for legal research and legal analysis and for conceptual integration.

- As a basis for a course that explores legal processes and their impact on social work practice. Programs that offer such courses typically focus on the interplay between social policy, social services, and the law.

- As a supplement to special topics courses, such as those that address the policy and practice aspects of, for example, child welfare, mental health, and juvenile justice.
- To provide supporting content for several foundation courses (e.g. social welfare policy and services, human behavior and the social environment, and practice), where an understanding of legal processes is important for effective practice.

Acknowledgments

The author acknowledges several people whose assistance helped produce this text. Rick Gaskins, Dean of the Graduate School of Social Work and Social Research and Director of the Law and Social Policy Program at Bryn Mawr College, reviewed a draft of Chapter 8 and, more importantly, provided encouragement not only during the writing of the manuscript but throughout my tenure at Bryn Mawr. I am also grateful to him for pointing Dr. Albert Roberts in my direction when Dr. Roberts first expressed Springer's interest in publishing a text on social work and law. Dr. Roberts also ultimately reviewed the manuscript and offered helpful advice, for which I thank him. Professor Al Alissi of the University of Connecticut, a longstanding source of encouragement and a fellow traveler along this sociolegal route, also read the manuscript at various stages of completion. Linda Stafford Burrows provided timely research assistance for the section of Chapter 13 which deals with child abuse and neglect. Sara Steber provided valuable information for Chapter 7, and her review of my subsequent efforts to illustrate institutional interdependence probably accounts for whatever insight the analysis provides. Ruth Ann Mattingly volunteered to use drafts of several chapters in her course on social work and the law. The feedback thus supplied was very helpful, and I thank her and her students. The editors at Springer, Barbara Watkins and Pamela Lankas, helped make the entire enterprise remarkably painless. And, finally, Theresa and Alexis supplied the type of patience and understanding that make this type of endeavor possible.

I would also like to acknowledge the assistance provided by Bryn Mawr College, through its Madge Miller Research Fund, which greatly facilitated the writing of this text.

An Introduction to
Legal Processes

1 Law and the Social Environment

CHARACTERISTICS OF LAW

To define law and whence it comes is a difficult task. Law is typically thought of as consisting of rules of indeterminate source. We invoke the rules when we feel we've been wronged and somehow, perhaps magically, they spring into existence. Given this result, the rules' origins seem irrelevant. This situation is neither good nor bad, *per se;* however, it does challenge us to think about the ends to which we assign the "law".

The search for a definition of the law may also be misleading; as in mistaking a shadow for the thing itself. Moreover, any definition is more likely to represent our hidden biases about law. Yet, the search is worthwhile if it deepens our appreciation of law in relation to society. Consider, for example, the following definitions supplied by Kidder (1983).

Law as a Modern Process

. . . definitions that are closest to our usual ways of thinking about law. Donald Black [1972] gives us: '*Law is governmental social control . . . the normative life of a state and its citizens.*' For him, law is a specialized form of social control, involving governments, definitions of citizenship, and formality. . . .

Law as All Forms of Social Control

Malinowski [1926, 1961] . . . [defined law as] '*a body of binding obligations regarded as rights by one party and acknowledged as the duty by the other, kept in force by the specific mechanism of reciprocity and publicity inherent in the structure of society'. . . .* Like Black's . . . [it], spells out the basic elements of his theory about how law works in society.

Law as Authorized Physical Force

E. Adamson Hoebel [1954] . . . insist[ed] that without physical force there is no law. His definition: *'A social norm is legal if its neglect or infraction is regularly met, in threat or in fact, by the application of physical force by an individual or group possessing the socially recognized privilege of so acting.'* . . . Hoebel's definition incorporates the concept of *social norm* . . . he is telling us that law, like other social norms, places demands on people to make choices of action they otherwise might not make.

Law, Coercion, and Specialization

Weber [1954] took great pains to include law in his general theory of society. . . . It may sound like Hoebel's . . . but it contains some subtle differences which show a different conception of law: *'An order shall be called law where it is guaranteed by the likelihood that (physical and psychological) coercion aimed at bringing about conformity with the order, or at avenging its violation, will be exercised by a staff of people especially holding themselves ready for this purpose.'* . . . Patriotism, economic incentives, and participatory goals are all used, as Weber's definition brings out, to obtain conformity with law.

Law as Justice

Philip Selznik [1961] . . . considers justice to be at the very center of any adequate definition. . . . If we define law as 'governmental social control', we cannot then distinguish between legal and illegal acts of government officials: *'The essence of legality lies not in the exercise of power and control, but in the predictable restraint on those using that power.'* . . . Law, then, is an organized way to produce justice.

Law as Custom Reinstituted

For Paul Bohannan [1967], *'Law is custom recreated by agents of society in institutions specifically meant to deal with legal questions.'* . . . Custom develops when isolated norms in a group become *institutionalized.* . . . Law is a later development made necessary by the growing inability of custom to support those institutions. Law [thus] *reinstitutionalizes* the norms of custom. [pp. 20–31]

These definitions imply that law cannot be understood apart from its place in the social order. The notion is not unfamiliar, and has been expressed in alternative perspectives on law and society, such as law as social control (Parsons, 1962), as the reconciliation of divergent social interests (Pound, 1943) or group interests (Cowan, 1958), as a weapon in social conflict (Turk, 1976), as something that can reflect the socialization of its principal technicians (Tapp & Levine, 1974), and as the end product of interconnected social systems (Vanyo, 1971). These viewpoints convey the myriad ways to express law's role in society. Moreover, they underscore that any "definition" of law must be sufficiently complicated to encompass varied characteristics.

SOURCES AND FUNCTIONS OF AMERICAN LAW

When we refer to the American legal system, we're really talking about the federal system and each of the fifty state systems. This may seem cumbersome, but one must remember that they are all very similar structurally. Each has a constitution as well as a mechanism for making, interpreting, and enforcing law.

The arrangement exists because of the way the U.S. Constitution assigns governmental powers to the three governmental branches: judicial, legislative, and executive. The legal rules that emerge from each are based on a different source of Constitutional authority. The concept of "authority to enact law" is important in our governmental scheme; it specifies each branch's scope, power and, ultimately, legitimacy (Freedman, 1978). There are four sources of authority for both federal and state systems, and each may be thought of as producing a "type" of law: constitutional, judicial or common law, legislative or statutory law, and administrative or regulatory law.

Constitutional Law: The U.S. Constitution is supreme in relation to the other "types". It is the foundation for all levels of the legal system. It articulates, among other things, the scope and functions of government; its counterpart is the state constitution.

Judicial or Common Law: Generally characterized as judge-made law, the common law is also referred to as decision making by *precedent* and is based on the notion that similar cases should be treated similarly. In this way a decision, once announced, guides a subsequent court when it decides an identical or similar situation.

Precedent also stipulates that judicial decisions be followed by so-called inferior courts; that is, a higher court's decision in a particular system (state or federal) will be followed by all lower courts.

Legislative or Statutory Law: Enacted by legislatures, this type appears as statutes or, on the local level, ordinances. The enactments can be repealed or amended and are interpreted by the judiciary to ensure their consistency with the federal constitution.

Administrative or Regulatory Law: To implement legislative goals, administrative agencies issue regulations that have the force of law. Regulations, however, must follow from the legislation's intent, and are invalid if they stray from it.

The arrangement may produce different types of law, but this does not mean that each is independent. The constitution structures the relationship between these sources of authority through its provisions for checking the power exercised by any one branch. The result is a significant degree of institutional interdependence. Mermin (1982) reflects below on this phenomenon.

Law and the Legal System: An Introduction*

Let me now explore one general aspect of this relation: What does law do for people in our society—or, putting it in terms of what the legal agencies are supposed to do or are trying to do (sometimes successfully), what are the social functions of our law?

You probably think first about the dispute-settling function. We do tend to think about the courts and their business of settling disputes. These may be disputes between private parties, or between a private party and a government unit or official, or between different government units or officials. Many government administrative agencies also engage in adjudicative dispute settling. But it is worth remembering that private individuals functioning in the area of labor arbitration and commercial arbitration already account for a larger number of dispute settlements per year than do all the courts of the nation. Here too, however, the courts play a role—they can be called on to enforce the arbitration award, and sometimes to enforce an agreement to arbitrate.

Another function we tend to think of right away is maintaining order, through the bulk of criminal law, against violence or aggravated harm to persons or property, by the threat of the penalties of imprisonment and/or fines. This of course includes the policing function as well as the court's role in trials and sentencing, and the operations of other officials such as

*From Samuel Mermin, Law and the Legal System: An Introduction, 2nd edition. pp. 5–8. © 1982 Little, Brown & Co., Inc., Boston, MA. Reprinted by permission of Little, Brown & Co.

prosecutors and parole and probation personnel. Maintaining order also involves protection (through sedition, treason, and related laws) against that extreme threat to order, the violent overthrow of government. Thus, the law legitimates certain uses of force by government but not (save for exceptional circumstances, such as legitimate self-defense) by private parties.

But there is much more to our legal system than settling disputes and maintaining order. For one thing, the legal system constitutes a framework within which certain common expectations about the transactions, relationships, planned happenings, and accidents of daily life can be met (and this force for predictability and regularity can itself be viewed as a species of maintenance of order). We expect that our customary ways of behavior will be facilitated and not disrupted by law without strong reason; we expect that those who have suffered personal injuries (particularly those who were without fault) will be compensated for their injuries under the laws of tort; that those who have made promises will be held to their promises (or, if not, be required to make recompense) under the laws of contract; that those who own property can get the law to enforce their expectations that they have exclusive rights in it and are free to dispose of it as they wish. All of these expectations have to be somewhat qualified since the rights involved (especially those of property) have been subjected to conditions and exceptions. That is, the nature of the expectations is partly a product of conditioning by the legal system, thereby illustrating what was referred to before as the interaction of law and society.

In both constitution and statute there are functions of yet another sort: provisions aimed at securing efficiency, harmony, and balance in the functioning of the government machinery. Here I am thinking of the constitutional separation of powers by which specific kinds of power are allocated to specific branches of government with an attempt to avoid undue concentration in any one branch. And I think of other provisions for planning the affairs of government—statutes such as the Full Employment Act and government reorganization acts, and the fiscal planning represented by budgets for the raising (taxation, borrowing) and spending of public money. I think of a different kind of planning too, exemplified by zoning and other land use controls, conservation laws, and environmental protections. I think also (because the legal machinery requires maintaining legal skills for its maintenance) of provisions governing the qualifications of lawyers, judges, and other government officials for their respective vocations. There are, moreover, measures that build into the system agencies to make continuing assessments and proposals for improvement of the system; e.g., the state legislative councils and judicial councils, the commissioners on uniform state laws, the federal judicial conferences, and the Administrative Conference of the United States.

In the Constitution can be seen another vital function of our law: Protection of the citizen against excessive or unfair government power.

This refers mainly to the Bill of Rights, which includes such basic rights as freedom of speech, press, and religion, the right to privacy and against unreasonable searches and seizure, the privilege against self-discrimination, and the right of jury trial for crime. (Remember that the "due process" clause is construed by the courts to assure both fair procedure and freedom from arbitrariness in the substance of government requirements.) A standard for equality of treatment applies to the states through the equal protection clause of the Fourteenth Amendment and is, to some uncertain extent, applicable to the federal government through the due process clause of the Fifth Amendment. (Also included in the due process protection against both governments are property rights, as well as life and liberty.)

Our legal system is concerned too with protecting people against excessive or unfair private power. In addition to antitrust law protection against private monopolistic power there are a number of specialized protections. For example, an employer's power is curbed by laws, such as those compelling the payment of minimum wages, or prohibiting discrimination in employment, or compelling collective bargaining with unions; a corporation's power in the sale of its securities is curbed by SEC requirements. Analogous restrictions apply through a host of regulatory laws and administrative commissions at both federal and state levels.

Somewhat overlapping in function with these laws are some that are aimed at assuring people an opportunity to enjoy the minimum decencies of life by protecting their economic and health status. These functions have been more prominent in the later history of our society. I have in mind laws on unemployment insurance, social security, Medicare, public housing, welfare, and antipoverty programs, as well as older statutes, like those on bankruptcy and garnishment. I would also include measures for psychic health, by which I mean not only government services for the poor who are mentally ill, but also to measures attempting to eliminate various external sources of psychic distress. These include laws and decisions discouraging discrimination, giving redress for injuries to reputation and invasions of privacy, enlarging opportunities for recreation, and reducing the pollution of air, water, and landscape.

One other point: Is there any sense in which it is true that law has an ethical or moral function? The answer, I think, is definitely yes. Most of the functions already mentioned have a clear ethical dimension. Thus, in settling disputes, the law aims at a result that is fair and socially desirable. A good deal of criminal law carries out ethical precepts of conduct — many of which are in the Ten Commandments. In tort law, many of the principles concerning either negligent or intentional infliction of injury may be traced to the Golden Rule. The obligation to keep one's promises is an ethical obligation. Similarly, the agencies I mentioned as being concerned with improving the legal system have had as goals not only increased efficiency but also more socially desirable results. Ethical or humanitarian motivation has been at least one of the sources of the mentioned legislation aimed at raising the standard of living of the disadvantaged, and legislation protecting people against unfair exercise of public or private power. Much legislation and general legal principles use explicitly ethical terms in laying down standards of conduct—phrases like "good faith," "not profiting by one's own wrong," "fair and equitable," "unjust enrichment." The Constitution itself, as we have seen, speaks in terms of equality and (as a judicial interpretation of "due process") fairness. Hence it is altogether misleading to say, as some have said, that legal duties have nothing to do with moral duties.

LIMITS ON THE LAW

That the law is expected to fulfill many roles has both positive and negative aspects—positive, because it can be responsive to evolving social needs; negative, because we may not like what we get. Consequently, we are left to determine the conditions under which we should use law to accomplish social goals. The task is easier said than done, however, because our society's divergent views on the law's social functions are difficult to consolidate and, more important, they change over time.

Can we then predict the conditions that will nurture a universally acceptable use of the law? Our efforts toward this end have lead to some flip-flopping, a going back and forth between treating legal rules as unchangeable or as malleable. A constantly changing social environment will challenge us to confront our preconceptions about the problems for which we seek legal solutions. But each problem is unique and must be understood on its own terms. As Mermin (1982) suggests:

> You have to investigate the significant facts in the particular problem and ask the questions relevant to the limits that may operate on the effectiveness of the proposed law or the proposed decision. Some relevant considerations are:
> (a) What is the strength of the values or attitudes or drives with which the law in question is inconsistent? . . . The problem is also complicated by the fact that reinforcement of or opposition to attitudes, drives, etc., may be received: (1) from the rest of an individual's value system . . . (2) from values and attitudes on the particular subject . . . (3) from his belief that the prohibited conduct works no serious harm to others. . . .
> (b) What techniques would be used to establish and enforce the prohibition or requirement in question? (1) Legislatures, courts, executives, and administrative agencies do not all have the same prestige, though

perhaps the ranking is different on different subjects and in different places. . . . (2) Is time allowed for a transition period, and does such allowances make acceptance more likely, or less so? . . . (3) Would enforcement personnel be enthusiastic, well financed, and really committed, or are they likely to be tolerant, apathetic, corrupt, or starved for funds? (4) Would enforcement be hampered for lack of complaints? . . . (5) Will there be a *perception* by potential violators, of the change in law or penalties, and also a perception of effective enforcement? (6) Is it possible to point to "models" of compliance . . .? (7) Would the law's expected benefits be outweighed by the costs, practical difficulties, and risks in administering it . . .?

(c) To what extent do we have the knowledge necessary to answer not only (1) the fact questions relevant to the consequences and desirability of the proposed law, but also (2) all of the other questions? The more you study the law's problems, the more you will appreciate the significance of our relative lack of the necessary reliable knowledge. . . . [56–57]

2 The Judicial Process

THE NATURE OF CASE LAW

Case Law and the Doctrine of Precedent

Courts hear an array of disputes, and resolve them by referring to rules gleaned from prior cases. The disputing parties end up in court because they cannot (or will not) resort to force, because they cannot reach a mutually acceptable compromise, because they feel entitled to their "day in court," or some combination of all of these. Motivation notwithstanding, they seek a court-imposed solution. In so doing, the parties may agree more or less with the judicial remedy, but their ultimate satisfaction with the outcome will depend on whether they feel they are treated fairly. And in our legal system, fairness is conveyed when similar disputes receive similar treatment.

This method of dispute resolution produces "case law": a system where the rules applied in a dispute today were not only gleaned from earlier disputes between A and B but may also become relevant to future conflicts between C and D. Case law development embodies the doctrine of precedent, which expresses the notion that similar cases should be handled similarly, regardless of the specific parties involved. Put simply, precedent focuses on consistency of result. "The force of precedent in law," according to Llewellyn (1930), "is heightened by . . . that curious, almost universal sense of justice which urges that all men are properly to be treated alike in like circumstances. As the social system varies we meet infinite variations as to what men or treatments or circumstances are to be classed as 'like'; but the pressure to accept the views of the time and place remains."

Despite its emphasis on "settled" rules, case law development is flexible. The flexibility is necessary to allow the court certain decision-making boundaries. For example, factual differences will emerge occasionally and prompt the court to "distinguish" between two apparently similar situations, or if the distinction is compelling, the court may even "overrule" a precedent. These results may seem contradictory, but as Bodenheimer et al. (1980) describe, they are really indications of a flexibility that stems from two sources.

> First, judges [decide cases] . . . according to the claims of the parties and the unique facts. . . . [Given two fact situations, there may be sufficient shades of differences that one side may argue that the similarity between their particular facts and previous facts is less than it appears, and there is really something unique about their case, enough to distance themselves from the facts for an earlier decision.]
>
> Lawyers call reliance on these differences as a means of avoiding the authoritative effect of the prior decision the process of "distinguishing" a precedent. [Theoretically] . . . virtually every precedent can arguably be "distinguished" from a subsequent case. . . .
>
> The problem of determining whether a preceding judicial decision is really "on point" and not factually distinguishable from the legal dispute in which it is cited as a precedent has two dimensions. It involves not only the question of what the facts were in the preceding case, but also which of the facts of the preceding case were actually relied upon by the court in deciding the case. It also involves the question whether the decision in the preceding case, if articulated in general terms which went beyond the facts actually then in issue, ought to be controlling in a subsequent case involving different facts. This second dimension calls for a determination of the "ratio decidendi" (a Latin phrase meaning "the reason for the decision") or the "holding" of the prior case.
>
> This leads us to the second fundamental reason for the flexibility of the authoritative force of precedent. Even when the controlling facts and "ratio decidendi" . . . are indisputably applicable to and dispositive of a subsequent lawsuit, an American court will not automatically follow precedent. . . . This is not to say that American courts never follow precedent. They almost always do, and they frequently invoke the doctrine of "stare decisis," which seems to say they must. . . . Even though the doctrine of *stare decisis* may be as important in America for its exceptions as for its rule, its exceptions are not without limit. . . . [pp. 62–64]

Case Law, Stare Decisis and the Court Hierarchy

The doctrine of *stare decisis* brings into focus the "binding effect" of judicial decisions. The term derives from a Latin phrase meaning "to stand by precedents and not to disturb settled points." It also emphasizes the way legal rules emerge as authoritative in a particular geographic area (a jurisdiction). Because similar cases may be brought before different judges, there must be some method of achieving uniformity. The American legal system responds to this problem by requiring lower courts to follow the rules announced by higher tribunals. The hierarchy for this process, illustrated in Figure 2.1, is outlined below.

Court systems exist at the federal and at the state level. Although each varies slightly, their hierarchy is similar. Lower level decisions can be reviewed by higher levels, and the process ends with some "court of last resort"; higher court decisions are built on lower tribunals. For example, a federal trial court is bound by the rulings of the federal court of appeals for its circuit. A state's highest appellate court, usually referred to as a Supreme Court, announces decisions that supply case law precedent for all lower state courts.

State Court Structure

"Inferior" or "petty" courts: The lowest court is designated to handle very minor disputes, usually involving small amounts of money. These "petty" courts generally take the form of a "Justice of the Peace," a "District Justice," or a "Municipal Court." Their jurisdiction (the matters they may hear) is cast in terms of the dollar amount in dispute; that is, the claims can only be heard by these courts if they don't exceed a certain dollar amount. (Small claims disputes are a prime example.) Though referred to as "inferior," they are the forum where most "everyday disputes" are heard. They thus provide necessary access for those who otherwise might be locked out of the civil process.

Trial courts of general jurisdiction: The next level is the court of general jurisdiction, the one empowered to hear all cases without regard to money limitations. Again, the names vary; some are referred to as "Superior Courts," others, "Courts of Common Pleas."

Appellate courts: These courts review lower court decisions. They are intermediary tribunals and are most often known as "Courts of Appeal." Their decisions are reviewed by the state's highest court.

Supreme Court: The state Supreme Court is the state's "court of last resort." It reviews all lower level decisions and announces the final word on the state's law.

Federal Court Structure

The federal hierarchy is like the state's in that there are trial and appellate levels. Unlike the states, however, each level is referred to by the same name in each of the country's geographical regions.

District Court: These are the federal trial courts. They are courts of general jurisdiction, although there are some cases that they alone can hear (e.g., so-called "federal questions" and disputes where the amount in controversy exceeds ten thousand dollars). There are ninety-five judicial districts in the United States.

Courts of Appeal: Known as Circuit Courts of Appeal, these intermediate appellate tribunals hear appeals from the District Courts. The country is divided into eleven circuits.

U.S. Supreme Court: The ultimate "court of last resort," the Supreme Court announces the "law of the land." It hears appeals from lower level federal courts and from state supreme courts. It may also hear, at its discretion, cases that petition for a "writ of certiorari."

Case Law and "Res Judicata," "Reversal," and "Overruling"

As the above suggests, judicial decisions influence both the immediate disputing parties and those who follow in their steps. The effect is best appreciated when understood in relation to several related concepts—*res judicata,* reversal, and overruling, which Jones, Kernochan, and Murphy (1980) discuss below.

Every final decision of an appellate court has a twofold impact or effect: (1) as an authoritative settlement of the particular controversy then before the court; and (2) as a precedent or potential precedent for future cases. A Latin tag has been attached by lawyers to each of these effects, *stare decisis,* as we have seen, to the impact of the decision as precedent, *res judicata* to its effect as a settlement of the immediate controversy. It is essential in legal analysis that these Latin terms and the concepts they symbolize not be confused. By way of illustration, let us suppose a simple case. *P,* a former surgical patient, sues the *D Hospital* to recover damages for injuries caused, according to *P's* allegations, by *D Hospital's* negligence in the maintenance of its operating room. The trial court judgment is in favor of the defendant, and this judgment is affirmed by the supreme court of the state, the court of last resort in the jurisdiction, on the ground, clearly stated in the opinion of the court, that a hospital is a "charitable corporation" and, as such, enjoys immunity from suits for negligence. This decision is a final and conclusive settlement of the controversy between *P* and *D Hospital;* the case, . . . is now *res judicata,* and the losing party, *P,* cannot have it tried, or bring his claim again.

    Now, to make plain the difference between *res judicata* and *stare decisis* as legal terms of art, let us suppose further that the same state

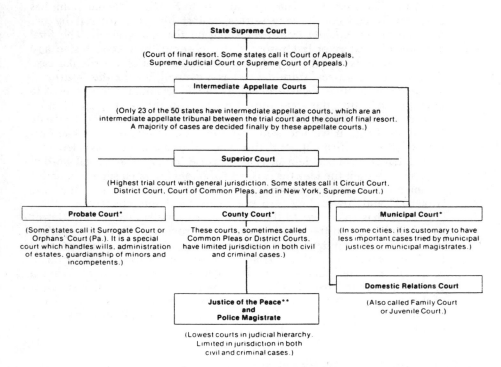

FIGURE 2.1 Hierarchy of state judicial systems

supreme court, two years later and in another hospital case, is persuaded that the principle of charitable immunity from suit for negligence is not a sound legal doctrine for present-day conditions and so "overrules *P v. D Hospital* and finds in favor of the injured plaintiff in the new case. This overruling decision is a deviation from the norm of *stare decisis*, of course, but American courts of last resort have never regarded precedents as absolutely binding—only as "generally" binding—and have reserved to themselves a largely undefined authority to overrule even clear precedents when considerations of public policy require a change in the case law.

What, however, of the particular claim of *P* against the *D Hospital?* Now that the supreme court of the jurisdiction has changed the law and flatly "overruled" the decision that was reached in *P*'s case two years ago, it might seem that *P* should be able to bring his suit again and prevail in his claim. The answer is clear, and adverse to *P*. His particular claim has been finally and conclusively settled against him; *P* is barred by the doctrine of *res judicata* from ever suing on that claim again. The final decision of a court of last resort is, we observe, more conclusive and permanent in its aspect *(res judicata)* as a settlement of a particular case than it is in its aspect *(stare decisis)* as a general law for the future.

One other nicety in legal terminology should be noted at this point. We have just said that the state supreme court, in the later hospital case, "overruled" its decision in *P v. D Hospital*. It would have been seriously inaccurate usage if we had said that the state supreme court had "reversed" *P v. D Hospital*. And this error in usage might have led to a substantial error in problem analysis, because "reverse," as a legal word of art, carries with it the idea that a court judgment has been set aside, and is no longer effective, as between the parties in controversy. In short, "reversal" and "overruling" are not to be used interchangeably. . . . "Reversal" has reference to the action of an appellate court on a lower court's judgment in the same particular controversy. When an appellate court reviews the judgment of a lower court in a case and concludes that the lower court reached an erroneous result in the case, the appellate court will "reverse," that is, set aside, the lower court's judgment. When a court of last resort "overrules" one of its past decisions, the conclusiveness of that earlier decision as a settlement of its particular controversy is not affected, but the overruled decision is no longer an authoritative precedent. [pp. 7–8]

Case Law; Ratio Decidendi and Dicta

In addition to the above, two other concepts shape case law development: *ratio decidendi* and *dicta*. They are important because they explicate the operation of precedent and *stare decisis* and shed light on the way law evolves. They are introduced and defined here, and not addressed in depth. Their meaning will become clearer when the sequence of cases in the latter part of this chapter is analyzed. Both concepts must be understood for what they have to say about the way judicial decisions become authoritative. As Bodenheimer (1974) states:

> [N]ot every statement made in a judicial decision is an authoritative source to be followed in a later case. . . . Only those statements in an earlier decision which may be said to constitute the *ratio decidendi* of that case are held to be binding, as a matter of general principle, in subsequent cases. Propositions not partaking of the character of *ratio decidendi* may be disregarded by the judge deciding the later case. Such nonauthoritative statements are usually referred to as *dicta*. . . .

17

. . . It is widely conceded, however, that not every proposition of law formulated by a court . . . possesses the authority belonging to the *ratio decidendi*. . . .

. . . [M]ost judges will hold that the *ratio decidendi* of a case is to be found in the general principle governing an earlier decision, as long as the formulation of this general principle was necessary to the decision of the actual issue between the litigants. Nonetheless, even though the majority of today's judges may theoretically agree on the basic method for finding the *ratio decidendi*, they may come to widely diverging conclusions in concrete cases calling for the application of this method. . . . [pp. 432–435]

THE ANALYSIS OF A JUDICIAL OPINION

The Structure of a Judicial Opinion

To comprehend the means by which a court arrives at a decision, one must analyze the judicial opinion to discover the court's rule selection and its reason for selecting one over another. Review the example of a judicial opinion in Figure 2.2. Note that it specifies the parties, the facts, the issues before the court, the lower court decisions, the court's decision or holding, and the court's reasoning for the decision.

Reading Judicial Opinions

Having explored the structural elements of an opinion, we turn now to its substance. What is the court trying to say, and why? The answers emerge from an understanding of, among other things, the dispute, the parties and their claims, the dispute's procedural route, the facts, and the court's judgment on them.

An understanding of an opinion begins with a firm grasp of its component parts. "Briefing" is a technique designed to break down an opinion into its multiple parts; it relies on a series of questions that may be used to capture the opinion's essential elements. To "brief" a case, then, involves formulating answers to the following questions:

- Who are the parties in the dispute? What does each want?
- On what legal theory does each base its claims?
- How was the dispute handled in lower courts? Who appealed and why?
- What are the facts, as the court describes them?

PARTIES TO SUIT

Volomino and Blasko v. Messenger Publishing Co.

HEADNOTES (SUMMARY OF POINTS OF LAW IN THE CASE)

1. In a defamation case, it is the function of the court, in the first instance, to determine whether or not the communication complained of is capable of a defamatory meaning.

2. Restatement, Torts, 614(1).

THE COURT'S HOLDING

3. In these actions of trespass for libel it was *Held* that the court below had properly determined that the articles and editorials constituting the alleged libels were not capable of the defamatory meaning pleaded by the plaintiffs.

4. A libel is a maliciously written or printed publication which tends to blacken a person's reputation or to expose him to public hatred, contempt, or ridicule, or to injure him in his business or profession.

DATE ARGUED

Argued March 25, 1963.

PLAINTIFF'S LEGAL THEORY

Trespass actions for libel.

Orders entered sustaining defendants' preliminary objections and complaints dismissed, opinion by Aldisert, J. Plaintiffs appealed.

OPINION AUTHOR

Opinion by Mr. Justice Eagen, April 16, 1963:

PROCEDURAL ROUTE

These actions of trespass seek damages for alleged libel. The court below sustained preliminary objections to the complaints in the nature of a demurrer. The plaintiffs appeal.

STATEMENT OF FACTS IN THE DISPUTE

Appellants are members of the Munhall Homestead Housing Association, a nonprofit private corporation, engaged in the business of maintaining and operating a housing project. They are also members of the corporate board of directors and serve as president and vice-president. The defendant is the publisher of a daily newspaper of general circulation. The alleged libel is based upon a series of articles and editorials published therein. The present actions are by the plaintiffs in their individual capacities. . . .

The lower court ruled that the published writings were not capable of the defamatory meaning the plaintiffs attribute to them and that no libel occurred. After a careful reading of the material complained of, we subscribe to this conclusion.

It is contended that certain portions of the publication involved necessarily lead, *inter alia*, to the conclusion that the plaintiffs have in their connection with the housing project cheated the public, violated the law and stole the election in which their corporate positions were attained. If this were true, libel would clearly be present. However, we find no such serious implications in the writings, nor are any extrinsic facts stated which change the critical but nondefamatory works into defamatory utterances. As the court below stated, any such conclusion as plaintiffs assert "requires an extravagant mental excursion." There is nothing in the publications complained, which suggests, intimates, or from which anyone reading them could infer, that the plaintiffs are guilty of the acts with which they were inferentially charged. In short, the publications are not libelous at all. A cause of action in libel is not pleaded by merely alleging that a publication is "scandalous, malicious, defamatory and libelous." This allegation in itself does not give to the language a construction which it will not bear. See, *Sarkees v. Warner-West Carp.*, 349 Pa. 365 37 A.2d 544 (1944). A libel is a maliciously written or printed publication which tends to blacken a person's reputation or to expose him to public hatred, contempt, or ridicule, or to injure him in his business or profession: *Schnabel v. Meredith*, 378 Pa. 609, 107 A.2d 860 (1954); *Cosgrove S. & C. Shop, Inc. v. Pane*, 408 Pa. 314, 182 A.2d 751 (1962). In a defamation case it is the function of the court, in the first instance, to determine whether or not the communication complained of is capable of a defamatory meaning: Restatement, Torts, 614 (1); *Boqash v. Elkins*, 405 Pa. 437, 176 A.2d 677 (1962); *Cosgrove S. & C. Shop v. Pane*, *supra*. The court below correctly concluded that the plaintiffs are reading into the publications a meaning that just is not there.

Source: 410 PA. 611 (1963)

FIGURE 2.2 Elements of a judicial opinion

ISSUE BEFORE *THIS* COURT

COURT'S DECISION ON THE ISSUE

RULE OF LAW GOVERNING THE CASE AND PRECEDENT

COURT'S DETERMINATION OF TERM "LIBEL" AND PRECEDENT

STATEMENT OF ITS FACT-FINDING ROLE

COURT'S HOLDING

- What is the legal issue the court is being asked to decide?
- What is the court's decision? (Also known as the *holding*, the decision will include a phrase such as "the court holds that . . .") Essentially, to "hold" is to "declare the conclusion of law reached by the court as to the legal effects of the facts decided" (Black, 1968).
- What reasons does the court offer to support its decision? What are its sources of authority (precedents)?
- How does the dissenting (or concurring) opinion, if there is one, depart from the majority?
- To what extent does the decision follow from the cited precedents? What guidance will the opinion offer future courts?

Each of the above questions can be answered after reading any opinion. (But don't be discouraged if you must re-read the case. Some opinions are very opaque; others, poorly written.) The goal is to understand its meaning, scope, and impact. The latter questions will be particularly helpful in assessing the opinion in relation to divergent rule interpretations and for reconciling an opinion with cases that precede or follow it.

THE JUDICIAL FUNCTION
AND THE DEVELOPMENT OF CASE LAW

Common Law Traditions

As we observed, case law evolves from the court's decision making by precedent. But what happens when the court encounters a situation where there are no prior rules to which it can turn? The lack of available precedent may make judicial decision making difficult, but judges *must* decide. Under these circumstances (also referred to as "cases of first impression"), the court determines the principles that, in its judgment, seem applicable and fashions them for the immediate facts. The impetus for such re-fashioning varies, but the primary aim is to reconcile the existent law with the court's view of the facts, the social context out of which they emerged and the extent to which the general legal principles apply to them. These judge-made rules are referred to as the common law. As Holtzoff (1966) points out:

Common law has been molded over the centuries by judges, step by step, growing from one specific case to another. . . . The analytical process by which it has evolved in the course of centuries is a triumph of inductive logic. . . . [A] judge determines on the basis of former precedents, social needs, and a sense of justice, in cases of first impression, what the governing rule of law should be. A judge may make law by building on prior material and may at times even modify it in the light of new requirements and changing conditions. His function of formulating law is, however, limited in the sense that he may not suddenly bring about far-reaching and drastic changes in basic theories, or adopt a novel approach or a new fundamental alteration in rights and liabilities. . . .

In this respect law formed by judges differs drastically from law enacted by legislators. Judges proceed gradually, as actual cases are presented to them. On the other hand, legislators are not restricted in this manner. They have the choice of either enacting detailed modifications in existing law, or proceeding without regard to prior legislation and making extensive changes, or even introducing new methods and novel approaches. . . . Once a statute is enacted by the legislature, it is rigid. The rule prescribed by it cannot be changed, except by subsequent action of the legislative body. By contrast the common law has the virtue of flexibility and capacity for continuous adjustment to shifting conditions and changing needs. Judges have it in their power by judicial decision in individual cases to make necessary modifications as time progresses. This process never stops or ends. [pp. 23–25]

The exercise of judicial creativity in the development of the common law may be an appropriate judicial function, but as Holtzoff states above, the opportunity to "create" new law does not mean that judicial law-making is unlimited. The development of common law occurs within the context of certain constitutional constraints, and these curb any tendencies toward excessive creativity. Notwithstanding, it is difficult to expose inappropriate judicial decision making. Judges are sufficiently aware of their role to avoid stepping beyond their constitutionally-defined functions, but they also have sole responsibility to find and apply the law. And to do this, they must reconcile the longstanding tension inherent in the judicial function, i.e., responsiveness versus constraint (Abraham, 1968).

Common Law and Legislation

A court can also turn to legislation in its search for legal doctrine. Indeed, legislation is frequently a "codified" version of prior common law rules. This method for rule selection also relies on the doctrine of precedent. The practice is not new, as Pound (1908) cites:

(1) They might receive it fully into the body of the law as affording not only a rule to be applied but a principle from which to reason, and hold it, as a later and more direct expression of the general will, of superior authority to judge-made rules on the same general subject; and so reason from it by analogy in preference to them. (2) They might receive it fully into the body of the law to be reasoned from by analogy the same as any other rule of law, regarding it, however, as of equal or coordinate authority in this respect with judge-made rules upon the same general subject. (3) They might refuse to receive it fully into the body of the law and give effect to it directly only; refusing to reason from it by analogy but giving it, nevertheless, a liberal interpretation to cover the whole field it was intended to cover. (4) They might not only refuse to reason from it by analogy and apply it directly only, but also give to it a strict and narrow interpretation, holding it down rigidly to those cases that it covers expressly. [pp. 383–386]

There are some instances, however, where both common law and legislation seem equally compelling. These cases are difficult to decide because the court may not simply resort to the assumption of legislative superiority, and is forced to confront its view of the judicial function. For example, the court may decide that the legislative rule is too ambiguous to apply—a situation that can arise with very "new" legislation. It may then determine that the best thing to do is apply the common law rules that preceded the legislation.

Judicial and legislative responsibilities occasionally overlap on a particular issue in a dispute. When this occurs, the court treats as irrelevant the fact that the legislature decided to address an issue on which it too is competent. The court's decision in these cases, and the rationale it offers, reveals a lot about its view of the relationship between common law and legislation. This concept may be difficult to grasp now in the abstract, but the series of cases that follow in the next section will concretely express these ideas. The *Pugh v. Holmes* decision, and the court's interpretation of the Rent Withholding Act will clarify the point.

CASE LAW DEVELOPMENT
AND THE LEGAL REASONING PROCESS

To make sense of case law development and synthesis requires the process of legal reasoning. What distinguishes this method from other ways of thinking? Is it really better, or merely different? And, in any case, why should social workers care about it?

On a practical level, "legal reasoning" can be thought of as "thinking like a lawyer." The non-lawyer reader may properly ask: Why should I want to do that? Will such habits, once begun, be difficult to break? Perhaps! The method, however, must be appreciated as a way of understanding how the legal system receives and resolves disputes. Lawyers operate the system, so it is not unusual to cast the problem-solving process in terms of "thinking like" its principal technicians.

We have seen that the legal system assumes that problem solving should be rational; every solution should be based on a reason. Legal reasoning, whether dealing with judicial decisions, legislation, or regulations, seeks to reconcile particular facts with general rules. It follows a clear pattern, i.e., problem solving by example, from case to case. But what is its impact? To what extent does the legal system's conduct match its rhetoric about rule-based decision making? These questions, though not new, are important because, as Levi (1949) suggests below, they help legitimize the way legal institutions address social problems. His analysis is both descriptive and critical. It shows the process of legal reasoning and the firm grasp it has on legal decision making, yet alerts us to the shortcomings as well.

An Introduction to Legal Reasoning*

It is important that the mechanism of legal reasoning should not be concealed by its pretense. The pretense is that the law is a system of known rules applied by a judge; the pretense has long been under attack. In an important sense legal rules are never clear, and if a rule had to be clear before it could be imposed, society would be impossible. The mechanism accepts the differences of view and ambiguities of words. It provides for the participation of the community in resolving the ambiguity by providing a forum for the discussion of policy in the gap of ambiguity. On serious controversial questions, rules make it possible to take the first step in the direction of what otherwise would be forbidden ends. The mechanism is indispensable to peace in a community.

The basic pattern of legal reasoning is reasoning by example. It is reasoning from case to case. It is a three-step process described by the doctrine of precedent in which a proposition descriptive of the first case is

*From Edward Levi, An introduction to legal reasoning, pp. 1–9. © 1949 University of Chicago; Chicago, IL. Reprinted by permission.

made into a rule of law and then applied to a next similar situation. The steps are these: similarity is seen between cases; next the rule of law inherent in the first case is announced; then the rule of law is made applicable to the second case. This is a method of reasoning necessary for the law, but it has characteristics which under other circumstances might be considered imperfections.

These characteristics become evident if the legal process is approached as though it were a method of applying general rules of law to diverse facts—in short, as though the doctrine of precedent meant that general rules, once properly determined, remained unchanged, and then were applied, albeit imperfectly, in later cases. If this were the doctrine, it would be disturbing to find that the rules change from case to case and are remade with each case. Yet this change in the rules is the indispensable dynamic quality of law. It occurs because the scope of a rule of law, and therefore its meaning, depends upon a determination of what facts will be considered similar to those present when the rule was first announced. The finding of similarity or difference is the key step in the legal process.

The determination of similarity or difference is the function of each judge. Where case law is considered, and there is no statute, he is not bound by the statement of the rule of law made by the prior judge even in the controlling case. The statement is mere dictum, and this means that the judge in the present case may find irrelevant the existence or absence of facts which prior judges thought important. It is not what the prior judge intended that is of any importance; rather it is what the present judge, attempting to see the law as a fairly consistent whole, thinks should be the determining classification. In arriving at his result, he will ignore what the past thought important; he will emphasize facts which prior judges would have thought made no difference. It is not alone that he could not see the law through the eyes of another, for he could at least try to do so. It is rather that the doctrine of dictum forces him to make his own decision.

Thus it cannot be said that the legal process is the application of known rules to diverse facts. It is, however, a system of rules; the rules are discovered in the process of determining similarity or difference. But if attention is directed toward the finding of similarity or difference, other peculiarities appear. The problem for the law is: When will it be just to treat different cases as though they were the same? A working legal system must therefore be willing to pick out key similarities and to reason from them to the justice of applying a common classification. The existence of some facts in common brings the general rule into play.

Therefore, it appears that the kind of reasoning involved in the legal process is one in which the classification changes as the classification is made. The rules change as the rules are applied. More important, the rules arise out of a process which, while comparing fact situations, creates the rules and then applies them. But this kind of reasoning is open to the charge that it is classifying things as equal when they are somewhat different, justifying the classification by rules made up as the reasoning or classification proceeds. In a sense all reasoning is of this type, but there is an additional requirement that compels the legal process to be this way. Not only do new situations arise, but in addition, peoples' desires change. The categories used in the legal process must be left ambiguous in order to permit the infusion of new ideas. And this is true even where legislation or a constitution is involved. The words used by the legislature or the constitutional convention must come to have new meaning. Furthermore, agreement on any other basis would be impossible. In this manner the laws come to express the ideas of the community and even when written in general terms, in statute or constitution, are molded for the specific case.

But attention must be given to the process. An argument as to whether the law is certain, unchanging, and expressed in rules, or uncertain, changing, and only a technique for deciding specific cases misses the point. It is both. Similarly it is not helpful to dispose of the process as a wonderful mystery possibly reflecting a higher law, by which the law can remain the same and yet change. The law forum is the most explicit demonstration of the mechanism required for a moving classification system. The folklore of law may choose to ignore the imperfections in legal reasoning, but the law forum itself has taken care of them.

What does the law forum require? It requires the presentation of competing examples. The forum protects the parties and the community by making sure that the competing analogies are before the court. The rule which will be created arises out of a process in which if different things are treated as similar, at least the differences have been urged. In this sense the parties as well as the court participate in the law making. In this sense, also, lawyers represent more than the litigants.

Reasoning by example in the law is a key to many things. It indicates in part the hold which the law process has over the litigants. They have participated in the law making. They are bound by something they helped to make. Moreover, the examples or analogies urged by the parties bring into the law the common ideas of the society. The ideas have their day in court, and they will have their day again. This is what makes the hearing fair, rather than any idea that the judge is completely impartial, for of course he cannot be completely so. Moreover, the hearing in a sense compels at least vicarious participation by all the citizens, for the rule which is made, even though ambiguous, will be law to them.

Reasoning by example shows the decisive role that the common ideas of the society and the distinctions made by experts can have in shaping the law. The movement of common or expert concepts into the law may be followed. The concept is suggested in arguing difference or similarity in a brief, but it wins no approval from the court. The idea achieves standing in the society. It is suggested again to a court. The court this time reinterprets the prior case and in doing so adopts the reflected idea. In subsequent cases, the idea is given further definition and is tied to other ideas which have been accepted by courts. It is now no longer the idea which was commonly held in the society. It becomes modified in subsequent cases. Ideas first rejected but which gradually have won acceptance now push what has become a legal category out of the system or convert it into something which may be its opposite. The process is one in which the ideas of the community and of the social sciences, whether correct or not, as they win acceptance in the community, control legal decisions. Erroneous ideas, of course, have played an enormous part in shaping the law. An idea, adopted by a court, is in a superior position to influence conduct and opinion in the community; judges, after all, are rulers. And the adoption of an idea by a court reflects the power structure in the community. But reasoning by example will operate to change the idea after it has been adopted.

Moreover, reasoning by example brings into focus important similarity and difference in the interpretation of case law, statutes, and the constitution of a nation. There is a striking similarity. It is only folklore which holds that a statute if clearly written can be completely unambiguous and applied as intended to a specific case. Fortunately or otherwise, ambiguity is inevitable in both statute and constitution as well as in case law. Hence reasoning by example operates with all three, there are important differences. What a court says is dictum, but what a legislature says is a statute. The reference of the reasoning changes. Interpretation of intention when dealing with a statute is the way of describing the attempt to compare cases on the basis of the standard thought to be common at the time the legislation was passed. While this is the attempt, it may not initially accomplish any different result than if the standard of the judge had been explicitly used. Nevertheless, the remarks of the judge are directed toward describing a category set up by the legislature. These remarks are different from ordinary dicta. They set the course of the statute, and later reasoning in subsequent cases is tied to them. As a consequence, courts are less free in applying a statute than in dealing with case law. The current rationale for this is the notion that the legislature has acquiesced by legislative silence in the prior, even though erroneous, interpretation of the court. But the change in reasoning where legislation is concerned seems an inevitable consequence of the division of function between court and legislature, and, paradoxically, a recognition also of the impossibility of determining legislative intent. The impairment of a court's freedom in interpreting legislation is reflected in frequent appeals to the constitution as a necessary justification for overruling cases even though these cases are thought to have interpreted the legislation erroneously.

Under the United States experience, contrary to what has sometimes been believed when a written constitution of a nation is involved, the court has greater freedom than it has with the application of a statute or case law. In case law, when a judge determines what the controlling similarity between the present and prior case is, the case is decided. The judge does not feel free to ignore the results of a great number of cases which he cannot explain under a remade rule. And in interpreting legislation, when the prior interpretation, even though erroneous, is determined after a comparison of facts to cover the case, the case is decided. But this is not true with a constitution. The constitution sets up the conflicting ideals of the community in certain ambiguous categories. These categories bring along with them satellite concepts covering the areas of ambiguity. It is with a set of these satellite concepts that reasoning by example must work. But no satellite concept, no matter how well developed, can prevent the court from shifting its course, not only by realigning cases which impose certain restrictions, but by going beyond realignment back to the over-all ambiguous category written into the document. The constitution, in order words, permits the court to be inconsistent. The freedom is concealed either as a search for the intention of the framers or as a proper understanding of a living instrument, and sometimes as both. But this does not mean that reasoning by example has any less validity in this field.

It may be objected that this analysis of legal reasoning places too much emphasis on the comparison of cases and too little on the legal concepts which are created. It is true that similarity is seen in terms of a word, and inability to find a ready word to express similarity or difference may prevent change in the law. The words which have been found in the past are much spoken of, have acquired a dignity of their own, and to a considerable measure control results. As Judge Cardozo suggested in speaking of metaphors, the word starts out to free thought and ends by enslaving it. The movement of concepts into and out of the law makes the point. If the society has begun to see certain significant similarities or differences, the comparison emerges with a word. When the word is finally accepted, it becomes a legal concept. Its meaning continues to change. But the comparison is not only between the instances which have been included under it and the actual case at hand, but also in terms of hypothetical instances which the word by itself suggests. Thus the connotation of the word for a time has a limiting influence—so much so that the reasoning may even appear to be simply deductive.

But it is not simply deductive. In the long run a circular motion can be seen. The first stage is the creation of the legal concept which is built up as cases are compared. The period is one in which the court fumbles for a phrase. Several phrases may be tried out; the misuse or misunderstanding of words itself may have an effect. The concept sounds like another, and the jump to the second is made. The second stage is the period when the concept is more or less fixed, although reasoning by example continues to classify items inside and out of the concept. The third stage is the breakdown of the concept, as reasoning by example has moved so far ahead as to make it clear that the suggestive influence of the word is no longer desired.

The process is likely to make judges and lawyers uncomfortable. It runs contrary to the pretense of the system. It seems inevitable, therefore, that as matters of kind vanish into matters of degree and then entirely new meanings turn up, there will be the attempt to escape to some overall rule which can be said to have always operated and which will make the reasoning look deductive. The rule will be useless. It will have to operate on a level where it has no meaning. Even when lip service is paid to it, care will be taken to say that it may be too wide or too narrow but that nevertheless it is a good rule. The statement of the rule is roughly analogous to the appeal to the meaning of a statute or of a constitution, but it has less of a function to perform. It is window dressing. Yet it can be very misleading. Particularly when a concept has broken down and reasoning by example is about to build another, textbook writers, well aware of the unreal aspect of old rules, will announce new ones, equally ambiguous and meaningless, forgetting that the legal process does not work with the rule but on a much lower level.

THE SYNTHESIS OF CASE LAW

Abolition of the *Caveat Emptor* Doctrine in Pennsylvania Landlord–Tenant Law

To know the law in a particular field, you must appreciate how all the related cases are put together. This task is accomplished by "synthesizing" the cases: looking for the strands that tie them together and understanding the factors that contributes to their growth and change.

The following cases span over forty years in the development of Pennsylvania landlord–tenant law. They were selected because the problem they describe is a familiar one. (Indeed, perhaps too familiar for some. Practically everyone has rented an apartment, and has an appreciation of the problems and prospects of dealing with landlords.) Essentially, they deal with the balance of power between landlords and tenants and the mutual rights and obligations on which their relationship is built. What can tenants really expect when they enter a lease agreement? If displeased with their rented premises, must they "take it or leave it?" Is the entire relationship "stacked" in favor of the landlord? The following cases illustrate the development of rules that govern these questions.

Specifically, they deal with the doctrine of *caveat emptor* in residential (as opposed to commercial) leases, its implications for legal duties between landlords and tenants, and its eventual displacement by the doctrine of "implied warranty of habitability." (These two concepts may seem foreign now, but the cases will explain them. As you will see, you are already more familiar with them than you realize.) Although the cases were actually decided between 1937

and 1979, the references to the assumptions underlying landlord–
tenant relationships date back to feudal property law and thus place
the cases on a doctrinal continuum that spans several hundred
years.

"Brief" each case after you read it. (Review the earlier section on
"Reading Judicial Opinions.") Analyze it both on its own merits and in
relation to those that precede it. As you read, consider Levi's discussion about legal rules, their development, and the conditions under
which they change.

HARRIS v. LEWISTOWN TRUST CO. 326 PA. (1937)

OPINION BY MR. JUSTICE DREW, March 29, 1937:

This is an action in trespass by Joseph R. Harris, a tenant, under a month-to-
month lease, and Sadie B. Harris, his wife, who was also his employee in a
beauty shop maintained by him on the demised premises. Damages are
sought for injuries sustained by her as a result of the collapse of a cellar
stairway. Named as defendants are the Lewistown Trust Company, indi-
vidually and as trustee, and the beneficial owners. A verdict was directed
against the husband because of his contributory negligence. Judgment *non
obstante veredicto* was entered against the wife. She alone has appealed.

Appellant places her principal reliance upon a promise by the agent of the
owner to repair. It is conceded such promise was made at the time of the
negotiation of the oral lease, and subsequently repeated, and that it was
never kept. The accident happened thirteen months after the tenant took
possession. The stairway was in an obviously defective and decayed condition. Of this the tenant was fully aware. The wife claimed that she had no
knowledge of it; that she had used the stairway but four times. We assume
for the purpose of this appeal that she was not guilty of contributory negligence, although there is evidence that she was. Giving her case the aid of
this assumption, we meet directly the question whether or not the owner is
liable in tort by reason of this promise.

The general rule in this country, and also in England, is that an agreement
to repair does not impose upon the owner a liability in tort at the suit of the
tenant or others lawfully on the land in the right of the tenant.

Fundamentally this view is based upon the conclusion that liability in tort
should follow as a legal incident of occupation and control. By the great
weight of authority, occupation and control are not reserved through an
agreement by the owner to repair.

There is no appellate decision directly on the point in this Commonwealth. We adopt the prevailing doctrine because it is sound in reason

and supported by a preponderance of juridical opinion in this country and in England.

We have held repeatedly that a tenant takes the property as he finds it, with all existing defects, which he knows or can ascertain by reasonable inspection. This is so even though the premises are in a condition called ruinous . . .

Where the entire possession and enjoyment of property are transferred by landlord to tenant, the rule of caveat emptor applies. As was said by Mr. Justice Sharswood in *Moore v. Weber*, "The lessee's eyes are his bargain. He is bound to examine the premises he rents, and secure himself by covenants to repair and rebuild."

A well-recognized exception to this rule exists where the landlord gives the tenant possession of land containing, to the landlord's knowledge, dangerous hidden defects unknown to the tenant and which by reasonable inspection he cannot discover. In such a case the landlord is guilty of active wrong doing, because he commits an act that almost inevitably draws the tenant into a hidden trap. This exception is inapplicable here. There was no hidden defect; the tenant had full knowledge of the condition of the stairs and freely admitted it. The case thus falls without the exception and within the general rule; and it is clear that the tenant, as plaintiff suing for his own injuries in trespass, could not recover.

Appellant insists she is entitled to recover on the authority of *Deutsch v. Max*. That, and the instant case, are in some respects very similar. There an employee of the tenant was injured by the collapse of an obviously defective wooden balustrade on a second-story porch. Here, a member of the family, who was also an employee of the tenant, was injured by the collapse of an obviously defective cellar stairway. In each case the tenant was fully aware of the dangerous condition. There was no promise to repair in that case, but existence of such a promise is of no consequence in tort actions as we have already pointed out. There can be no doubt that in the *Deutsch* case, under circumstances in which the tenant could not have recovered, his employee was nonetheless permitted to recover against the owner. The result there professedly rested upon the principle that where "a landlord lets premises in a *ruinous condition or in a condition amounting to a nuisance*, the landlord is liable for injuries resulting therefrom."

The doctrine of "condition amounting to a nuisance," as mentioned in the *Deutsch case*, does not apply as between landlord and tenant: *Jackson v. Public Service Co.*

The doctrine of "condition amounting to a nuisance" is confined to third persons or strangers to the premises, those "either the owners or occupants of nearby property, persons temporarily on such property, or persons on a neighboring highway or other public places"

From what has been said it is clear that our decision in *Deutsch v. Max* cannot be followed. It is a bar to a proper decision in this case. For this

reason it is now necessary to overrule it. There being no liability on defendants in this action, the judgment of the court below must be affirmed.

Judgment affirmed.

HAYDEN v. SECOND NATIONAL BANK OF ALLENTOWN
331 PA. 29 (1938)

OPINION BY MR. JUSTICE DREW, May 9, 1938:

The action is trespass by mother and father to recover damages for the death
of their son and the destruction of the father's automobile; defendant's
affidavit of defense raising questions of law was sustained and judgment
entered in its favor. Plaintiffs appeal.

We take the facts from the statement of claim. On February 9, 1935, the
son went to get his father's car from the public garage building in Allentown
in which it was stored. The car was on the third floor, and the son was taken
up in an elevator, the only means of access to the upper floors "for persons
with automobiles." It was operated by an employee of the tenant–proprietor
of the garage, who was in possession under a lease from the defendant bank,
the owner of the building. Instead of waiting for the son to return and drive
the car on to the elevator, the operator, without closing the elevator shaft
doors and without giving any warning, proceeded to the fourth floor. Plaintiffs' son, believing that the elevator car was in place at the third floor
landing, drove toward the elevator shaft and, "while in the process of
carefully driving upon what appeared to be the elevator car in place," drove
into the open shaft, plunged to the bottom, and was killed.

Defendant did not build the garage building. At the time it acquired title,
the elevator was not equipped with any automatic locking device that would
prevent the elevator from being moved until the shaft doors were securely
closed; nor did defendant equip the elevator with any such device prior to its
lease of the premises.

The general rule is that the landlord who is entirely out of possession and
control is not liable for bodily harm caused to the tenant and those upon the
leased premises in the latter's right by reason of any dangerous condition
existing when the tenant took possession. In other words, such a landlord
owes no duty to persons coming upon the premises for conditions present at
the time of the tenant's entrance. To this rigid rule of non-liability there are
but two exceptions: (1) when the landlord conceals or fails to disclose
dangerous conditions of which he has knowledge and of which the tenant is
unaware and cannot be expected to discover, and (2) where the landlord,
who knows or should know of dangerous conditions, leases premises for a
purpose involving the admission of many persons and has reason to believe
that the tenant will not first correct the conditions. These principles were

recently reviewed at length in *Harris v. Lewistown Trust Co.*, and from them we have no intention to depart. Their application to the present case makes it clear that defendant owed no common law duty to plaintiffs' son. It is not contended that the landlord delivered possession of the premises to the tenant at a time when they contained concealed dangers known to the landlord and unknown to the tenant. Plaintiffs' contention that defendant is subject to liability under the second exception is untenable.

In this disposition of the case no problem of proximate causation arises. Judgment affirmed.

KOLOJESKI v. JOHN DEISHER, INC. 429 PA. 191 (1968)

OPINION BY MR. JUSTICE O'BRIEN, March 15, 1968:

Madeline Kolojeski, a two-year old child, died, allegedly as the result of lead poisoning caused by the ingestion of lead base paint, which had chipped and peeled from the woodwork of the living room of the apartment occupied by the minor decedent and her parents. The decedent's mother, as administratrix of the decedent's estate, and the decedent's mother and father in their own right, commenced wrongful death and survival actions against appellee, John Deisher, Inc., the rental agent of the owners of the building in which the apartment was situated, and the owners themselves, Nazareno Pomponi and Virginia Pomponi. The defendants–appellees filed preliminary objections to the complaint in the nature of a demurrer. The court below sustained the demurrer and dismissed the complaint. This appeal followed.

Appellants' occupancy of the premises commenced on or about April 22, 1964, when they entered into a month-to-month lease with appellee, Deisher. The complaint alleges that on or about January 4, 1966, some 20 months after appellants had gone into occupancy of the premises, the minor decedent consumed pieces of paint which had peeled from the living room woodwork, thereby sustaining injuries which resulted in her death on January 6, 1966. Appellants alleged that appellees were negligent in failing to maintain the premises in proper living condition; failing to inspect the premises adequately to insure the safety of the tenants; failing to notify the tenants of the dangerous substance with which the living room woodwork had been painted; having caused the living room woodwork to be painted with a toxic substance; and failing to remove and remedy the condition of the woodwork, and permitting the paint to become decayed, chipped, and peeling. Reduced to its essentials, the complaint alleges that appellees were negligent in allowing the living room woodwork paint job to deteriorate to the point where paint peeled and fell therefrom; and in using lead base paint, which is poisonous if consumed. We are in agreement with the court below that no cause of action has been stated.

In *Lopez v. Gukenback,* this court summarized the general liability of a landlord to his tenant for injuries received by the tenant on the premises. We there said: "(1) In the absence of any provision in the lease, a landlord is under no obligation to repair the leased premises, to see to it that they are fit for rental or to keep the premises in repair: (citing cases); (2) a tenant takes the premises as he finds them and the landlord is not liable for existing defects of which the tenant knows or can ascertain by a reasonable inspection: (citing cases); (3) a landlord out of possession, however, may be liable (a) where he conceals a dangerous condition of which he has knowledge and of which the tenant has no knowledge or cannot be expected to discover, and (b) where he knows or should know of a dangerous condition and leases the premises for a purpose involving a 'public use' and has reason to believe the tenant will not first correct the condition: (citing cases) . . ." There is nothing in the complaint to indicate that the landlord was under any duty to make repairs. Without such a duty, we have no option but to agree with the court below that "no liability on the part of defendants can be predicated upon their failure to repair the premises or in allowing the paint to peel."

Appellants' only possible basis for recovery must arise from the use by appellees of lead-base paint. Such use would support liability only if such use constituted the creation of a dangerous condition of which appellees had knowledge and of which appellants had no knowledge. In this connection, appellants cite a New York decision which we, as did the court below, find to be inapposite. The decision in that case was bottomed on the violation of a law requiring the landlord to make repairs. No such situation exists here. Although the situation is tragic, we cannot help but agree that the use of lead-base paint in these circumstances cannot constitute actionable negligence. The court below aptly stated: "Plaintiffs have cited no judicial decisions in this jurisdiction or any statute or ordinance which would justify a conclusion that the use of a lead-base paint constitutes negligence . . . In the absence of compelling authority we cannot find that the use of lead-base paint constitutes negligence, as we take judicial notice that the use of such paint is common and widespread." Were we to conclude otherwise, we would be required to ascribe to appellees a knowledge and expertise not ascribable, at least at the time of this incident, to people without special training or experience. . . . Judgment affirmed.

REITMEYER v. SPRECHER 431 PA. 284 (1968)

OPINION BY MR. JUSTICE JONES, July 1, 1968:

This appeal presents a narrow, albeit an important, issue: is a landlord subject to liability in tort for physical harm caused to his tenant by a defective condition of the leased premises, which existed when the written lease was executed and which the landlord orally promised the tenant, when the lease was executed, that he would repair?

This matter comes before us on two pleadings, i.e., a complaint in trespass and preliminary objections thereto, in the nature of a demurrer, which alleges that the complaint facts do not set forth a cause of action.

Meda Reitmeyer and Joe Reitmeyer (Reitmeyers) executed a printed lease for one of four row houses the owner of which was Harold Sprecher. Allegedly, the rear porch floor of the leased premises (approximately three feet above ground, access to which is by three wooden steps) was defective where the wooden porch floor overhung the top step and, allegedly, such defect was known to Sprecher. At the time of execution of the lease and, in consideration thereof, allegedly, Sprecher orally promised to repair promptly or to provide promptly the materials to repair the leased premises including specifically repair of the rear porch floor and steps and, in reliance upon such promise, Reitmeyers executed the lease and took possession of the premises. Sprecher subsequently repeated the original oral promise to make repairs to the premises. Approximately two months after execution of the lease and the entry of Reitmeyers into possession of the premises, Mrs. Reitmeyer fell and injured herself as a result of a defect in the rear porch floor. Sprecher had not made any repairs nor had he provided materials for repairs as promised.

Reitmeyers instituted an action of trespass against Sprecher in the Court of Common Pleas of Union County by the filing of a complaint to which Sprecher filed preliminary objections. The court sustained the preliminary objections and dismissed the action. From that order the instant appeal stems.

Thirty-one years ago, on *substantially* similar facts, in *Harris v. Lewistown Trust Co.*, 326 PA. 145, A. 34 (1937), we held that a promise on the part of a landlord to repair the premises, made at the time of negotiation of the lease and subsequently repeated, which was not performed, did not impose upon the landlord a liability *in tort* at the suit of the tenant for injuries sustained by the tenant.

Counsel for Reitmeyers frankly concedes that, unless we now overrule *Harris*, *Harris* governs the instant situation and requires affirmance of the court below. What counsel for Reitmeyers urges is that *Harris* be reconsidered and overruled and that we adopt 357 of Restatement 2d, Torts, which enunciates a view contrary to that expressed by this Court in *Harris*.

Section 357, supra, provides:

"Where Lessor Contracts to Repair. A lessor of land is subject to liability for physical harm caused to his lessee and others upon the land with the consent of the lessee or his sublessee by a condition of disrepair existing before or arising after the lessee has taken possession if (a) the lessor, as such, has contracted by a covenant in the lease or otherwise to keep the land in repair, and (b) the disrepair creates an unreasonable risk to persons upon the land, which the performance of the lessor's agreement would have prevented, and (c) the lessor fails to exercise reasonable care to perform his contract." Counsel for Reitmeyers argues that, although the majority of the jurisdictions of the American courts still adhere to the *Harris* view and reject the Restatement view, as of 1964 "An increasing minority of the courts, by now only slightly less in number, have worked out a liability in tort for such injuries to person or property, finding a duty arising out of the contract relation."

We must recognize the fact that, since the time when *Harris* was decided, critical changes have taken place economically and socially. Aware of such changes, we must realize further that most frequently today, the average prospective tenant vis-a-vis the prospective landlord, occupies a disadvantageous position. Start necessity very often forces a tenant into occupancy of premises far from desirable and in a defective state of repair. The acute housing shortage mandates that the average prospective tenant accede to the demands of the prospective landlord as to conditions of rental, which, under ordinary conditions with housing available, the average tenant would not and should not accept.

No longer does the average prospective tenant occupy a free bargaining status and no longer do the average landlord-to-be and tenant-to-be negotiate a lease on an "arm's-length" basis. Premises which, under normal circumstances, would be completely unattractive for rental are now, by necessity, at a premium. If our law is to keep in tune with our times we must recognize the present day inferior position of the average tenant vis-a-vis the landlord when it comes to negotiating a lease.

In the case at bar, it is *alleged* that, as an inducement to the execution of the instant lease for premises, which were obviously in a defective condition, the landlord promised the tenant to remedy this defective condition and, in reliance upon that promise a lease was negotiated.

Under the instant circumstances, a duty on the part of the landlord arose to repair and render safe the defective condition of the premises and if, as alleged, physical harm was caused to the tenant, by a breach of the landlord's promise to repair, liability in tort on the part of the landlord should arise. As we said in *Evans v. Otis Elevator Co.*, "It is not the contract per se which creates the duty; it is the law which imposes the duty because of the nature of the undertaking in the contract." Such holding is based upon the common sense of the situation and is in line with the most rudimentary principles of justice.

To the extent that *Harris v. Lewistown Trust Co. and Hayden v. Second Nat. Bank of Allentown* are in conflict with the Restatement 2nd, Torts, 357, they are hereby expressly overruled. We adopt Section 357 of Restatement 2d, Torts, as the sound and sensible approach to the instant problem.

Order reversed.

PUGH v. HOLMES 486 PA. 272 (1979)
OPINION

LARSEN, Justice.

Eloise Holmes, appellee, had been pursuant to an oral month-to-month lease, renting a residential dwelling in Chambersburg in Franklin County at the rate of $60.00 per month from November, 1971 until recently. Her landlord, appellant J. C. Pugh, instituted two separate landlord–tenant actions against appellee before a justice of the peace, the first resulting in a judgment for unpaid rent (for the period from September, 1975 through June, 1976) and the second resulting in a judgment for unpaid rent (for the period from June, 1976 through August, 1976) and for possession of the premises. Following Mrs. Holmes' appeals to the Court of Common Pleas of Franklin County, appellant filed separate complaints, the first seeking unpaid rent and the second seeking both unpaid rent and possession. In both actions, appellee filed answers asserting a defense of the landlord's alleged breach of an implied warranty of habitability. Additionally, in the second action, appellee asserted a set-off due in an amount, which she claimed she had spent to repair a broken lock after having given appellant notice and a reasonable opportunity to repair the lock. Appellee also filed a counterclaim for the cost of repairing other allegedly defective conditions of which she had given appellant notice. Appellant filed preliminary objections to the answer and counterclaim, which the Court of Common Pleas sustained, finding that appellees' answer failed to set forth a legal defense to the landlord's actions, and that the counterclaim failed to set forth a legal cause of action.

On appeal, the Superior Court, by opinion of President Judge Jacobs, reversed and remanded. By order dated July 20, 1978, this Court granted appellant's petition for allowance of appeal.

I. Doctrine of *Caveat Emptor* Abolished/Implied Warranty of Habitability Adopted

The doctrine of *caveat emptor* comported with the needs of the society in which it developed. However, we find that the doctrine of *caveat emptor* has outlived its usefulness and must be abolished, and that, in order to keep in step with the realities of modern-day leasing, it is appropriate to adopt an implied warranty of habitability in residential leases. The rule of *caveat emptor*, as applied to landlord–tenant relationships, developed in England in the sixteenth century and was adopted in the nineteenth century as the law of this Commonwealth in *Moore v. Weber*, Moore held "The rule here, as in other cases, is *caveat emptor*. The lessee's eyes are his bargain. He is bound to examine the premises he rents, and secure himself by covenants to repair." In the primarily agrarian society in which the doctrine developed, the law viewed the lease transaction as a conveyance of land for a term, and the focal interest in the conveyance was the land—any shelters or structures existing on the land were "incidental" concerns. The rent was viewed as "coming out of the land" itself, not from the dwelling or the dweller.

The feudal landlord

"had no obligations to the tenant other than those made expressly, and the tenant's obligation to pay rent was independent of the landlord's (covenants) . . . The doctrine of *caveat emptor* was fully applicable. The tenant's only protections were to inspect the premises before taking possession or to extract express warranties from the landlord. It was assumed that landlords and tenants held equal bargaining power in arranging their rental agreements, and that the agrarian tenant had the ability to inspect the dwelling adequately and to make simple repairs in the buildings, which possessed no modern conveniences such as indoor plumbing or electrical wiring. As agrarian society declined and population centers shifted from rural to urban areas, the common law concepts of landlord–tenant relationships did not change. Despite the facts that the primary purpose of the urban leasing arrangement was housing and not land and that the tenant could neither adequately inspect nor repair urban dwelling units, landlords still were not held to any implied warranties in the places they rented and tenants leased dwellings at their own risk."

As stated by appellee, "times have changed. So has the law." (Brief for appellee at 3). Today, the doctrine of the implied warranty of habitability has attained majority status in the United States, the doctrine having been embraced by the appellate courts and/or the legislatures of some 40 state jurisdictions and the District of Columbia. The warranty recognizes that the modern tenant is not interested in land, but rather bargains for a dwelling house suitable for habitation.

"Functionally viewed, the modern apartment dweller is a consumer of housing services. The contemporary leasing of residences envisions one person (landlord) exchanging for periodic payments (rent) a bundle of goods and services, rights and obligations. The now classic description of this economic reality appears in *Javins v. First National Realty Corp.* When American city dwellers both rich and poor, seek 'shelter today, they seek a well known package of goods and services—a package which includes not merely walls and ceilings, but also adequate heat, light and ventilation, serviceable plumbing facilities, secure windows and doors, proper sanitation, and proper maintenance.' "

Moreover, prospective tenants today can have vastly inferior bargaining power compared with the landlord, as was recognized in *Reitmeyer v. Sprecher*. In Reitmeyer this Court stated:

"Stark necessity very often forces a tenant into occupancy of premises far from desirable and in a defective state of repair. The acute housing shortage mandates that the average prospective tenant accede to the demands of the prospective landlord as to conditions of rental, which, under ordinary conditions with housing available, the average tenant would not and should not accept. No longer does the average prospective tenant occupy a free bargaining status and no longer do the average landlord-to-be and tenant-to-be negotiate a lease on an 'arm's-length' basis."

The Superior Court correctly observed that to join the trend toward an implied warranty of habitability would not be a complete and sudden break with the past, but would be the "next step in the law which has been developing in the Commonwealth for a number of years." Pennsylvania courts have held that a tenant's obligation to pay rent was mutually dependent on express covenants of a landlord to repair and that a material breach of the landlord's covenant to repair relieved a tenant from his obligation to pay rent. *McDanel v. Mack Realty Company*. In *Reitmeyer v. Sprecher*, supra, recognizing the contractual nature of modern leasing and the severe housing shortage resulting in unequal bargaining power, this Court adopted 357 of the Restatement (Second) of Torts and imposed liability on a landlord who had breached a covenant to repair a dangerous condition on the premises, which breach resulted in injury to the tenant.

Given the foregoing considerations and authority, we affirm the Superior Court's holding that a lease is in the nature of a contract and is to be controlled by principles of contract law. The covenants and warranties in the lease are mutually dependent; the tenant's obligation to pay rent and the landlord's obligation imposed by the implied warranty of habitability to provide and maintain habitable premises are, therefore, dependent and a material breach of one of these obligations will relieve the obligation of the other so long as the breach continues.

II. Adoption of Implied Warranty of Habitability: A Proper Judicial Function

Appellant does not argue that an implied warranty of habitability does not comport with current understanding of the landlord–tenant relationship. In light of the overwhelming authority in favor of the warrant, he would be hard pressed to do so. Rather, the thrust of appellant's argument is that the establishment of an implied warranty of habitability is the setting of social policy, which is a function of the legislature. Specifically, appellant maintains that, because the legislature has acted in the field via the Rent Withholding Act, Act of January 24, 1966, P.L. 1534, as amended, 35 P.S. 1700-1 (1977), the courts are prohibited from further development of common law solutions to landlord–tenant/habitability problems. We cannot accept this position.

The Rent Withholding Act (hereinafter the Act) provides: "Notwithstanding any other provision of law, or of any agreement, whether oral or in writing, whenever the Department of Licenses and Inspections of any city of the first class, or the Department of Public Safety of any city of the second class, second class A, or third class as the case may be, or any Public Health Department of any such city, or of the county in which such city is located, certifies a dwelling as unfit for human habitation, the duty of any tenant of such dwelling to pay, and the right of the landlord to collect rent shall be suspended without affecting any other terms or conditions of the landlord–tenant relationship, until the dwelling is certified as fit for human habitation or until the tenancy is terminated for any reason other than nonpayment of rent. During any period when the duty to pay rent is suspended, and the tenant continues to occupy the dwelling, the rent withheld shall be deposited by the tenant in an escrow account in a bank or trust company approved by the city or county as the case may be and shall be paid to the landlord when the dwelling is certified as fit for human habitation at any time within six months from the date on which the dwelling was certified as unfit for human habitation. If, at the end of six months after the certification of a dwelling as unfit for human habitation, such dwelling has not been certified as fit for human habitation, any moneys deposited in escrow on account of continued occupancy shall be payable to the depositor, except that any funds deposited in escrow may be used, for the purpose of making such dwelling fit for human habitation and for the payment of utility services for which the landlord is obligated but which he refuses or is unable to pay. No tenant shall be evicted for any reason whatsoever while rent is deposited in escrow."

Initially we note the Act is applicable only to cities of the first three classes and so is, by its terms, not applicable to the case at bar. Nevertheless, we must consider appellant's contention that, by acting *at all*, the legislature has precluded the judiciary from common law development in the landlord–tenant/habitability area.

The Act does not purport to be the exclusive tenant remedy for unsavory housing, nor does it attempt to replace or alter certain limited and already existing tenant remedies such as constructive eviction. Neither can mere enactment of the Rent Withholding Act signal a legislative intent to remove from the courts the authority to fashion new remedies where appropriate in the landlord–tenant field.

Caveat emptor was a creature of the common law. Courts have a duty "to reappraise old doctrines in the light of the facts and values of contemporary life—particularly old common law doctrines which the courts themselves have created and developed." *Favins v. First National Realty Corp.*, quoted in *Albert M. Greenfield & Co., Inc. v. Kolea*. And when a rule has been duly tested by experience and found inconsistent with the sense of justice or the social welfare there should be little hesitation in "frank avowal and full abandonment." Cardozo, *The Nature of the Judicial Process,* cited in *Grif-fith v. United Airlines, Inc.* We have followed these principles recently in several decisions which are clearly founded on a realization of, and adaption of the law to correspond to, changing social policy. *Ayala v. Philadelphia Board of Education* (governmental immunity abolished) and *Flagiello v. Pennsylvania Hospital* (immunity for charitable institutions abolished).

In reappraising antiquated laws, it is entirely proper to seek guidance from policies underlying related legislation.

"(C)ourts, in assessing the continued vitality of precedents, rules and doctrines of the past, may give weight to the policies reflected in more recent, widespread legislation, though the statutes do not apply—treating the total body of the statutory law in the manner endorsed long ago by Mr. Justice Stone "as both a declaration and a source of law, and as premise for legal reasoning" (*The Common Law in the United States,* 50 Harv.L.Rev. 4 13 (1976)." Introduction to Restatement (Second) of Property, Landlord and Tenant.

The purpose of the Act is to restore substandard housing to a reasonable level of habitability as swiftly as possible and to deter landlords from allowing their property to deteriorate into a condition unfit for habitation. The adoption of the implied warranty of habitability is consistent with this policy.

Appellate courts of other jurisdictions have considered and rejected the argument that a state's rent withholding act or other statutory remedies precluded judicial adoption of the implied warranty of habitability. In *Boston Housing Authority v. Hemingway,* the Massachusetts Supreme Court reviewed the overwhelming support from other jurisdictions which have judicially sanctioned the implied warranty and stated "All of these decisions are predicated on the implied assumption that remedial legislation designed to promote safe and sanitary housing does not preclude the courts from fashioning new common law rights and remedies to facilitate the policy of safe and sanitary housing embodied in the withholding statutes." We conclude, therefore, that the Rent Withholding Act is not the exclusive tenant remedy for a landlord's failure to maintain the leased premises in a habitable state nor does it preclude judicial development of common law landlord and tenant obligations, rights and remedies. To the contrary, the Act supports the adoption of the implied warranty of habitability.

III. Breach of the Implied Warranty of Habitability

Appellant also asserts that the Superior Court erred by failing to establish definite standards by which habitability can be measured and breach of the warranty ascertained. We disagree—the parameters of the warranty were adequately defined by the Superior Court.

"The implied warranty is designed to insure that a landlord will provide facilities and services vital to the life, health, and safety of the tenant and to the use of the premises for residential purposes. This warranty is applicable both at the beginning of the lease and throughout its duration."

In order to constitute a breach of the warranty the defect must be of a nature and kind, which will prevent the use of the dwelling for its intended purpose to provide premises fit for habitation by its dwellers. At a minimum, this means the premises must be safe and sanitary—of course, there is no obligation on the part of the landlord to supply a perfect or aesthetically pleasing dwelling. "Materiality of the breach is a question of fact to be decided by the trier of fact on a case-by-case basis." Several factors (not exclusive) are listed by the Superior Court as considerations in determining materiality, including the existence of housing code violations and the nature, seriousness, and duration of the defect.

Additionally, we agree with the Superior Court that, to assert a breach of the implied warranty of habitability, a tenant must prove he or she gave notice to the landlord of the defect or condition, that he (the landlord) had a reasonable opportunity to make the necessary repairs, and that he failed to do so.

Appellant would require that a determination breach of the implied warranty be dependent upon proof of violations of the local housing codes. We decline to accept this argument as it would unnecessarily restrict the determination of breach. The Supreme Court of Massachusetts was asked to define their implied warranty of habitability by reference to a housing code of statewide applicability, but declined to do so. In *Boston Housing Authority v. Hemingway,* that court stated:

"The State Sanitary Code minimum standards of fitness for human habitation and relevant local health regulations provide the trial court with the threshold requirements that all housing must meet. Proof of any violation of these regulations would usually constitute compelling evidence that the apartment was not in habitable condition, regardless of whether the evidence was sufficient proof of a constructive eviction under our old case law. However, the protection afforded by the implied warranty or (sic) habitability does not necessarily coincide with the Code's requirements. There may be instances where conditions not covered by the Code regulations render the apartment uninhabitable. Although we have eliminated the defense of constructive eviction in favor of a warranty of habitability defense, a fact situation, which would have demonstrated a constructive eviction, would now be sufficient proof of a material breach of the warranty of habitability, regardless of whether a sanitary code violation existed or not."

Other courts have likewise concluded that the existence of housing code violations is only one of several evidentiary considerations that enter into the materiality of the breach issue. This reasoning is even more persuasive in Pennsylvania where there is no statewide housing code and where many municipalities have not promulgated local housing regulations.

In this case, appellee alleged ten specific defective conditions including a leaky roof, lack of hot water, leaking toilet and pipes, cockroach infestation, and hazardous floors and steps. If proven on remand, these conditions would substantially prevent the use of the premises as a habitable dwelling place and could justify a finding by the trier of fact that a breach of the implied warranty of habitability had occurred.

For the foregoing reasons, we overrule all cases inconsistent with this opinion, affirm the order of the Superior Court with the aforementioned modifications, and remand to the Court of Common Pleas of Franklin County for proceedings consonant with this opinion.

AN INTRODUCTION TO THE CIVIL PROCESS

The decisions that courts announce begin with a single dispute: landlord versus tenant, debtor versus creditor, husband versus wife, professional (lawyer, social worker, doctor, etc.) versus client, employer versus employee—the variations are almost limitless. Having explored above the process by which courts decide these disputes, we turn now to the stages through which they got to court. You are already a little familiar with the stages as a result of analyses of the previous cases. They are, in short, the route the dispute travels on its way to judicial resolution: One party complains, the other responds, they both come to trial and present evidence to support their version of the truth, the judge announces a reasoned decision (that may be appealed) and the decision becomes another rule of law in a long line of legal doctrine.

A full treatment of the civil process is beyond this text's scope. Civil procedure typically occupies a prominent spot in the law school curriculum, but no attempt will be made here to replicate all of that content. There is simply too much for our purposes. Instead, we will excerpt from this tremendous body of knowledge and present the pattern of stages for getting *civil* disputes to court. (The *criminal* process is described briefly in a later chapter.)

The Structure of a Civil Lawsuit

To begin, let's examine a concrete problem:

Black has just departed from Gimbels with her shiny new toaster. She climbs into her Camaro and drives home excitedly, thrilled by the prospect of consuming large quantities of toasted bread, waffles, and pizza. She travels the ten blocks to her apartment, pulls into her driveway, darts from the car (barely stopping to turn off the motor), ascends the stairs, two at a time, to her fourth floor apartment, thrusts open the door, streaks past her roommate and into the kitchen, unwraps the toaster, grabs two slices of bread, and inserts them into the new appliance. While the bread toasts, she walks across the kitchen to get the apple butter she plans to spread lavishly on the toast.

Yummy!

Suddenly overwhelmed by the aroma of burning toast, she whips around to discover what is wrong, only to witness a small fire consuming the new toaster and inching up the kitchen wall. A little internal voice tells her to quickly grab the fire extinguisher mounted on the wall next to the flaming toaster. She reaches to grab it, but the flames have grown and she burns her hand. She manages to hold onto the extinguisher, however, and rapidly reads the operating instructions and douses the flames.

"Is something burning?", her roommate asks from the adjacent room?

She thinks to herself, Just me and my toast, but responds "It's all under control now, but we're back to frozen pizza for breakfast."

What can she do now?

Although state legislation provides for the replacement of defective consumer products, Black wants to sue to recover damages for the personal injury she suffered. She visits an attorney, Ms. Green, to investigate the likelihood of a successful suit against Sunglow, the toaster manufacturer. Attorney Green thinks the case has merit; she believes Black and is satisfied that everything she has told her can be proved at trial. Ms. Green decides to represent Ms. Black. The case will proceed through the following stages.

PRE-TRIAL STAGE

1. Who will Black sue?
   The manufacturer, Sunglow Toasters. The company has its headquarters in the same state as Ms. Black.
2. On what legal theory will Black sue?
   Green, after researching the state law, informs Ms. Black that she may have a *cause of action* based on negligence theory. The facts, as represented by Black, appear to entitle her to a legal remedy.
3. Where will Black bring her suit?
   Because both Black and Sunglow reside in the same state (and there is no federal law issue involved), the suit can be brought in a state court. This court is said to have *jurisdiction* over the parties (Black and Sunglow) and

the subject matter (state laws on manufacturer negligence and product liability). Having jurisdiction over the defendant (Sunglow) is especially important because the court cannot render a valid judgment against a defendant unless it has such jurisdiction.

4. Black files a *complaint.*
   Black, through her attorney, will begin the suit by *serving* a *summons* and *complaint* on the defendant. The complaint is part of the *pleadings,* which are designed to identify the issues in the case and to specify all the facts necessary to state the plaintiff's (Black) cause of action or the defendant's *defense.*

5. Sunglow *answers* the complaint.
   Sunglow receives Black's complaint, and it must *answer* to avoid a *default judgment* (an automatic "win" for Black). The answer can be used in several ways: (1) to deny Black's allegations (e.g. Sunglow claims Black's facts are wrong); (2) to assert an *affirmative defense* (e.g. Sunglow admits the toaster was defective, but states that Black knew about the defect almost immediately after purchasing it, and used it anyway instead of informing the dealer at Gimbels); or (3) to serve a *motion to dismiss* (e.g. Sunglow asserts that Black has no legitimate legal theory on which to obtain a legal remedy. [There are other grounds for this motion, but this example will suffice for our purposes.]).

6. Black's *reply* to Sunglow's answer.
   Black will reply to Sunglow's answer if: (1) it contains a *counter claim;* (2) it asserts an affirmative defense; (3) it contains a motion to dismiss; or (4) the court orders Black to reply.

7. The parties proceed to *discovery.*
   Discovery allows each side to obtain relevant information about the litigation. The activity saves time and costs and can narrow the precise issues on which both sides disagree. Discovery devices include, for example, written *interrogatories, depositions,* or physical or mental examinations of persons.

8. The parties attempt to settle before trial.
   Both sides determine whether it is in their interest to settle the dispute without trial. If they can't agree, they proceed to trial.

THE TRIAL STAGE

9. The parties select a jury.
   Not all cases are jury cases. When one arises, the parties, through *voir dire,* select the members.

10. The parties present their opening arguments.
    Both sides state the facts they intend to prove at trial. The plaintiff presents first.

11. The parties present their cases.
    The plaintiff begins by introducing appropriate evidence and examining

witnesses. *Direct examination* involves questioning one's own witnesses; *cross-examination,* the other side's.
12. Motions to dismiss or for *directed verdict.*
    Following the plaintiff's presentation, the defendant may request a *motion to dismiss* or for a *directed verdict.* Both imply that the plaintiff has failed to prove her facts. The plaintiff, too, may make such motions after the defendant's presentation. If all motions are denied, both sides move to the next step.
13. Both sides present their closing arguments to the jury.
14. *Charge to the jury.*
    The *charge to the jury* is the judge's instructions on the applicable law. Often both sides will submit charges they want the judge to use, and (s)he can decide whether to use them. The jury uses the judge's instructions in their deliberations.
15. *Verdict* of the jury.
    The jury's verdict is the result of its deliberations. It is typically a *general verdict,* which announces the verdict on all issues.
16. The court enters its *judgment* on the case.
    The trial court's *judgment* is the final statement on the dispute. It states the rights and responsibilities for each. (It may be a written opinion.)

APPEALS STAGE

17. Filing for *appeal,* submission of accompanying *briefs,* and oral argument.
    The losing party may notify the court of its intention to seek a review of the decision by a higher tribunal. The party bringing the *appeal* (the *appellant*) files a *brief* (an argument on the lower court's error in the interpretation of the law) with the higher court. The party against whom the appeal is brought (the *appellee*) will file a reply brief. Both sides then make their oral argument to the appellate court and then await its decision.
18. Decision of appellate court.

3 The Legislative Process

LEGISLATIVE AUTHORITY, STRUCTURE AND FUNCTION

State and federal legislatures have similar structures. Both have two chambers (Nebraska, with only one chamber, is the exception among the states), which provide for different tenures (e.g. the U.S. Senate members are elected for six-year terms; House members, for two years). There are currently 100 members of the U.S. Senate and 435 members of the U.S. House of Representatives. The size for each state chamber varies. Both exercise their law-making authority as stated in the state or federal constitution. For example, Article One of the U.S. Constitution defines the scope of Congressional law-making authority: "All legislative Powers herein granted shall be vested in a congress of the United States, which shall consist of a Senate and House of Representatives. . . . [It] shall make all Laws which shall be necessary and proper for carrying into Execution [their enumerated] Powers, and all other Powers vested by this Constitution in the government of the United States, or in any Department or Officer thereof" (U.S. Constitution, Article I).

The authority to act, however, does not speak to the issue of competency—Can an institution do well what is has the exclusive power to do? This question is important because legislatures are increasingly called on to enact public policy that incorporates our full range of social values. We tend to turn to them to address numerous social problems, but in so doing we threaten to strain their competency. The prospect is both positive and negative. On the one hand, legislatures are perceived as the rule-making mechanism closest to the people and, consequently, express the vagaries of public opinion (Hurst, 1982). (Consider, for example, the diversity among state legislatures when all attempt to address identical social problems.) On the other hand, legislatures are also forums for compromise (Dworkin, 1979; Nunez, 1972). The rules that emerge typically reflect the negotiations among diverse and competing interests. Thus, one of the most attractive legislative features (representation of public interests) can produce two seemingly incompatible tendencies: receptivity to evolutionary social norms and a narrowing of that receptivity caused by the need to reach a consensus on competing normative views.

Finally, the legislative function also incorporates a concern for implementation of legislative goals (Baum, 1980; Sabatier & Mazmanian, 1980). Legislatures must rely heavily on administrative agencies for policy implementation, so the connection between legislative intention and implementation can not be overstated.

THE DESIGN OF LEGISLATION

Some Preliminary Considerations

Our examination of the law-making process will begin with several questions that defy easy answers: How do problems get to government? What happens once they get there? What difference does it make? (Jones, 1980) It is difficult to resist the temptation to advance several straightforward answers. But once we assess the questions in light of our experiences (actual or in terms of what we read in newspapers), their complexity quickly surfaces. The focus shifts then from the search for a simple response to a recognition that complicated questions require similarly complicated responses. Put another way, there are certain "initial realities", according to Jones (1977), that should inform our understanding of lawmaking. They include:

1. Events in society are interpreted in different ways by different people at different times.
2. Many problems may result from the same event.
3. People have varying degrees of access to the policy process in government.
4. Not all public problems are acted on in government.

5. Many private problems are acted on in government.
6. Many private problems are acted on in government as though they were public problems.
7. Most problems aren't solved by government though they are acted on there.
8. "Policy makers are not faced with a *given* problem."
9. Most decision making is based on little information and poor communication.
10. Programs often reflect an attainable consensus rather than a substantive conviction.
11. Problems and demands are constantly being defined and re-defined in the policy process.
12. Policy makers sometimes define problems for people who have not defined problems for themselves.
13. Many programs are developed and implemented without the problem ever having been clearly defined.
14. Most people do not maintain interest in other people's problems.
15. Most people do not prefer large policy change.
16. Most people cannot identify a public policy.
17. All policy systems have a bias.
18. No ideal policy exists apart from the preferences of the architect of that system.
19. Most decision making is incremental in nature (Jones, 1977; p. 8)

Although other factors interact with these "initial realities" to influence law making, the above are among the most prominent. Collectively, they shed light on some of the conditions that shape the law-making process and on the process by which government receives and responds to problems.

How to Read a Statute or Bill: Before beginning our examination of the stages of the law-making process, we will turn our attention to the components and structure of a statute or bill. You will find several features in almost every bill or statute, whether state or federal. These elements can be seen in figures 3.1 and 3.2 below.

- *Identifying designation:* House or Senate Bill number or Public Law number. Both state and federal bills or statutes have similar designations.

- *Title:* the legislation's subject—"A Bill to . . ."; "An Act to . . ."
- *Enacting clause:* a statement that the legislature adopts as law the language that follows this clause—"Be it enacted by . . . that . . ." Essentially, that which follows this clause is the law the legislature wishes to enact.
- *Purpose or findings:* the facts and issues that comprise the reason for the legislation; the "evil" the legislation seeks to address. Because it follows the "enacting clause", the purpose is part of the legislation and is frequently codified as such.
- *Definitions:* terms that have special meanings within the statute.
- *Purview:* the body of the law; it contains the substantive provisions, the available remedies under, and provisions for administrative implementation or enforcement.

How can one make sense of these elements? The analytical process is similar to the one described for the analysis of judicial opinions. The component parts must be understood to really grasp the whole document. Naturally, the actual text of the legislation is the logical place to begin the analysis. But the text (either by design or as a result of compromise among legislative members) is not always transparent. How then can one uncover the legislature's design? While no perfect formula exists for statutory analysis, Statsky (1984) offers the following guidelines.

Statutory text is unclear: the ambiguity is sometimes by design; but more often than not it is due to poor draftsmanship or the limitations of language. The search for meaning will *require* interpretation.

Legislative intent will always be beyond our grasp: under the best circumstances intent will be elusive. The documents that comprise the legislative trial can put "intent" within our reach, but on the more complicated issues, it can easily elude our grasp.

Statutes should be read one word at a time: Speed reading is out. Proceed through them line by line, attending to each punctuation mark and qualification.

"Brief" each statute: "Briefing" techniques are as relevant here as in judicial opinions. The goal is the same: To better grasp the whole by analyzing its component parts. The briefing should allow you to know: the citation, the parties to whom the statute is addressed, the references to related legislation, the conditions that make the statute operative, the conduct explicitly included or excluded, the mandatory or discretionary provisions, the penalties, and the general purpose of the statute. [pp. 43–62]

Act 1984-132   LAWS OF PENNSYLVANIA

No. 1984-132

AN ACT

HB 1551

Prohibiting persons from refusing to provide property or services to individuals who do not possess credit cards; providing for enforcement of the act; providing remedies; and imposing civil penalties.

The General Assembly of the Commonwealth of Pennsylvania hereby enacts as follows:

Section 1. Short title.
This act shall be known and may be cited as the Cash Consumer Protection Act.

Section 2. Definitions.
The following words and phrases when used in this act shall have the meanings given to them in this section unless the context clearly indicates otherwise:
"Credit card." A device or instrument which entitles the holder to obtain money, goods, services or anything of value on credit.
"Person." An individual, corporation, trust, partnership, limited partnership, incorporated or unincorporated association or other entity.

Section 3. Refusal to provide property prohibited.
It shall be unlawful for any person to refuse to rent or sell property or services to any individual for the reason that the individual does not possess a credit card. Nothing in this section requires the acceptance of any particular form of payment.

Section 4. Reasonable security authorized; excessive security prohibited.
(a) Demand for security.—A person may, prior to providing property or services to an individual who does not possess a credit card, demand and receive reasonable security from the individual to secure payment for the property or services requested. Reasonable security may take the form of a payment in cash on account reasonably related to the value of the property or services to be provided or any other appropriate assurance.
(b) Excessive security prohibited.—Demanding or receiving an unreasonable or excessive amount of security is unlawful.

Section 5. Injunctive relief.
Whenever the Attorney General or a district attorney has reason to believe that any person is violating or is about to violate section 3 or 4 and that proceedings would be in the public interest, the Attorney General • • •

Section 10. Effective date.
This act shall take effect in 60 days.

APPROVED—The 6th day of July, A. D. 1984.

DICK THORNBURGH

Act Number in
Pennsylvania
Legislature

Chamber of Origin and
Number for Original Bill
(useful to begin search for
legislature history)

Title

Short Title

Definitions

Substantive Provisions
of the Act

Effective Date

Date Bill was
Signed into Law by
Governor Thornburgh

Volume and Page Where Act can be Found in U.S. Statutes-at-Large

Public Law 98-377
98th Congress

An Act

To provide assistance to improve elementary, secondary, and postsecondary education in mathematics and science; to provide a national policy for engineering, technical, and scientific personnel; to provide cost sharing by the private sector in training such personnel; to encourage creation of new engineering, technical, and scientific jobs; and for other purposes.

Aug. 11, 1984
[H.R. 1310]

Session of Congress and the 377th Law Enacted in that Session

Be it enacted by the Senate and House of Representatives of the United States of America in Congress assembled, That this Act may be cited as the "Education for Economic Security Act".

Title

Education for Económic Security Act.
20 USC 3901 note.

Marginal Notes Refer to United States Code (title and section)

STATEMENT OF PURPOSE

SEC. 2. It is the purpose of this Act to improve the quality of mathematics and science teaching and instruction in the United States.

20 USC 3901.

Purpose of the Act

DEFINITIONS

SEC. 3. For the purpose of this Act—
(1) The term "area vocational education school" has the same meaning given that term under section 195(2) of the Vocational Education Act of 1965.
(2) The term "Director" means the Director of the National Science Foundation.
(3) The term "elementary school" has the same meaning given that term under section 198(a)(7) of the Elementary and Secondary Education Act of 1965.
(4) The term "Governor" means the chief executive of a State.
(5) The term "Foundation" means the National Science Foundation.
(6) The term "institution of higher education" has the same meaning given that term by section 1201(a) of the Higher Education Act of 1965.
(7) The term "local educational agency" has the same meaning given that term under section 198(a)(10) of the Elementary and Secondary Education Act of 1965.
(8) The term "secondary school" has the same meaning given that term under section 198(a)(7) of the Elementary and Secondary Education Act of 1965.
(9) The term "Secretary" means the Secretary of Education.
(10) The term "State" means each of the several States, the District of Columbia, the Commonwealth of Puerto Rico, Guam, American Samoa, the Virgin Islands, the Trust Territory of the Pacific Islands, and the Northern Mariana Islands.
(11) The term "State agency for higher education" means the State board of higher education or other agency or officer primarily responsible for the State supervision of higher education, or, if there is no such officer or agency, an officer or agency designated for the purpose of this title by the Governor or by State law.

20 USC 3902.

20 USC 2461.

Definitions

20 USC 2854.

20 USC 1141.

20 USC 2854.

LEGISLATIVE HISTORY—H.R. 1310 (S. 1285):

HOUSE REPORTS No. 98-6, Pt. 1 (Comm. on Education and Labor) and Pt. 2 (Comm. on Science and Technology).
SENATE REPORT: No. 98-151 accompanying S. 1285 (Comm. on Labor and Human Resources).
CONGRESSIONAL RECORD:
  Vol. 129 (1983): Mar. 2, considered and passed House.
  Vol. 130 (1984): June 6, 26, S. 1285 considered in Senate.
             June 27, considered and passed Senate, amended, in lieu of S. 1285.
             July 25, House concurred in Senate amendment.
WEEKLY COMPILATION OF PRESIDENTIAL DOCUMENTS, Vol. 20, No. 33 (1984): Aug. 11, Presidential statement.

The Legislative History for the Act.

FIGURE 3.2 Elements of a statute

The above "how-to" scheme is straightforward and will yield valuable information about the statute or bill. The surface picture, however, masks the underlying forces that account for the final language. One can read the "purpose and findings" section—but what can it really tell us about intentions? One may have similar reservations about the "definitions" section, which tries to anticipate all the possible cases to which the act's substantive provisions will apply, but even this attempt can fall short. Thus, to "read" a statute or bill is to appreciate its explicit language *and* the history of debates (over wording, over purposes, over scope, etc.) that preceded the final language. In sum, *reading* a statute or bill can involve *interpreting* it.

STAGES IN THE LAW-MAKING PROCESS: ENACTING SUBSTANTIVE LEGISLATION

The law-making process unfolds in several stages. We will examine these stages below by following the le₅slative trial of a particularly controversial Pennsylvania bill—Senate Bill 742 (1981). The examination depicts the state law-making process, which is comparable to the federal process. Other state legislatures go through similar stages.

Stage One: Introduction of the Bill

The subject matter (abortion) of Senate Bill 742 had surfaced in three earlier House bills: HB 1725 (An act regulating abortions); HB 1727 (An act amending Title 42 [Judiciary and Procedure] of the Pennsylvania Consolidated Statutes, further providing for death actions and actions for wrongful birth and wrongful life); and HB 1728 (An act amending The Administrative Code of 1929, approved April 9, 1929 [P.L. 177, No. 175], further providing for powers and duties of the Advisory Health Board). Each was referred to the House Health and Welfare Committee, from which they failed to emerge. Senate Bill 742 was introduced on April 28, 1981 as:

An Act amending Title 18 (Crimes and Offenses) of the Pennsylvania Consolidated Statutes, regulating abortions and further providing that certain competition between individuals and the promotion of such competition be unlawful, and providing penalties. More below, in Echenbarger's account, on the apparently peculiar content of the bill.

Stage Two: Referral to a Committee of the Chamber of Origin

The bill was referred to the Senate Judiciary Committee. It originated in the senate, so it was considered there first. This is also the point at which the committee chairperson consults with the bill sponsor(s) to determine the best time for committee hearings, but he/she retains the ultimate decision. These hearings provide an opportunity for the public to testify about the proposed bill. Members of the public register as "witnesses" (either as opponents or proponents). The witnesses can be questioned by the Committee members. This is also the stage at which amendments to the proposed bill can be made.

Stage Three: The Committee Reports to its Full Chamber

Senate Bill 742 was reported out of the Judiciary Committee, which presented it to the full senate for consideration. A bill may go through several "readings" or considerations before it is voted on by the full chamber. During these considerations, the bill may be amended from the floor. Senate Bill 742 went through three considerations, which produced an amended version that the full senate ultimately passed by a 44 to 4 vote. It was now ready to be considered by the other chamber, the House.

Stage Four: Referral to Appropriate Committee in Other Chamber

A bill becomes law only after it has been passed by both chambers of the legislature. (Nebraska is an exception because it only has one chamber.) A bill passed in one chamber goes on to be introduced in the second, which puts it through the same process. Senate Bill 742 was referred to the House of Representative's Judiciary Committee, which discussed it and reported it to the full House.

Stage Five: Committee Reports to the Full Chamber

Senate Bill 742 was reported to the House as committed. Essentially, the House Judiciary Committee made no changes in the bill they received from the Senate.

Stage Six: Consideration and Debate by the Chamber

A bill reported out of committee must be considered by the full chamber, which will debate it and, perhaps, amend it before voting

on it. Senate Bill 742 was first considered, then tabled and subsequently removed, and then reconsidered a second time and
amended.

The Bill, together with its amendments was again tabled, but was
subsequently resurrected for a third consideration. This third consideration resulted in further amendments, which the House ultimately accepted, following which the bill was passed by a 132 to 61
vote.

Stage Seven: Referral of Bill Back to Chamber of Origin

If a bill passes in the second chamber, but in an amended version,
then the chamber of origin must concur in those changes. If there is
no concurrence, then a conference committee (composed of members
from each chamber) will be appointed to put the bill in a mutually
acceptable form. The bill will die if the conference committee fails to
reach agreement. Senate Bill 742, as amended, was sent back to the
Senate, which concurred in the House amendments by a 29 to 21
vote.

Stage Eight: Bill Signed by Each Chamber

The Senate signed the bill on December 15, 1981; the House, on December 16th.

Stage Nine: Referral to the Governor

The signed bill was sent to the Governor. If he failed to sign it within
ten days, it would automatically take effect. He could also veto it
within the specified time. Three days before the deadline, the governor vetoed Senate Bill 742, which was returned to the Senate along
with the governor's veto message and tabled. The governor's veto
message on the bill follows:

> To the Honorable, the Senate of the Commonwealth of Pennsylvania:
> I have before me for action Senate Bill 742, Printer's No. 1535, which
> would establish a number of detailed procedures and requirements with
> respect to the performance of medical abortions. What this bill would do is
> erect a series of hurdles, which would have to be cleared by a pregnant
> woman interested in obtaining an abortion. . . . The U.S. Supreme Court
> has recognized the interest of a state in reasonably regulating abortion in
> ways related to maternal health and well-being, and for the purpose of

protecting the "potentiality of human life." I believe that many provisions of the bill, as I have indicated, are consistent with those interests and are reasonable, particularly with regard to those women who, because of their circumstances, would benefit from the guidance and protection afforded by them.

On the other hand, I am concerned that other provisions, and to some extent, the overall tone and tenor of the bill, would have the effect of imposing an undue and, in some cases, unconstitutional burden upon even informed, mature adults intent upon obtaining an abortion under circumstances in which the U.S. Supreme Court has determined they are entitled to do so. . . . Likewise, I am concerned that some of the detailed, complex and burdensome requirements of the bill, accompanied as they are by severe criminal sanctions, could well foster an atmosphere in which many physicians would be deterred from providing the kind of abortion-related medical services to which the U.S. Supreme Court has held their patients are constitutionally entitled. This could well disrupt the traditional doctor–patient relationship and impinge upon the right of physicians to practice. Of even greater concern is the potential for more experienced and conscientious physicians to refrain from involvement in even medically necessary abortions, and to abandon the field to marginal practitioners. It could even lead to a resurgence of "back alley" abortions, which no thoughtful person would wish to happen. . . .

Accordingly, and after extensive consideration and deliberation, I am returning this bill without my signature. . . .

The above stages represent the essential components of the law-making process. But this skeletal description merely introduces the context within which the legislature tried to codify a troublesome moral and social problem. William Echenbarger's (1982) account below of how Senate Bill 742 almost became law puts flesh on the skeletal description.

The Life and Death of Senate Bill 742*

The Pennsylvania Abortion Control Bill of 1981 actually got started inside the Cambria County War Memorial arena in Johnstown, Pa., on a Saturday night last March.

This aging hockey rink had heretofore been best known as the location for the movie Slapshot, but on this particular night a boxing ring was set up over the ice for the First Annual Central Pennsylvania Toughman Contest. Dangling a $1,000 first prize, promoters had lured two dozen local men to slug it out.

*From William Echenbarger, "The Life and Death of Senate Bill 742". *The Philadelphia Inquirer,* 306 (31) pp. 16–19, 23–27. © 1982 The Philadelphia Inquirer, Phil., PA. Reprinted by permission of The Philadelphia Inquirer, Jan. 31, 1982.

Ronald Miller, 23, an ex-Marine and unemployed construction worker, was one of the contestants, and at 169 pounds he was also probably the lightest. (The posted weight range was 175 to 400 pounds.) Nevertheless, he knocked out his first opponent. He also won his second bout by a knockout, but relentless pain seared his abdomen at the end of it, and Miller himself was knocked out in his third fight. Blood gushed from his mouth and nose as he left the ring and he began vomiting in the locker room. He was rushed to the hospital, but at 9:15 Sunday morning Miller died from a brain hemorrhage.

In the ensuing outrage, state Sen. Mark Singel, a Democrat from Johnstown, introduced legislation on April 28 that would ban "toughman" promotions in Pennsylvania. Since it was the 742d bill offered in the Senate during the 1981–82 session, it was designated Senate Bill 742. And since the measure would amend the state's criminal code, it was referred to the Senate Judiciary Committee, which approved it. On July 1 the Senate passed it by a vote of 44–4—though not before one of the four dissenters, Sen. Milton Street of Philadelphia, made a case for freedom of choice: "I don't think we should be in the business of regulating individuals."

That was the first time this point about how far the state should go in regulating individuals was made in connection with Senate Bill 742, but it would not be the last. That's because this seemingly simple nine-paragraph bill would ultimately have added onto it, as an amendment, the 31-page abortion control act.

It may not seem, at first, that boxing and abortion have much to do with each other, and in fact this circumstance did bother some of the legislators. But stranger things than that took place during the eight tumultuous days last month [December, 1981] when the Pennsylvania General Assembly—a collection of insurance brokers, farmers, lawyers, teachers and laborers—grappled with the question of when life begins. With a deluge of words and an occasional droplet of sense, the lawmakers soared to the imponderable and dived to the unfathomable. Throughout, the process that repelled Bismarck a century ago was never more manifest.

A careful inspection of what happened is instructive not only because it shows how a political body sought to deal (or to avoid dealing, as the case often was) with the most complex ethical and scientific dilemma of our time. For one thing, since the bill was ultimately vetoed by Gov. Thornburgh, the issue will be coming up again this year.

For another, this was the first test in the nation for legislation that had been specially prepared with the help of a Chicago organization called Americans United for Life, a sort of anti-abortion think tank. A team of lawyers there had set out to design a bill that would be as restrictive as possible, yet would still conform with court decisions holding that a woman, under most circumstances, has a constitutional right to have an abortion if she so desires.

The lengthy legislation doesn't lend itself easily to summarizing, but among other things it would require a 24-hour "cooling off" period for women seeking abortions; allow any individual to go into court for an injunction against a woman seeking an abortion; require minors to have the consent of both parents for an abortion; define a fertilized egg as a human being; prohibit the use of public funds and public hospitals for most abortions; and prohibit private insurers from including abortion coverage in their standard policies. Most of the regulatory burden would fall upon doctors, who would risk seven-year jail terms and $15,000 fines for violations.

Our story begins about 8 a.m. on Dec. 8, [1981] the day the Toughman Bill is scheduled to come up for a final vote on the House floor. A car carrying two men is crossing the Taylor Bridge over the Susquehanna River, whose sparkling shallowness at this point in its flow toward the Chesapeake has seemed symbolic, to some, of much that goes on in the state's capital. Above the water, embryonic winter is scheming with autumn to produce squally winds, and the driver grips the steering wheel tightly and squints into the orange morning sun.

Harrisburg, when seen from the west, has a skyline of sorts. Progress has been through the city several times, leaving a trail of multistory parking garages and vacant lots. The resulting serrated effect brings to mind a mouth deformed by missing teeth. But the dominant feature is the Capitol dome, which juts up into the sky like a nurturing breast, and it is toward the dome that the two men are heading.

Both are lawyers in their mid-30s, and each is a member of the state House of Representatives. Both are Republicans. And they share a passionate belief: Abortion is murder. They have acted on this conviction by cosponsoring the abortion control legislation in Pennsylvania, so that, among its other names, it is known as the Freind–Cunningham Bill. But beyond these affinities, the two men are strikingly different in appearance, background and temperament.

Rep. Gregg Cunningham, the driver, is from State College in north-central Pennsylvania. He is single and a Baptist. He is tan, bushy-browed, and when he smiles there are teeth that bite an apple every day. He could pass for television's version of an FBI agent. His passenger is Rep. Stephen Freind (pronounced "friend") from Havertown. He is Catholic, married, and has five young children. Freind is pale, about six inches shorter than Cunningham, and fidgety. Freind actually was an FBI agent, back during the same period when Cunningham was flying combat missions over Vietnam.

They differ, too, in personal style. Cunningham emits a reserved, Cromwellian air, appearing to some as though he is waiting for a vacancy to open up in the Holy Trinity. Freind, in contrast, is passionate, likeable—as spontaneous and candid as a hiccup.

They have been eagerly awaiting this day for months. To be more precise, what they have been waiting for is the arrival on the floor of the House of a bill—any bill—that amends Pennsylvania's criminal code.

The reason for this is that the abortion legislation they are sponsoring also involves amending the criminal code, and that connection, they believe, will be sufficient to allow the two pieces of legislation to be linked by the amendment process. (Their efforts to move their legislation in the usual manner through the committees of the House had been thwarted when the bill was defeated in the Public Welfare Committee in October.)

Because it is a special day, both men have forsaken cherished habits. For the first time in several years, Freind has spent a night away from home, sleeping on the couch in Cunningham's apartment in suburban Harrisburg. Cunningham has not run his customary five miles this morning. It also happens that this day is the Feast of the Immaculate Conception. Freind and Cunningham stop at St. Patrick's Cathedral, a half-block from the Capitol, to pray for success.

About the same time, a solitary figure is walking along Third Street toward the Capitol, clutching the lapels of his overcoat to keep out the wind. The sunlight is warming, but it mocks his mood. He knows what Freind and Cunningham will seek to do—it has not been exactly a secret—and it bothers him.

Rep. Joseph Hoeffel, 31, is a Democrat from the Republican stronghold of Montgomery County—a posture that has required him to cast his votes carefully. A non-churchgoer, Hoeffel is thinking rather than praying, and his emotions are mixed. The idea of abortion disturbs him. He is the father of a 2-year-old daughter, and his wife is due to give birth in June. He believes that, in an abortion, whatever is being aborted is some sort of life. But he's not sure just what kind, and for this reason he believes that the final decision ought to rest with the individual rather than the state. Consequently, he has prepared a substitute amendment that would convert the Freind–Cunningham bill into a very mild regulatory act with light penalties.

Hoeffel, who got his degree in English from Boston University and had been in hospital administration before becoming a legislator, is not a lawyer. But he can read, and he has spent much of the summer reading court decisions on abortion. He feels he is well prepared to debate. He wonders, though, if his colleagues are prepared to listen. Hoeffel will meet this morning in his office with a number of other legislators who oppose the Freind–Cunningham legislation, but he already knows from previous conversations that it will be difficult to get any sense of unity on tactics.

This is partly because of a feeling that defeat is inevitable. The ad hoc group formed to oppose the Freind–Cunningham bill, called Pennsylvanians for the Right to a Private Life, has been making contacts with individual legislators during the last several weeks, but they know they are not matching the volume of calls and letters that are coming in in favor of the bill. Morgan Plant, the coordinator for the group, complains, "We don't have priests thundering from the pulpit every Sunday, and we don't have churches where people can be handed letters to sign."

But the problem is more complexed than that. The pro-choice people simply cannot match the passion of the anti-abortionists, who sincerely believe they are seeking to stop the murder of babies. Things look murkier from the other side. While some authorities contend that the total effect of the bill would be to restrict drastically the availability of abortions in the state, the bill's provisions, considered one at a time, don't seem all that awful. After all, this isn't a bill to ban abortions; it is simply to eliminate abuses. Who wanted to be in favor of abuses?

As Hoeffel enters the Capitol and heads for the final strategy meeting, faraway bells are bonging out Christmas carols.

After the Mass at St. Patrick's, Freind and Cunningham arrive at the Capitol and make quick stops at their own small legislative offices. Freind's office on the third floor of the Capitol is disarrayed. A Pisa of old newspapers threatens to topple a half-cup of last week's coffee, and a chair for visitors is occupied this morning by a box filled with file folders. Cunningham's office also brims, but everything is neat. On his desk there are perhaps 30 detailed models of military jet aircraft precisely lined up on plastic stands.

Both offices are small, and for months legislators who call themselves "pro-life" have been meeting in the more commodious office of Rep. Martin P. Mullen (D., Philadelphia), a senior legislator who, part in derision, part in affection, is known as "St. Martin." During his 26 years as a legislator, Mullen has crusaded against birth control, pornography, divorce and abortion. Again this morning the group is gathered there.

About a dozen legislators, including two Philadelphia Republicans— Frances Weston and Joseph Rocks—are present, as are a priest, a minister and several antiabortion activists. There is little strategy to discuss. Like Ms. Plant's operatives, lobbying groups backing the Freind-Cunningham bill have been canvassing the legislators. They know that if they can force the House to a simple vote on the legislation, it will pass. They also anticipate most of the stratagems and procedural moves that opponents can make to avoid such a vote, and believe these can be thwarted.

It will turn out that there is one possible method of assault that they have not anticipated, but for the moment Freind is buoyed and confident. "I felt just like I did back at St. Lawrence's Grade School in Upper Darby just before the kickoff," he said later. "I felt that the education I received there, the discipline and the faith, had prepared me for this. I never felt closer to the Church."

At the conclusion of the meeting the group kneels on the orange carpet and recites prayers together. The final prayer, offered by Freind, is the same one Notre Dame football teams use, "Our Lady of Victory, pray for us."

The principal work place of the 193 men and 10 women in the Pennsylvania House of Representatives is surrounded by French marble that was taken from quarries in the Pyrenees mountains 75 years ago. The quarries were owned by an order of French monks, who, for some reason lost to history, donated the marble, and were not cut in on the extensive graft connected with construction of the building.

Deep red carpet covers the entire floor of the House, which slopes up toward the rear. The desks are arranged in neat concentric arcs from front to rear, and there is a maroon swivel chair in front of each desk. On each is a tiny wired box with three buttons. There is a green button on the left (for a yes vote), a black button in the middle (to summon a page), and a red button on the right (for a no vote).

High up on each side wall are big boards listing the names of each member, Alden to Zwikl; Republicans on top, Democrats below; with a red light and a green light beside each name to indicate how the legislator voted. On most occasions, when the vote is along party lines, the outcome is a foregone conclusion. But on the tricky skirmishes involving the abortion bill the legislators will be peering up at the board after each vote, waiting to see the result.

As members drift into the chamber today there is the hyperkinetic conviviality of a Shriners convention, which gives way, as always, to the first order of business: prayer. Then, after the clerk reads a series of routine transactions in a murmurous monotone, House Speaker Matthew J. Ryan, seated atop an alter-like dais in the front of the chamber, calls up House Bill 742.

Freind and Cunningham are standing by a microphone near the rear of the chamber on the Republican side, to the Speaker's right, but the floor is first given to Rep. Russell Letterman (D., Centre). Letterman, a barber in private life, mildly surprises everyone by offering an amendment to the Toughman Bill that actually has to do with boxing. It is quickly approved.

Now, at last, Ryan initiates the customary responsive litany with Freind.

RYAN: The chair recognizes the gentlemen from Delaware, Mr.
            Freind. For what purpose does the gentleman rise?
FREIND: Mr. Speaker, I offer an amendment to Senate Bill 742.

Freind, vested but unjacketed, hands his amendment to a page. Ryan designates the proposal Amendment A4911, and then recognizes Rep. Hardy Williams (D., Philadelphia), who challenges the amendment on the ground that it is not germane to the original bill. Abortion, he suggests, has nothing to do with boxing. Freind responds that the amendment is germane because it, like the original bill, would add new sections to the Pennsylvania Criminal Code. Ryan at this point interrupts the discussion to welcome visitors to the House gallery. "The chair is pleased to welcome to the House a group of executives from the Jones & Laughlin Steel Co." Members applaud.

Many opponents of the Freind–Cunningham proposal feel that the germaneness issue, rather than the Hoeffel amendment, is their best bet to block the bill. There is actually a rule in the House that any amendment to a bill must have something to do with the bill it is being attached to. The rule is designed to prevent legislators from doing just what Freind and Cunningham are doing—circumventing the committee system.

But over the years, the House interpretation of germaneness has been steadily expanded by those bent on circumventing committees. Pennsylvania's current no-fault automobile insurance law, for instance, began in the House as an amendment to a bill requiring auto insurers to notify policyholders of cancellations. Nonetheless, a vote on germaneness often provides legislators with a way to duck issues—as in this case, where those who fear voter repercussion for opposing the abortion measure directly can stop it by casting a vote that is intended not to kill the abortion bill, but rather to preserve the committee system.

Williams continues to wave the House rule book and demand a roll call on the germaneness issue. (Behind him, Rep. Charles Laughlin, a Beaver County Democrat, appears to be asleep, snoring softly through slightly parted lips.) Ryan obliges and calls for the vote. There are staccato clicks of members pushing buttons. Green and red lights flash on the tote boards. By a vote of 114 to 81, the House determines that the amendment is germane.

Next Rep. John S. Davies (R., Berks) will ask for a vote on whether or not the amendment meets the requirement of the state constitution that "no bill shall be altered or amended on its passage through either house as to change its original purpose." But this is something of a charade. The opponents of the Freind–Cunningham bill have already seen that they do not have the votes to win this kind of procedural maneuver. Nonetheless, Davies, Williams and Freind debate the constitutional issue for about half an hour, during which time members are milling in the aisles, giving the House the air of a commuter station at rush hour. Many lawmakers are returning from the cafeteria with hot dogs and milkshakes.

Far more intriguing than the action on the floor is a phone call that House Republican Leader Samuel Hayes of Blair receives from one of Gov. Thornburgh's aides. The aide says that Thornburgh does not want the abortion bill to reach his desk. Undoubtedly speaking the same thoughts that are running through many legislators' heads, the aide reminds Hayes that the abortion issue is a politician's nightmare—a no-win proposition because no matter which side you take, the other side gets very mad at you. Hayes responds that there doesn't seem to be any way to stop the bill now, but he'll try.

Back on the floor the undercurrent of talk and movement has grown so strong that Ryan tries to interrupt Freind long enough to restore order. But Freind can't hear Ryan. Almost no one can hear Freind. Ryan bangs his wooden gavel until it shatters into three pieces. The House then votes that the amendment is constitutional.

Ryan next welcomes to the House two special guests who are allowed to sit in chairs on the floor with members, Rep. Freind's father and 12-year-old son. He also announces that he has given permission to WCAU television to do 10 minutes of silent filming. Members remove their feet from desks and generally straighten up.

By the time Hoeffel gets a chance to introduce his omnibus amendment to the Freind–Cunningham proposal, the sun is warming the west side of the Capitol dome. Citing the court decisions he has studied all summer, Hoeffel argues that the proposal is unconstitutional and would "create a whole new area of government intrusion into private decision-making." On the Republican side of the aisle, it is now Rep. Fred Noye of Perry County who seems to have fallen asleep. His chin rests lightly on his chest, and his glasses have slipped to the end of his nose.

The opposition is predictable and *pro forma*. Freind argues that his measure is constitutional. Mullen says simply that "the issue here is saving babies." Minutes later Hoeffel is looking around in amazement. No one is rising to support him. Ryan orders a roll call and the Hoeffel substitute amendment is swamped on a vote of 152–44. Freind and Cunningham smile.

As twilight draws its diaphanous curtain over Harrisburg, the bill is ready for a final vote. But there's a Democratic fund-raising dinner tonight that will provide money for legislators' re-election campaigns, and the House adjourns about 5:30 p.m.

Hoeffel and the other opponents of the Freind-Cunningham bill take advantage of the reprieve, and regroup during the night. When the House convenes Wednesday morning, there is another series of attempts to dilute A4911. But one by one they fall, and the membership becomes increasingly res . . . Ryan breaks two more gavels trying to restore order.

Amidst the cacaphony, a number of lawmakers are agonizing over how to vote on the final bill. One of them, Rep. Thomas Michlovic (D., Allegheny), voices his frustration in a floor speech. "Mr. Speaker, I don't know about the rest of you, but I feel rather inadequate about making this kind of decision. We're deciding when life begins and whether that life shall be a person under the law and whether persons involved in aborting that life shall be considered criminals under the law. I feel the weight of that decision, Mr. Speaker, and frankly I could use some help." But very few of Michlovic's lawmaking brethren hear the speech because there is too much noise in the chamber.

Then, late in the afternoon, Mullen makes a slight misstep in debating a motion that would send the entire bill back to the House Judiciary Committee. "Nothing will be served by putting this off to another day," he says. "If you're not intelligent enough to vote on this by now, you ought to resign."

This remark infuriates several members. Rep. Walter DeVerter (R., Mifflin) is shaking with rage when Ryan finally recognizes him. "I think Mr. Mullen owes each and every member of this House an apology," says DeVerter, who then slams the microphone down on the adjustable stand.

Mullen sort of apologizes, saying he didn't mean to insult anyone's intelligence. Freind, still standing at the microphone on the Republican side, senses that the mood of the House has shifted, almost as if a weather front has moved through. Lawmakers are getting angry that they are being put through this uncomfortable procedure.

The motion to send the bill back to committee is defeated, but a few moments later it is clear that there is support for the next amendment offered by Freind's opponents. This amendment would delete the provision that would permit anyone to seek a court order against any woman planning an abortion. Hoeffel says the provision is "an invitation to every fanatic in this state who wants to take people to court, who wants to file petitions, who wants to harass women, to harass doctors, to harass clinics."

Cunningham, whose role to this point has been largely to feed Freind information for debate, takes the microphone to defend the provision. "This section protects the lives of babies who are born alive when an abortion is improperly performed. Once that baby is killed or allowed to die, no legal action is going to bring that baby back to life."

But this amendment passes, 137–55, and the House cheers. Another amendment also succeeds, changing the legislation so that now minors need the consent of one parent, rather than two, to have an abortion.

And then, out of nowhere, comes a real shocker for both sides. Rep. Harry Bowser (R., Erie), a farmer in his second House term who seldom makes speeches, seeks Ryan's attention. His voice quavering slightly, Bowser says: "Nobody ever told me I was anointed when I was elected. What right do I have to force this thing on people when I don't know whether they want it?" He introduces a proposal to submit the entire abortion issue, as raised by Freind and Cunningham, to a public referendum next year. Eureka! Suddenly, legislators see a way to avoid committing themselves on the abortion issue. Let the voters decide!

After 45 minutes of debate, the Bowser amendment passes, 102–89. Cheers roll through the chamber. Ryan breaks another gavel. Freind lights a Winston as Mullen rushes across the chamber to confer with him and Cunningham. Up in the visitor's gallery, Howard Fetterhoff, chief lobbyist for the Pennsylvania Catholic Conference, runs to a telephone. Ms. Plant and her pro-choice people, who are also in the gallery, sit tight.

Neither side, after all, can really anticipate what would happen in a referendum. Public opinion polls show that sentiment in the state is fairly evenly divided. But Fetterhoff has decided that there is no need to have a referendum. The votes are there to get the bill passed tonight—if he can just get the issue to a vote. Quickly, he and his aides identify about a dozen "pro-life" lawmakers who voted for the Bowser amendment. They call field workers in each of their home districts, who in turn put in calls to the targeted legislators. Soon pages are summoning the lawmakers to answer telephone calls outside the chamber.

By 10:15 the Catholic Conference lobbyists have completed their work, and a motion is made to reconsider the vote on the Bowser amendment. "Mary, don't let us down now. We've come too far," Freind prays to himself. Ryan orders a roll call. Ten legislators change their votes from yes to no, and the Bowser amendment dies after a life of one hour.

Now the end comes quickly. Amendment A4911 is formally approved as part of Senate Bill 742, and at 11:45 p.m. Ryan orders a roll call on the amended bill. It passes on a vote of 132–61. Of the 10 women legislators, five vote for the bill, five against it. Of the 92 Catholic legislators who are present, 85 vote for the bill, seven against it. DeVerter votes against it. So does Michlovic. Bowser votes yes.

Midnight in the Capitol Rotunda. Two hundred feet above is the interior of the dome with a circular painting entitled "The Spirit of Religious Liberty." On the ground floor, the lights of the official state Christmas tree, a 30-foot white spruce, have been turned off. But at the top of the marble staircase, television lights glare as Freind and Cunningham hold a news conference. Freind is red-eyed and disheveled, Cunningham shaven and composed. Freind is asked how he feels. "It was the most difficult emotional experience I've ever been through with the exception of watching my wife give birth to our five children."

Cunningham is asked if the bill is a message to the doctors of Pennsylvania. "Please be advised that we are not trying to give a message to anyone." But Freind disagrees. "Look, we can't stop abortions. The message we're sending to doctors is this: 'We can't stop you from performing abortions. We wish we could, and we hope to God that someday we'll get the Human Life Amendment (to the U.S. Constitution) so we can. But until that time there are going to be regulations you'll have to follow if you're going to perform abortions'. That's the message."

Lobbyist Fetterhoff is waiting for Freind in his office. The two embrace tearfully. Freind's father, who is also there, tells his son, "I've always been proud of you. Now I'm really proud of you."

The next crisis point for the bill occurs on Tuesday, Dec. 15, when the amended Toughman Bill comes up for approval in the State Senate.

In the morning George H. Seidel, Thornburgh's director of legislative relations, tells Senate Republicans the same thing that Rep. Hayes was told: Thornburgh does not want the bill to reach his desk. But Senate President Pro Tempore Henry Hager (R., Lycoming) and Senate Republican Leader Robert Jubelirer of Blair doubt they can stop it, and they are worried about the divisive effect the abortion bill is having on the Republican senators.

Freind and Cunningham have worked over the weekend for a vote today. Among other things, they have threatened Republican legislative leaders that if Senate Bill 742 does not come up for a vote, they will rally anti-abortion forces to block a number of important budget proposals sought earnestly by Thornburgh. Budget votes normally take place along straight party lines, with no regard for their merit (or lack of it). A defection by a handful of Republicans could bring about their defeat.

This is real political hardball, and Freind will be attacked for it in the House Republican caucus that afternoon. Jubelirer himself says that when he heard Freind was willing to block the budget to get the bill, "I was so angry that if someone had touched me they'd have singed their finger." But Freind is angry too. "There are guys in here who have held up budgets for studded tires or a bridge in their districts," he tells the caucus. "I've never done that, and I never will. But this issue is too important to me."

In the Senate Republican caucus, Jubelirer suggests that the Senate, in effect, should pass the Bowser amendment, and submit the abortion issue to the voters in a referendum. Sen. Clarence D. Bell (R., Delaware), who is closing out an undistinguished 20-year Senate career, objects to Jubelirer's idea. Jubelirer, his voice rising, thinks he should at least be allowed to propose the referendum. Bell retorts that Jubelirer is trying to manipulate him.

Jubelirer shrieks: "Goddamit, Clarence, I'm not trying to manipulate you!"

Bell screams: "I don't have to take this s— from you or any punk like you!" He storms out of the caucus room.

The next combatants in the caucus are Hager and Sen. Edward Helfrick (R., Northumberland). Helfrick seldom speaks in caucus, but he is one of the Senate's most ardent anti-abortionists, and today he is screaming at Hager for supporting Jubelirer's referendum idea. Helfrick calls Hager "a deceitful person who will have the blood of children on your hands."

The Senate Democratic caucus that same afternoon is much calmer. For one thing, most members favor Senate Bill 742, and even some of those who don't are enchanted by the prospect of handing Thornburgh the political dilemma of deciding whether to sign the bill. The referendum idea is considered—and rejected. Several Democratic senators who face re-election next year are appalled at the idea of a referendum on abortion alongside their names on the primary ballot, and the most vocal among them is Sen. Francis Lynch (D., Philadelphia). Philadelphia Democrats thrive on low, controlled turnouts in primaries, and Lynch clearly believes that the abortion issue would bring out dangerous numbers of free-thinkers and libertines on election day.

One Democratic senator, however, is unequivocally against the bill. Sen. Vincent Fumo (D., Philadelphia) tells his colleagues he thinks the bill is abominable, and he tells them not to fear the wrath of the Catholic lobby. "Last time we had an abortion fight, I got telegrams from all over the place. Three of them came from my neighbors. I went to them and said, 'Hey, why are you sending me a telegram?' They said, 'We didn't send you any telegram. We just signed a petition in the back of the church.'"

The caucuses break up and the Senate convenes about 5:30 p.m. It will take the Senate one hour to do what took the House 22 hours.

The principal work place of the 49 men and one woman in the Senate of Pennsylvania is surrounded by Irish Connemara marble. There are stained-glass windows partially covered by gold velvet drapes, and chandeliers dangle from the gilded ceiling like earrings.

The referendum issue comes up first, but is defeated easily, 20–28, and Lt. Gov. William Scranton, the presiding officer, calls up Senate Bill 742. There is a saying in the Senate, which is far more genteel than the House, that "the minority will have its say; the majority will have its way." Today the majority, those supporting Senate Bill 742, is indeed content to sit back and let the minority do the talking.

The most emotional is Jubelirer, who two years ago survived a bitter election campaign in which anti-abortion activists attacked his previous stands on the issue. ("Thump, thump, thump," went one radio advertisement. "This is the heartbeat of a fetus. We need money for highways and schools, but Senator Bob Jubelirer wants to spend your tax money to kill that fetus.")

Jubelirer's speech lasts about 30 minutes, but the gist of it is that "this bill attempts to . . . impose religious views upon the people of this Commonwealth. . . ." While he speaks, Sen. James A. Romanelli (D., Allegheny) is sitting on his desk reading the sports pages of the Pittsburgh Post-Gazette. Sen. Tim Shaffer (R., Butler) has put both feet on his desk and leaned back in his chair, staring at the ceiling. At one point late in the speech Lynch emerges from the rear antechamber, whistling loudly. He cups his hand to his mouth in mock chagrin, strolls to his desk, sits down and lights a cigarette.

The final speaker on Senate Bill 742 is Sen. Henry Messinger (D., Lehigh), who looks like a conservative farmer but in fact is one of the Senate's few certifiable liberals. Waving his copy of Senate Bill 742 as though it were a battle flag, Messinger says: "I wish everyone would read this bill and look at some of the ridiculous parts, like the sentence I am going to read. 'Fertilization: The fertilization of an ovum by a sperm . . . which shall be deemed to have occurred when the head of the sperm has penetrated the cell membrane of the ovum and the process of development . . .' and so on and so on."

"I want to be the inspector to find out when that sperm cell has penetrated the cell membrane because unless we know that has occurred, we do not know whether this woman is pregnant or not, and somebody has to know it because they have to report things. This is so highly insulting to women that I just wonder what attitude men legislators and men priests and men ministers really have toward women and the rights of women. I think they believe that life begins at conception and ends at birth and that during the process of development the fetus has more rights than a living person."

In the Senate, the roll is actually called. No electronic gadgetry here. Forty-nine deep male voices and one female voice (that of Sen. Jeanette Reibman (D., Northampton)) respond as they are called. When they are finished the yeas are 29, the nays 21. Reibman has voted no. Of the Senate's 16 Catholic members, 15 have voted for the bill. Fumo is the only Catholic who votes no.

Thornburgh is attending a fund-raising dinner at the Union League in Philadelphia when he is advised that Senate Bill 742 is on its way to his desk. He is not pleased.

The next day, Friday, Thornburgh meets in the formal dining room of the Governor's Home with his most trusted advisers—Jay C. Waldman, general counsel; Richard Stafford, secretary for legislative affairs; and Paul Critchlow, press secretary.

The four review a poll taken last August showing that sentiment in

Pennsylvania on the abortion issue is nearly evenly divided. Thornburgh is reported to be dismayed over the emotional polarity surrounding Senate Bill 742: Sign it and you've reduced Pennsylvania women to state-regulated incubators; veto it and you have the blood of murdered children on your hands.

By the beginning of Christmas week, speculation is rampant that the governor will sign. Waldman, Stafford and Critchlow have all advised him to sign. But on Wednesday, Dec. 23, about 5 p.m., Thornburgh pokes his head into Waldman's office and says he's decided to veto.

There is a final half-hour meeting in the governor's office, then Thornburgh signs a seven-page veto message built on one basic idea. It says that while the governor is personally opposed to abortion, Senate Bill 742 would place undue and in some cases unconstitutional burdens on women seeking abortions. The press is handed copies of the veto message about 6 p.m. Thornburgh declines to discuss it further. The matter, an aide says, is simply too sensitive to be discussed extemporaneously.

Freind has waited most of the afternoon at his home legislative office in Havertown. About 6:05 p.m. he receives a call from Fetterhoff, who tells him of the veto. Freind will say later that he felt as if someone had kicked him in the stomach. He is bitter. He is also determined to try again.

For now, it might be noted that there is no law against having "tough-man promotions" in Pennsylvania.

STAGES IN THE LAW-MAKING PROCESS:
APPROPRIATING FOR LEGISLATION

The federal enactment process is comparable to the one described above. Both are concerned with defining and shaping the substance of legislation. There is another related, post-enactment process, however, that is particularly important at the federal level: the authorization–appropriation process. (States also appropriate funds to implement legislative goals, but the federal process, owing to its mechanism for authorization, is slightly more comprehensive.) Hetzel (1982) describes this process, which he labels the "two-congress procedure," in detail below.*

The factor that differentiates the work of these two Congresses is the committee system. While one committee is responsible for substantive legislation in a particular field, an entirely different committee, composed of different members and often possessed of a different philosophy, is responsible for providing funds for that same legislation.

*From Otto J. Hetzel; Legislative Law and Process, pp. 813–814. The Michie Company. © 1980 The Michie Company, Charlottesville, Virginia. Reprinted by permission.

Although the development of regulatory legislation is an important function of Congress, the creation and funding of federal programs constitutes an even more important part of the work that Congress performs. Congress determines the actual level of funding for a program by a separate appropriation act enacted after the measure creating the program has become law. . . .

. . . Once approved by Congress and signed by the President, these [laws, which have an accompanying recommended price tag that has been prepared by the subcommittee of origin for the law] become the authorizing legislation for a specific program and the budget authority for federal expenditures for that purpose.

The executive branch agency that will be responsible for administering the program now becomes involved. The agency studies the legislation and develops plans to implement the new program. Legislative hearings are again held at the subcommittee level, usually with testimony from the administering agency, but this time before an appropriations subcommittee. This second bill is the appropriations bill. It specifies how much money is to be made available by the Treasury to carry out the purposes of the first act. Such amounts may be less than that authorized but may not exceed the authorization. From the subcommittee, the bill goes to the committee, the entire house, the other house, and the President as before.

The procedure for considering appropriations is much the same as that for considering authorizations. One of the important differences, however, lies in the interrelation of the actions of the two houses. Traditionally, all appropriations bills originate in the House of Representatives. Most of the initial work and study must necessarily be done there. The Senate, therefore, often functions as a sort of court of last resort. Supporters of programs that were cut from appropriations bills in the House press their case in the Senate. The Senate also examines the appropriations bills to determine if cuts should be made from the House version.

While bills containing authorizations tend to focus on one program or a group of related programs, appropriations bills almost always group together programs by the same administrative agency and often combine appropriations for several different agencies in one bill. . . . Serious dispute between the two chambers . . . is almost preordained. Conference committees established to resolve these differences hold considerable power in molding federal policy and programs.

The "two Congress" procedure gives the chief executive additional power. Unlike the governors of some states, the President does not have the power to "item veto" certain aspects of an appropriations bill while approving the remainder. Nevertheless, the President has power to veto or threaten to veto the entire bill if he objects to specific parts of it.

4 The Interpretation of Legislation

"Legislative intent" is a well-traveled road, complete with unexpected detours, poor design, misleading guideposts, inadequate illumination, and numerous points still "under construction". The statutory interpretation literature contains numerous references to "legislative intent," as though it was easily accessible to even the most amateur investigator. But sit through any legislative body of your choice, and you are certain to depart convinced that the only discernible intention is to compromise. Clearly, the exchanges thus witnessed can not be the stuff of which monolithic intentions are made, at least not "intent" as that term is normally understood.

Why then, the preoccupation with "legislative intent"? Primarily, because our Constitutional scheme for separating governmental functions defines the branch's relation to each other. For example, courts, when applying a legislative rule, may search for its intent, but not because they really care about the underlying motivation. Rather, the search is the method by which the court remains within its particular function; it thus defers to legislative wisdom because legislatures, not courts, make law. Administrative agencies resort to similar constitutionally-inspired restraints. They may issue regulations, but only those that express the enabling legislation's purposes will be legally valid. An agency doing otherwise is acting *ultra vires* (beyond its scope of authority). Thus, the search for "legislative intent" is a method both courts and agencies use to contain possible impulses to act beyond their constitutionally-granted authority.

The search for intent is particularly compelling because the application of a statute can be adversely affected if competing or contradictory meanings are assigned to it. It is also important because of the relative "superiority" of statutes in relation to common law. Courts, for example, interpret a statute's meaning against a very complicated background, including the documents compiled in the legislative history, the court's assessment of the social–political climate that gave rise to the statute, the so-called "evil" the legislation was designed to remedy, and the court's view of its law-making function. The executive branch (administrative agencies) is similarly confounded by the task of uncovering legislative intent. Considerations similar to those facing courts guide regulatory interpretation, although the executive branch's concern with statutory *implementation* gives it a relatively unique vantage point. Administrative agencies also work with established programs that to some extent represent the agency's interpretation of intent.

IDENTIFYING LEGISLATIVE INTENT

Legislation is more authoritative than case law in that it is the starting point for the court's search for a legal rule, and unlike case law, a judge can not "overrule" a legislative rule or change statutory language. The courts' deference to legislation further underscores its unique function: to interpret, and not make law. The three basic approaches, according to Bodenheimer, et al. (1980), that courts adopt are: the literal plain-meaning approach; the qualified plain-meaning approach; and the social-purpose approach. These are not necessarily exclusive or exhaustive. Rather, they illuminate the court's orientation to legislation. The *plain-meaning* approach emphasizes giving meaning to whatever is plainly expressed, with no concern for the effect. The *qualified plain-meaning* approach attempts to read the statutes as a whole and thereby give it meaning, unless such a broad construction produces inconsistency or absurdity. The so-called *social-purpose* approach is built around four considerations: (1) the common law prior to the legislation in question; (2) the "mischief" or "defect" not addressed by the common law; (3) the text of the legislation that has been enacted to remedy the defect; and (4) the lawmakers' intent, in terms of the public good they sought to advance by enacting the remedial legislation.

Constraints on Judicial Interpretation of Legislation

Courts rely on certain "rules of thumb" to make sense of legislation. These devices are helpful, and are used in conjunction with the aforementioned approaches. The techniques are numerous, so no attempt will be made here to illustrate them all. Rather, the following examples, "canons of construction" supplied by Llewellen (1950), will sufficiently illustrate the tension a judge experiences when interpreting legislation.

> When it comes to presenting a proposed statutory construction in court, there is an accepted conventional vocabulary. As in argument over points of case law, the accepted convention still, unhappily, requires discussion as if only one single correct meaning could exist. Hence there are two opposing canons on almost every point. . . . [pp. 395–396]

Thrust	*Parry*
1. A statute cannot go beyond its text.	To effect its purpose a statute may be implemented beyond its text.
2. Statutes are to be read in the light of the common law and a statute affirming the common law rule is to be construed in accordance with the common law.	The common law gives way to a statute which is inconsistent with it and when a statute is designed as a revision of a whole body of law applicable to a given subject it supersedes the common law.
3. Where design has been distinctly stated, no place is left for construction.	Courts have the power to inquire into real (as distinct from ostensible) purpose.
4. Titles do not control meaning; preambles do not expand scope; section headings do not change language.	The title may be consulted as a guide when there is doubt or obscurity in the body; preambles may be consulted to determine rationale, and thus the true construction of terms; section headings may be looked upon as part of the statute itself.
5. If language is plain and unambiguous it must be given effect.	Not when literal interpretation would lead to absurd or mischievous consequences or thwart manifest purpose.

Though courts can resort to the above "rules" of construction (and Llewellen goes on to describe over forty additional ones), they must ultimately decide. The canons may help keep them from straying too far afield. The task becomes difficult, however, when sensitive social problems find their way into court, as the following opinion dealing with "affirmative action" illustrates. As you read it, consider the way the court searches for legislative intent and the manner in which it describes legislative documents.

UNITED STEELWORKERS OF AMERICA v. WEBER
443 U.S. 193 (1979)

Mr. Justice Brennan delivered the opinion of the Court.

Challenged here is the legality of an affirmative action plan—collectively bargained by an employer and a union—that reserves for black employees 50% of the openings in an in-plant craft training program until the percentage of black craftworkers in the plant is commensurate with the percentage of blacks in the local labor force. The question for decision is whether Congress, in Title VII of the Civil Rights Act of 1964 . . . left employers and unions in the private sector free to take such race-conscious steps to eliminate manifest racial imbalances in traditionally segregated job categories. We hold that Title VII does not prohibit such race-conscious affirmative action plans.

In 1974, petitioner United Steelworkers of America (USWA) and petitioner Kaiser Aluminum and Chemical Corp. (Kaiser) entered into a master collective-bargaining agreement covering terms and conditions of employment at 15 Kaiser plants. The agreement contained . . . an affirmative action plan designed to eliminate conspicuous racial imbalances in Kaiser's then almost exclusively white craftwork forces. Black craft-hiring goals were set for each Kaiser plant equal to the percentage of blacks in the respective local labor forces. To enable plants to meet these goals, on-the-job training programs were established to teach unskilled production workers (black and white) the skills necessary to become craftworkers. The plan reserved for black employees 50% of the openings in these newly created in-plant training programs.

This case arose from the operation of the plan at Kaiser's plant in Gramercy, La. Until 1974, Kaiser hired as craftworkers for that plant only persons who had had prior craft experience. Because blacks had long been excluded from craft unions, few were able to present such credentials. As a consequence, prior to 1974 only 1.83% (5 out of 273) of the skilled craft workers at the Gramercy plant were black, even though the work force in the Gramercy area was approximately 39% black.

Pursuant to the national agreement Kaiser altered its craft-hiring practice in the Gramercy plant. Rather than hiring already trained outsiders, Kaiser established a training program to train its production workers to fill craft openings. Selection of craft trainees was made on the basis of seniority, with the proviso that at least 50% of the new trainees were to be black until the percentage of black skilled craft workers in the Gramercy plant approximated the percentage of blacks in the local labor force. . . .

The complaint alleged that the filling of craft trainee positions at the Gramercy plant pursuant to the affirmative action program had resulted in junior black employees' receiving training in preference to senior white employees, thus discriminating against respondent and other similarly situated white employees in violation of . . . Title VII. The District Court held that the plan violated Title VII, entered a judgment in favor of the plaintiff class, and granted a permanent injunction prohibiting Kaiser and the USWA "from denying plaintiffs, Brian F. Weber and all other members of the class, access to on-the-job training programs on the basis of race." A divided panel of the Court of Appeals for the Fifth Circuit affirmed, holding that all employment preferences based upon race, including those preferences incidental to bona fide affirmative action plans, violated Title VII's prohibition against racial discrimination in employment . . . We granted certiorari. . . . We reverse.

We emphasize at the outset the narrowness of our inquiry. . . . *The only question before us is the narrow statutory issue of whether Title VII forbids private employers and unions from voluntarily agreeing upon bona fide affirmative action plans that accord racial preferences in the manner and for the purpose provided in the Kaiser–USWA plan* [emphasis supplied]. . . .

. . . Respondent argues that Congress intended in Title VII to prohibit all race-conscious affirmative action plans. Respondent's argument rests upon a literal interpretation of 703 (a) and (d) of the Act. Those sections make it unlawful to "discriminate . . . because of race . . ." in hiring and in the selection of apprentices for training programs. . . .

Respondent's argument is not without force. But it overlooks the significance of the fact that the Kaiser–USWA plan is an affirmative action plan voluntarily adopted by private parties to eliminate traditional patterns of racial segregation. In this context respondent's reliance upon a literal construction of 703 (a) and (d) . . . is misplaced. . . . It is a "familiar rule, that a thing may be within the letter of the statute and yet not within the statute, because not within its spirit, nor within the intention of its makers." . . . The prohibition against racial discrimination in 703 (a) and (d) of Title VII must therefore be read against the background of the legislative history of Title VII and the historical context from which the Act arose. . . . Examination of those sources makes clear that an interpretation of the sections that forbade all race-conscious affirmative action would "bring about an end completely at variance with the purpose of the statute" and must be rejected. . . .

Congress' primary concern in enacting the prohibition against racial discrimination in Title VII of the Civil Rights Act of 1964 was with "the plight of the Negro in our economy." 110 Cong[ressional] Rec[ord] 6548 (1964) (remarks of Sen. Humphrey). Before 1964, blacks were largely relegated to "unskilled and semiskilled jobs." *Ibid.* (remarks of Sen. Humphrey); *id.*, at 7204 (remarks of Sen. Clark); *id.*, at 7379–7380 (remarks of Sen. Kennedy). Because of automation the number of such jobs was rapidly decreasing. See *id.*, at 6548 (remarks of Sen. Humphrey); *id.*, at 7204 (remarks of Sen. Clark). As a consequence, "the relative position of the Negro worker [was] steadily worsening. In 1947 the nonwhite unemployment rate was only 64 % higher than the white rate; in 1962 it was 124 % higher." *Id.*, at 6547 (remarks of Sen. Humphrey). . . . Congress considered this a serious social problem. As Senator Clark told the Senate:

> The rate of Negro unemployment has gone up consistently as compared with white unemployment for the past 15 years. This is a social malaise and a social situation which we should not tolerate. That is one of the principal reasons why the bill should pass. *Id.*, at 7220.

Congress feared that the goals of the Civil Rights Act—the integration of blacks into the mainstream of American society—could not be achieved unless this trend were reversed. And Congress recognized that that would not be possible unless blacks were able to secure jobs "which have a future." *Id.*, at 7204 (remarks of Sen. Kennedy). . . . As Senator Humphrey explained to the Senate:

> What good does it do a Negro to be able to eat in a fine restaurant if he cannot afford to pay the bill? What good does it do him to be accepted in a hotel that is too expensive for his modest income? How can a Negro child be motivated to take full advantage of integrated educational facilities if he has no hope of getting a job where he can use that education? *Id.*, at 6547. . . .

These remarks echoed President Kennedy's original message to congress upon the introduction of the Civil Rights Act in 1963.

> There is little value in a Negro's obtaining the right to be admitted to hotels and restaurants if he has no cash in his pocket and no job. 109 Cong. Rec. 11159.

Accordingly, it was clear to Congress that "[t]he crux of the problem [was] to open employment opportunities for Negroes in occupations that have been traditionally closed to them," 110 Cong. Rec. 6548 (1964) (remarks of Sen. Humphrey); and it was to this problem that Title VII's prohibition against racial discrimination in employment was primarily addressed.

It plainly appears from the House Report accompanying the Civil Rights Act that Congress did not intend wholly to prohibit private and voluntary affirmative action efforts as one method of solving this problem. The Report provides:

> No bill can or should lay claim to eliminating all of the causes and consequences of racial and other types of discrimination against minorities. There is reason to believe, however, that national leadership provided by the enactment of Federal legislation dealing with the most troublesome problems *will create an atmosphere conducive to voluntary or local resolution of other forms of discrimination*. H.R. Rep. No. 914, 88th Cong., 1st Sess., pt. 1, p. 18 (1963). (Emphasis supplied.)

Given this legislative history, we cannot agree with respondent that Congress intended to prohibit the private sector from taking effective steps to accomplish the goal that Congress designed Title VII to achieve. The very statutory words intended as a spur or catalyst to cause "employers and unions to self-examine and to self-evaluate their employment practices, and to endeavor to eliminate, so far as possible, the last vestiges of an unfortunate and ignominious page in this country's history," . . . cannot be interpreted as an absolute prohibition against all private, voluntary, race-conscious affirmative action efforts to hasten the elimination of such vestiges. It would be ironic indeed if a law triggered by a Nation's concern over centuries of racial injustice and intended to improve the lot of those who had "been excluded from the American dream for so long," 110 Cong. Rec. 6552 (1964) (remarks of Sen. Humphrey), constituted the first legislative prohibition of all voluntary, private, race-conscious efforts to abolish traditional patterns of racial segregation and hierarchy. . . .

We need not today define in detail the line of demarcation between permissible and impermissible affirmative action plans. It suffices to hold that the challenged Kaiser–USWA affirmative action plan falls on the permissible side of the line. The purposes of the plan mirror those of the statute. Both were designed to break down old patterns of racial segregation and hierarchy. Both were structured to "open employment opportunities for Negroes in occupations which have been traditionally closed to them." 110 Cong. Rec. 6548 (1964) (remarks of Sen. Humphrey).

At the same time, the plan does not unnecessarily trammel the interests of the white employees. The plan does not require the discharge of white employees and their replacement with new black employees. . . . Nor does the plan create an absolute bar to the advancement of white employees; half of those trained in the program will be white. Moreover, the plan is a temporary measure; it is not intended to maintain racial balance, but simply to eliminate a manifest racial imbalance. Preferential selection of craft trainees at the Gramercy plant will end as soon as the percentage of black skilled craft workers in the Gramercy plant approximates the percentage of blacks in the local labor force. . . .

We conclude, therefore, that the adoption of the Kaiser-USWA plan for the Gramercy plant falls within the area of discretion left by Title VII to the private sector to voluntarily adopt affirmative action plans designed to eliminate conspicuous racial imbalance in traditionally segregated job categories. Accordingly, the judgment of the Court of Appeals for the Fifth Circuit is reversed.

The above decision demonstrates why the court's hold on legislative intent is so tenuous. It may have relied heavily on legislative documents in its search for statutory meaning, but obviously even these can yield divergent interpretations. Do these complications then call a halt to the use of legislative intent? No, not necessarily. Given our constitutional framework, if legislative intent did not exist, something like it would be invented. The search for intent, albeit frustrating occasionally, is not a lost cause, as Nunez (1972) suggests below. Compare his description of legislative intent with the method the Supreme Court used in the above case.

THE NATURE OF LEGISLATIVE INTENT AND THE USE OF LEGISLATIVE DOCUMENTS AS EXTRINSIC AIDS TO STATUTORY

Interpretation: A Re-examination*

Having drafted and interpreted numerous pieces of legislation and observed a state legislature "making up its mind," I have slowly reached the conclusion that the concept of legislative intent, as discussed in the legal profession, is a fiction. A convenient legal fiction, and perhaps necessary to help smooth over the rough or thin spots in a statute, but a fiction nevertheless.

After a review of the literature on legislative intent and on the use of extrinsic aids to ascertain legislative intent, I came to realize that much of the confusion surrounding the concept of legislative intent, even among scholars, is caused by the misconception that legislative intent is a single entity which must be proven to exist or not exist. In truth, there is not one, but three legislative intents, two of which can usually be proven to

---

*From Richard Nunez, "The nature of legislative intent and the use of legislative documents." *California Western Law Review, 9,* pp. 128–135. © 1972 California Western School of Law, San Diego, CA. Reprinted by Permission.

exist, while one is most often created by legal fiction. [I will try to] lay out in a systematic pattern the three legislative documents as extrinsic aids in finding specific legislative intent.

The necessity of hunting for legislative intent arises under two circumstances: first, when an administrator or court cannot read the statute and grasp its simple meaning because of shoddy draftsmanship or language errors, and second, when the statute is understandable but the case at hand was not anticipated at the time the statute was enacted. In either situation, whether due to defective drafting or unexpected problems, the search for legislative intent is a search for some evidence, intrinsic or extrinsic, that can be used as the basis for the statement: "The legislature intended. . . ." Once this intent is discovered, the problem at hand can be solved.

A more precise examination reveals that the concept of legislative intent subdivides into three major categories. The three intents, ranked from the most general to the most specific, are:

1. Legislative intent concerning solution of a general social problem. For example, a statute enacted in response to the pollution problem is not intended to be used with respect to other social problems in which pollution plays an insignificant role. Mr. Justice Cardozo, speaking of the importance of the larger social problem, stated that "the meaning of a statute is to be looked for, not in any single section, but in all the parts together and in their relation to the end in view."

2. Legislative intent concerning the general purposes of a specific statute. For example, a Selective Service statute intended to recruit men for military service is not intended to be employed to suppress political dissent. "[T]he general purpose is a more important aid to the meaning than any rule which grammar or formal logic may lay down."

3. Legislative intent concerning the meaning of a specific statutory word or phrase. It is this category that is usually thought of when the words "legislative intent" are debated. There is often a need to know whether the statute covers the particular case in mind, or whether the administrator possesses the specific power he wishes to exercise. Because most of the debate in the profession is focused upon this single category of legislative intent, the debaters are pressed to prove the existence or nonexistence of this single category of intent. If, in the debate, the concept of intent in this category is rejected, than all legislative intent is apparently rejected, and the legislative process appears as a mindless operation.

At the beginning of each debate on the existence or nonexistence of legislative intent, we should start with these questions: Which intent? At what level of generality? Are we interested in the larger social policy, the general purpose of the statute, or the meaning of specific words?

It is possible for a legislature to have a clear and discernible intent concerning the social policy and the general purpose of the statute, and yet not have devoted a single moment of thought to the specific meaning of a word or phrase. Among the documents there may be evidence of specific intent; most often there is none. If the specific legislative intent does not exist and yet we act as though it does, we are acting upon a legal fiction. And even when legislative intent exists on a higher level of generality, it is still likely to be a legal fiction when applied to a word or phrase.

Where does the researcher turn for evidence of legislative intent? Simply answered: Anywhere. Chief Justice Marshall stated: "Where the mind labors to discover the design of the legislature, it seizes everything from which aid can be derived. . . ." Mr. Justice Frankfurter was almost as broad, asking only that the evidence be relevant: "If the purpose of construction is the ascertainment of meaning, nothing that is logically relevant should be excluded."

Such statements open up a wide range of evidence that can be brought forward to "prove" the legislative intent. However, all evidence is not equally reliable. Evidence can be grouped into three major categories that vary in degree of reliability; statisticians would say these categories were based on the "hardness" of the evidence. The "hardest" evidence is internal evidence derived from within the statute itself, such as the definition section, the preamble, or the explicit recitals of policy. This is the type of evidence Mr. Justice Holmes relied upon: "We do not inquire what the legislature meant; we ask only what the statute means."

The second category of evidence is legislative evidence, such as transcripts of debates, minutes of committee hearings and reports of legislative investigating committees. . . .

The last category, the "softest" evidence, is non-legislative evidence, which is evidence not produced by the legislative process, and generally includes journal articles, restatements of the law, [etc.]. . . .

REFINING INTENT: RESPONSES TO JUDICIAL INTERPRETATIONS OF LEGISLATION

Though the above discussion addresses opportunities for and limits on a judge's ability to interpret legislation, (s)he eventually decides. In the case of the U.S. Supreme Court, its decisions are the "law of the land". A rule thus announced will exist until it is "overruled" by a higher tribunal or until the legislature acts to limit or otherwise clarify the rule through new legislation. This rule-modification/correction feature may seem cumbersome, but it works very effectively, as the following illustrates.

Battle Lines Drawn Again on Rights Bill

New battle lines emerged January 24 over the scope of legislation to shore up four of the nation's major civil rights laws, and they are almost identical to those staked out when a similar bill was considered by the 98th congress.

The legislation is designed to overturn a February 28, 1984, Supreme Court decision, *Grove City College v. Bell*, which narrowed coverage of a law banning sex discrimination in federally assisted education programs. The ruling was expected to affect laws barring discrimination based on race, age and handicap as well.

Both the Reagan administration and the nation's leading civil rights groups want the decision overturned, but they continue to disagree on how to do it.

Rep. Augustus F. Hawkins, D–Calif., on January 24 introduced legislation (HR 700) supported by civil rights lobbyists, which would make clear that discrimination is prohibited in any institution receiving federal funds. . . .

Also on January 24, Senate Majority Leader Robert Dole, R-Kan., introduced a more limited bill (S 272) supported by the Reagan administration.

The Court Case: In the *Grove City* case, the court ruled by 6–3 that Title IX of the 1972 Education Act Amendments barred sex discrimination only in a "program or activity" receiving federal aid, not the entire institution. The other three rights laws have the same "program or activity" language, and lawyers said they too would be affected by the court's decision.

Since the ruling, the Department of Education has ended or restricted the focus of about 60 anti-bias lawsuits. . . .

Civil rights attorneys contend that the court misread the law, and that congress intended to prohibit discrimination in any institution receiving federal funds, in spite of the "program or activity" language.

New Language: Hawkins' bill . . . defines the term "program or activity" in each of the four statutes to make clear that entire institutions are coerced. . . . [It] spells out what "program or activity" means in a school or university, a state or local government, a corporation, partnership or other private organization. . . .

Dole's bill also amends all four civil rights statutes. But it expressly overturns the *Grove City* reading of "program or activity" only for educational institutions. For all other entities, the bill says the civil rights laws should be construed as they were prior to the Supreme Court's ruling. Dole said this "grandfather clause" was designed to "ensure that the *Grove City* case does not serve as a precedent for judicial interpretations of civil rights coverage in other areas . . . that such coverage is to be as broad as it was before the case was decided." . . . (Congressional Quarterly Weekly, January 26, 1985) [p. 147]

The above excerpt reports on Congressional attempts to limit a Supreme Court decision. On the one hand, the Court must interpret federal legislation in the light of its understanding of the underlying purpose; and generally, Congress will not act to refine or redefine the law after every decision that construes statutory meaning. (It would be foolish to do so, and would make the "separation of powers" doctrine seem ridiculous.) On the other hand, however, there are instances where the Congress decides that the Supreme Court has strayed so far away from statutory intentions that it feels compelled to reinforce the Court's original goals. Such was the case in the Congressional reaction to the aforementioned *Grove City* decision. Consider the goals suggested by the text of the bills subsequently introduced to refine Congressional intentions. The title of the bills, rather than their full text, is presented below to illustrate the direction of the legislation.

H.R. 700

A BILL TO RESTORE THE BROAD SCOPE OF COVERAGE AND TO CLARIFY THE APPLICATION OF TITLE IX OF THE EDUCATION AMENDMENTS OF 1972, SECTION 504 OF THE REHABILITATION ACT OF 1973, THE AGE DISCRIMINATION ACT OF 1975, AND TITLE VI OF THE CIVIL RIGHTS ACT OF 1964. [REFERRED TO THE COMMITTEES ON EDUCATION AND LABOR AND THE JUDICIARY] (131 Cong. Rec. 166 (1985)).

S. 272

A BILL TO CLARIFY THE MEANING OF THE PHRASE "PROGRAM OR ACTIVITY" AS APPLIED TO EDUCATIONAL INSTITUTIONS THAT ARE EXTENDED FEDERAL FINANCIAL ASSISTANCE, AND FOR OTHER PURPOSES. [REFERRED TO THE COMMITTEE ON LABOR AND HUMAN RESOURCES] (131 Cong. Rec. 632 (1985)).

The differences in wording in the two bills notwithstanding, they share a common goal: to respond to a judicial decision that appears to have strayed too far from legislative intentions. But what is likely to result? What will their ultimate language look like? How will the court deal with legislative intent, given the circumstances under which the legislation was proposed, debated, and enacted? On the one hand, it is clear that these legislative initiatives are the equivalent of *underlying for emphasis,* in which case there is no problem with intent. On the other hand, given what we know about judicial interpretation of legislation, there is no guarantee that a single uniform view of intent will emerge.

Institutional Interdependence

The *Weber* and *Grove City* cases not only illustrate the vagaries of exposing legislative intent, they illuminate the subtle balance of powers that is at the heart of our system of government. This feature is also important because it demonstrates the degree of institutional interdependence that occurs in the formulation and implementation of public policy. The interdependence simply means that legal institutions (1) are aware of developments beyond their individual scope and (2) rely on this awareness to correct perceived defects or errors.

For example, the *Weber* decision can be thought of as a reaction to Title VII of the Civil Rights Act of 1964 and its related regulations pertaining to affirmative action programs. It was also an attempt to clarify the scope of such programs, particularly in the aftermath of *Regents of University of California v. Bakke*. In *Bakke*, the U.S. Supreme Court found unconstitutional the affirmative action program at the University of California at Davis Medical School because it appeared to set up two distinct tracks for admission to the school, and the only apparent difference between the two routes was the applicant's race. Mr. Allan Bakke charged that he would have been admitted to the medical school but for the program's existence. The school responded that the program relied on a classification scheme that allowed race to be considered as one of the many factors that go into an admissions decision, and did so to accomplish a legitimate purpose, i.e., to increase the number of minority physicians. The Court agreed and disagreed with both parties. They ordered Bakke admitted to the medical school because the program, *as then structured*, seemed to use race as the *sole* criterion for participation in the school's affirmative action program; the effect was to exclude Bakke. On the other hand, the Court found that race could be *one of the factors* considered for participation in such programs, provided there were other accompanying purposes, such as seeking to remedy past historical racial discrimination. The decision, understandably, produced a certain degree of confusion. The *Weber* decision, therefore, provided an opportunity to clarify the legislative goals of Title VII of the Civil Rights Act and the related regulations in relation to the purpose and scope of affirmative action programs. The Court, through its decision, thus "heard" the confusion within the legislative and executive branches, and responded in a way that supplied some clarity but did not upset the balance among the institutions.

The *Grove City* case seems to exemplify a similar reaction to the scope of the Civil Rights Act, particularly Title IX, which prohibits sex discrimination in federally funded programs. The U.S. Supreme Court construed Title IX and its accompanying regulations very narrowly, and thereby produced a result arguably inconsistent with Congress' intent on the matter. Congress "heard" the decision, was alerted to the possible regulatory consequences, and responded to correct the imbalance. It assumed that the decision, if left unchecked, would steadily erode the purpose and vitality of the Civil Rights Act. This anticipated erosion would unfold in the form of future judicial decisions, legislative amendments and the regulations issued to enforce them.

5 The Implementation of Legislation and Legislative Advocacy

A Conceptual Framework for Analyzing the Implementation of Legislation

Ultimately, the lawmaking process culminates in a statute that is implemented by an administrative agency. Although the point is perhaps obvious by now, the link between the lawmaking stages and law implementation cannot be overstated. Logic may suggest the latter follows the former, but experience has repeatedly shown that implementation is less than logical.

How then can we construct a bridge between legislative intent and implementation? To what extent can we effectively link the two? Sabatier and Mazmanian (1980) have considered these questions and concluded that policy outcome is dependent on an array of variables that interact with the lawmaking process. Their analysis pulls together these variables in a coherent framework, which they suggest captures the conditions that link the two. They argue that "[i]mplementation is the carrying out of a basic policy decision, usually made in a statute . . . that . . . "structures" the implementation process. . . . In our view, the crucial role of implementation analysis is to identify the factors that affect the achievement of statutory objectives throughout this entire process. These can be divided into three broad categories: (1) the tractability of the problem(s) being addressed by the statute; (2) the ability of the statute to favorably structure the implementation process; and (3) the net effect of a variety of "political" variables on the balance of support for statutory objectives." [p. 541]

The Sabatier and Mazmanian framework stresses the importance of

being aware of the implementation apparatus *prior to* the enactment
of legislation. In this way, they argue, one can effectively match
legislative outcomes with legislative intent. In short, one can structure the implementation process to ensure policy outcomes that
reflect a predesigned orientation. Their conceptual framework thus
prods the would-be advocate to keep in mind the array variables in
the aforementioned three categories, which they have identified as
contributing to implementation.

First, regarding the question of tractability, Sabatier and Mazmanian suggest that not all problems are equal; some are inherently more
difficult than others. This proposition has an intuitive appeal; one can
readily identify examples of "hard" versus "easy" problems. The authors then go on to specify certain factors that contribute to placing
problems in one of these two groups. For example, if the problem
defies change, is misunderstood or ill-defined, or if the technology
does not exist to institute the anticipated behavioral changes, then
the problem can be thought of as a "hard" one. They also suggest that
factors, such as the size and diversity of the group whose behavior is
to be changed also contribute to the determination of tractability.

Second, regarding the statute's ability to structure implementation, Sabatier and Mazmanian hold that the statute can organize the
means through which policy goals are realized.

> They argue, "A statute" constitutes the fundamental policy decision being
> implemented in that it indicates the problem(s) being addressed and
> stipulates the objective(s) to be pursued. It also has the capacity to
> "structure" the entire implementation process through its selection of the
> implementing institution; through providing legal and financial resources
> to those institutions; through biasing the probable orientations of agency
> officials; and through regulating the opportunities for participation by
> non-agency actors in the implementation process. To the extent that the
> statute stipulates a set of clear and consistent objectives, incorporates a
> sound theory relating behavioral change to those objectives, and then
> structures the implementation process in a fashion conducive to obtaining
> such behavioral changes, the possibilities for obtaining statutory objec-
> tives are enhanced. . . . [p. 542]

Finally, regarding so-called non-statutory variables that effect implementation, essentially, these are a manifestation of the fact that
statutory implementation unfolds within a dynamic and unpredict-
able context. This context represents an array of activities and ideas
that supply the lifeblood for policy outputs. The authors suggest that

factors, such as changes in technology, media representation of the problem, public response, constituency groups, and support by officials contribute to the extent to which policy outcomes match policy objectives. The proposed factors are not exhaustive, and others may come to mind. The important point, however, is that statutory goals are framed within and interact with a larger context; and this interaction shapes the scope of goals that are ultimately implemented.

The practical implications of this conceptual framework are perhaps most apparent in, for example, Echenbarger's account of the defeat of a state anti-abortion bill (see Chapter 3). One could easily describe and explain those events in the terms that Sabatier and Mazmanian have supplied. Their framework might also be a useful context for the tactics and roles that follow in the next section.

LEGISLATIVE ADVOCACY ROLES AND TECHNIQUES

Our previous exploration of lawmaking and implementation has lead us to an inquiry into possible social work roles in shaping and carrying out policy initiatives. The profession's commitment to its conceptualization of advocacy has typically thrust it into the legislative arena. Under what conditions will these efforts be successful? We will examine below two viewpoints on the means by which social workers may influence lawmaking. The first explores the role of the lobbyist; the second, tactics for legislative advocacy. The two are related, but distinguished by the activities required to put them into effect. We will look first at Patterson and Jewel's (1977) description of lobbyist roles, followed by Patti and Dear's (1981) empirically-based tactics for legislative advocacy.

Lobbyist Roles

Following are some general forms that, according to Patterson and Jewel (1977), lobbying can take. Though not addressed to social workers explicitly, we can consider whether there are some instances when they too rely on these approaches. The key issue, as a practical matter, is the conditions under which the various roles can contribute to effective social work advocacy. Without offering any judgment on this issue, the roles are presented below to stimulate your thinking about their applicability.

The Role of the Lobbyist*

The role of the lobbyist, like other political roles, is likely to be played in somewhat different forms by different actors. That is to say, in playing the lobbyist role, individuals give that role various orientations. Five distinct lobbyist role orientations can be identified for analysis here: the contact man, the campaign organizer, the informant, the watchdog, and the strategist.

The Contact Man: The contact man plays a classic role as a lobbyist. He is the legislative representative who conceives his job to be that of making crucial contacts with the members of the legislative group. He devotes his time and energies to walking the legislative halls, visiting legislators, collaring them in the halls, establishing relationships with administrative assistants and others of the legislators' staffs, cultivating key legislators on a friendship basis, and developing contacts on the staffs of critical legislative committees. . . . The contact man believes that the legislative goals of his organization can best be achieved through personal influence and personal contact with legislators. When faced with a legislative problem for his group, the lobbyist with a contact-man orientation is likely to propose as the solution personally contacting as many members of the legislative body as possible and directly presenting the interest group's case.

All lobbyists may make contacts with legislators, but the contact man is a lobbyist for whom this is the primary or most salient orientation. There are important differences in the ubiquity with which this role is played, differences between national and state legislative systems and differences among groups. At the national level, the complexity of legislative life has made contact work relatively impractical, and Washington lobbyists reported spending relatively little time in face-to-face contacting. A lobbyist before Congress is likely to spend more time in face-to-face contact in the early stages of his career and then simply maintain his contacts by letter or telephone, although fence-mending personal calls are usually required to maintain continuous contact.

Although Washington lobbyists reported spending relatively little of their time in direct contact work, more than 80% said they preferred direct methods, even though they were not able to employ them extensively. Contact work is probably much more pervasive at the state level, where access to legislators is easier.

The Campaign Organizer: The campaign organizer's conception of his role as a lobbyist is different from the contact man's conception. Although he may make some contacts, this is not, for him, the important part of his job. He conceives his job to be that of organizing mass grassroots support for his organization's legislative program. He believes

---

that his most important contacts are with leaders in the field and with rank-and-file members of his organization. He feels that the most effective lobbying for his group's program is achieved by demonstrating mass support for that program among the members of his organization "back home" who are the legislator's constituents. When a problem in legislative strategy is raised, the campaign organizer's solution is to map out a nationwide or statewide campaign from the grass roots, utilizing television and radio programs, fact sheets on specific legislation for workers in the field, millions of leaflets for field distribution, delegations to the capitol, and letters to legislators. He sees the value of personal contact but regards it as merely routine and by no means the most significant part of his own job. . . .

The Informant: The informant is a lobbyist who conveys information to legislators without necessarily advocating a particular position or program. He may lobby only by testimony, presenting information in his area of expertise to a legislative committee. He differs from the contact man in that his lobbying is often public and his contacts are frequently collective rather than individual. He may simply provide informational services for legislators.

The Watchdog: This is the lobbyist who conceives his job as that of scrutinizing closely the legislative calendars and watching legislative activity carefully, usually from a distance. His job is to be alert to developments in the legislative system that might affect his client group. Whenever legislation that affects his employer is proposed or introduced, his job is to signal his group so that it can attempt to bring pressure on legislators. He is a listening post for his organization, staked out in the capital to keep alert to developments that might affect his client. In performing this role, he may seldom enter the legislative halls or talk to individual members; he may never leave his office downtown in the capital city. . . .

The Strategist: A few lobbyists specialize in the formulation and development of legislative strategy; thus, their orientation with regard to lobbying is a strategy-formulating one. The strategist plans legislative campaigns to be executed by other lobbyists. He may advise other lobbyists concerning legislative strategy and thus act as a "lobbyist's lobbyist."

These role orientations are not mutually exclusive. A contact man plans strategy; a campaign organizer makes contacts; both alert their groups to action and convey factual information. These are analytically distinct orientations in the sense that it is possible to type lobbyist roles in terms of the primacy and saliency of the lobbyist's approach to his job.

Legislative Advocacy Tactics

Patti and Dear (1981) provide seven empirically-based tactics for influencing the lawmaking process. The tactics are drawn from their study of the Washington state legislature and should highlight some of the factors that contribute to effective legislative advocacy. They are practical and essentially self-explanatory.

1. *Introduce the bill early in the session or, ideally, before the session has begun*. The authors suggest this allows the advocate to get a head start on the competition for the legislators attention. It also provides important extra time for additional research to ensure the bill is effectively drafted.

2. *Have more than one legislator sponsor a bill*. The strategy broadens the base of support and, according to the authors, can increase the likelihood that the bill will be reported out of committee—and a reported bill has a better chance of making its way through the process.

3. *Try to obtain the sponsorship of the majority party or, if possible, bipartisan sponsorship*. They conclude that bipartisan sponsorship can be particularly rewarding: it extends the influence and makes the proposal acceptable to a wider (in terms of numbers and ideology) range of legislators.

4. *Try to obtain the support of the governor and relevant state agencies*. The chief executive can throw considerable weight behind a bill he/she supports. The state agency, as an extension of the executive, also exerts enormous influence of the legislation it will be charged to implement. The authors suggest that the support of both increases the bill's chances for passage.

5. *Seek influential legislators to sponsor your bill and try to get them to exert their influence in support of it*. The legislative structure has its own hierarchy, which an advocate can effectively use to pinpoint the key members of the assembly. Knowledge of the committee structure and the seniority system, therefore, is important. But the authors are quick to emphasize that the selected legislator must be ready to use his/her apparent influence in support of your bill.

6. *Press for open committee hearings on the bill and be prepared to offer testimony at them*. Hearings not only offer an opportunity to argue the merits of your bill; they also provide important public exposure. The authors suggest that these hearings also expose potential allies and opponents. Finally, they can be used to educate legislators as well as the public by providing expert testimony on the bill's merits and consequences.

7. *Be prepared to use the amendatory process to advance the bill.*
Given the high degree of compromise that occurs in the legislature, this process may offer invaluable opportunities to promote your bill. The opportunity is not cost-free, however, and there may be some reworking of your original proposal. The authors suggest you consider the extent to which you are willing to live with the changes that may follow from this process. [pp. 99–117]

The above tactics promote, but can not guarantee, a favorable outcome. The authors identify several related factors that challenge even the best advocacy strategies. They present them as dilemmas, and leave them as questions that we must wrestle with. Not surprisingly, there are no easy answers; notwithstanding, they must be faced directly.

• If the advocate has the skill and resources necessary to mobilize an active constituency around a measure, it may be feasible to pursue legislation that calls for far-reaching change at considerable cost.
• In some cases the advocate may wish to proceed with a more ambitious proposal to dramatize an issue or to introduce a policy principle into legislative consideration. In this instance, the purpose is not to achieve immediate success, but to establish a basis for future advocacy.
• When the advocate is pressing several proposals, it may be wise to defer introducing ambitious measures to conserve legislative cooperation and support for measures that stand some chance of passage.
• When the advocate is interested in building a reputation as a political realist, it may be necessary to focus on bills that have some prospect of succeeding. This can help establish the credibility that is often an important asset in advocating for major change.

6 The Administrative Process

Administrative agencies, which exist at local, state, and federal levels, implement legislative goals. The legislature has lawmaking authority, but it must turn to the administrative agency to implement its statutory objectives. This is not to suggest, however, that these agencies lack constraints. The reverse is true: They operate within the context of the enabling legislation that governs their activities.

Administrative agencies promulgate (issue) regulations to inform those governed by the regulations of new standards of conduct to which they must conform. These new standards also influence the conduct of agency officials, who must keep abreast of regulatory changes that effect the programs they administer. Thus, both agency officials and those effected by agency decisions must recognize the interaction between legislative goals and the accomplishment of those goals through agency regulations.

KEY FEATURES OF ADMINISTRATIVE AUTHORITY

Administrative agency authority must be understood within the context of our Constitutional provision for separation of governmental powers. Ours is a republican form of government; it is a government of the people through their representatives, and derives its power and authority from the people. We have expressed in our Constitution our collective will about the distribution of governmental functions necessary to ensure some connection between the exercise of authority and the people from whom that authority emanates. Gov-

ernmental power, consequently, is distributed among three independent departments: the legislative (which enjoys lawmaking authority),
the judicial (which is responsible for law interpretation), and the
executive (which assumes the law enforcement function).

An agency must carry out its statutory mandate within the context
of the authority delegated to it by the legislature. The regulations
thus promulgated have the force of law. And when it exceeds its
statutory authority, its conduct is *ultra vires* and void. Here, again,
we note the tension created by, on the one hand, our need to
reconcile the administrative process with the separation of powers
doctrine and, on the other hand, our determination to have some
governmental institution handle complex social problems. The dilemma then can be viewed in the light of a longstanding problem:
How to blend legislative, judicial, and executive functions in one
institution.

The delegation of authority is not unlimited, however. Agency
conduct must be gauged against the enabling legislation's original
intent and related policy goals. An agency, consequently, can only
make and enforce such rules as are necessary to put into effect
legislative policy. Congress and state legislatures retain jurisdiction
over delegated authority through mechanisms such as legislative
oversight, budget appropriations, confirmation power over executive
branch officials, and its ability to rescind the delegation.

The link between legislative goals and administrative enforcement
then is forged by certain constitutional requirements about the
interrelations among our three branches of government. This interdependence, albeit occasionally cumbersome and complicated, is
essential. This feature is also incorporated in the functioning of administrative agencies. They mirror the constitutional tripartite powers because they must somehow blend all three functions. And as
Robinson and Gellhorn (1977) note below, the task is formidable.

Tripartite Powers in Administrative Government*

Our tripartite constitutional system of checks and balances roughly assigns
lawmaking power to the legislature, law-enforcing power to the executive,
and law-deciding power to the judiciary. Administrative agencies do not
fit neatly into any one of these governmental groupings; their functions
overlap into each. . . .

*From Glen O. Robinson and Ernest Gellhorn, The Administrative Process, pp. 25–33.
© 1972 West Publishing Co., St. Paul, MN. Reprinted with permission of West Publishing Co.

The soundness and constitutionality of this combination of powers in administrative agencies (in contrast to their functional division by the Constitution) was once seriously questioned as being logically and legally indefensible. The attack assumed, erroneously, that each governmental function is both readily distinguishable and mutually exclusive. Neither premise is sound. Many, perhaps even most traditional government bodies perform all three functions. For example, at the turn of the century Congress passed the Sherman Antitrust Act prohibiting any "restraint of trade" tending substantially to reduce competition. This law was passed by the legislature. However, the latter did not decide whether an agreement by two steel companies to fix the prices at which they would sell steel was an unlawful restraint. (The legislature could have decided that question by specifying that price-fixing is an unlawful restraint, but it did not do so.) The executive branch, acting through the Justice Department, may decide this "lawmaking" question by issuing rules against price-fixing and by prosecuting the two steel companies in our example who elected not to observe them (charging them with creating an unlawful restraint on trade). If the steel companies then decide to dispute the question, a court will "make the law," in the manner of a common law court; except that its decision will be announced as in favor of the government or of the steel companies. The nub of the matter is that at each level, be it the legislature, the executive, or the judiciary, the governmental body announces a "rule" that involves lawmaking. Its rule governs past transactions making it, in effect, retroactive. In other words, the executive and the judiciary constantly engage in lawmaking; hence it is incorrect to assert that this function is in the exclusive domain of the legislature. . . .

The constitutional division of power then does not mean that only the legislature, in contrast to the executive or judiciary, can "make the law." In the same vein, administrative agencies engage in lawmaking whenever they issue rules, enforce them, or adjudicate disputes. This does not suggest that the principle of separation of powers embodied in the Constitution is irrelevant and has no meaning in administrative law. Its great end is the dispersal of governmental authority to prevent absolutism. As Professor Jaffe observes, "Its object is the preservation of political safeguards against the capricious exercise of power; and, incidentally, it lays down the broad lines of efficient division of function." Judicial Control of Administrative Action 32 (1965). The legislature is the most "competent" lawmaking body of government and has basic responsibility for writing the law; the courts have similar responsibility for deciding controversies. However, the Constitution is not an organization chart locking government into boxes drawn two centuries ago. When the legislature determines that an administrative agency is the best means for regulating an industry, for distributing licenses or for managing government lands, it is not straight-jacketed by governmental theories current in 1789.

The operation of the typical agency is similar to that of any ongoing enterprise. Plans are made, information sought, negotiations conducted or directions given, and specific decisions are made and implemented. Time is spent on personnel, budgets, and priorities as well as on regulatory functions, and mostly as a matter of routine. As we noted earlier, formal processes are a readily identifiable but only occasional result. They draw much of the attention of administrative law, but their practical significance should be placed in context. This is not to say that formal hearing procedures and practices are insignificant; their ultimate availability may in fact be the determining force for informal procedures. . . .

Administrative Methods

Agencies are given, by statute, a mandate to fulfill. The statutory delegation also sets out how public policy is to be formally articulated and implemented. Three basic methods are generally employed: prosecution, adjudication, and rule making.

Prosecutions: The most common method relied upon to enforce agency policy is to have the agency directly (or indirectly, by referring the matter to the Justice Department) prosecute violators in court. Thus, the Cost of Living Council or the Environmental Protection Agency assure compliance with price controls or pollution requirements by seeking judicially imposed civil fines, injunctions and criminal penalties. In this circumstance the administrative agency is not distinctive from local prosecutors or the Justice Department, itself an administrative agency. In other words, administrative enforcement often is not distinctive.

Adjudications: Agencies are also frequently authorized to adjudicate and decide a matter without initial reliance on judicial authority. These administrative counterparts to judicial trials are called adjudications. At first glance many appear to be merely carbon copies of judicial trials. They are usually open to the public and conducted in an orderly and dignified manner, though not necessarily with the formality of a judicial trial. Typically, the proceeding is initiated by the agency's filing of a complaint in a manner similar to the procedure followed in a civil action. Following the respondent's answer, discovery and pre-hearing conferences may be held. At the trial an administrative law judge presides by conducting the hearing and ruling on all motions. The agency is represented by counsel who presents evidence in either written or oral question-and-answer form in support of the complaint. The respondent then presents his case in the same fashion. Witnesses may be cross-examined, objections may be raised, and rulings issued. The parties usually submit briefs and proposed findings to the law judge. They may also make oral argument. Shortly after the hearing ends, the judge renders a decision, usually supported by findings and a written opinion. If neither agency counsel nor respondent objects, the recommended order is customarily adopted by the agency. If there are exceptions, the agency will review the decision in the manner of an appellate court through the submission of briefs and oral argument by both parties. In general, therefore, a lawyer experienced in litigating cases in state or federal courts will not find an administrative hearing strange or unfamiliar. The parties are represented by counsel; the administrative judge is treated with deference; and the evidence is received in the usual question-and-answer form. On the other hand, variations from this general pattern are neither uncommon nor insignificant. Many adjudicatory hearings are conducted informally without the presence of attorneys and by hearing officers without legal training. In some instances, an action may be initiated by a private party rather than by the agency, such as the granting of a license or the approval of a rate request. In addition, an administrative hearing is tried to the trial judge and never to a jury. Since many of the rules governing the admission of proof in judicial trials are designed to protect the jury from unreliable and possibly confusing evidence, these rules need not be applied with the same vigor in proceedings solely before a judge or trial examiner. Consequently, the rules of evidence applied in jury trials presided over by a judge are frequently inapplicable in an administrative trial. The trial examiner decides both the facts and the law to be applied. He is usually a lawyer and is often an expert on the very question he must decide. Courts, on the other hand, accept whatever cases the parties present. Consequently, their familiarity with the subject matter is accidental. Agencies, however, usually select their cases. Administrative trial judges and agency chiefs are either experts or at least have a substantial familiarity with the subject matter since their jurisdictions tend to be restricted. And agencies are usually staffed by experts whose reports, commonly relating to matters adjudicated before the agencies, are made available to administrative judges and commissioners alike.

Another and more significant distinction between judicial and administrative adjudications is that agency hearings tend to produce evidence of general conditions as distinguished from facts relating solely to the respondent. This difference is attributable to one of the original justifications for administrative agencies—the development of policy. Administrative agencies more consciously formulate policy than do courts. Consequently, administrative hearings require that the hearing officer consider the impact of his decision on the general public interest as well as on the particular respondent. Testimonial evidence and cross-examination therefore often play less decisive roles in many administrative hearings.

Rule making: Perhaps the most distinctive administrative procedure (especially as compared to the judicial process) is rule making, whereby the agency formally seeks to develop and articulate policy, which it will apply in the future. This procedure is wholly separate from adjudication. Adjudication applies (and sometimes develops) policy to a set of past actions and results in an order against (or in favor of) the injured party. The focus of rule making is wholly prospective. And where the rule is substantive (also called legislative or prescriptive) the agency will usually give interested and affected persons notice and an opportunity to be heard before the rule is finally announced. Acting as a quasi-legislative body, agencies issue three types of rules: procedural, interpretative, and substantive. [These three types are defined in the section below that deals with the rule-making process.] . . .

Judicial Review

Court review scrutinizes the fairness of agency procedures and the authority for an 'agency's substantive decisions. The availability and scope of review has a direct bearing not only on the matter under review, but also on general agency procedures and substantive policies. The procedural elements of most adjudicative hearings—insuring that the affected party is given notice, the opportunity to be heard, and the occasion to test unfavorable evidence—stem from constitutional standards and statutory requirements pressed on agencies during judicial review of their final orders.

The major point to note is that regardless of the form of the order or the procedure relied upon, a significant administrative sanction generally cannot be imposed without an opportunity for judicial review. There are of course exceptions. Review may not be available until after a fine or tax is paid or interim license suspended. The discretionary decision of whether to prosecute, which is usually not reviewable, may work a hardship equal to any other. The thrust of current developments, however, is to narrow the exceptions, to open up additional avenues for judicial review, and to require that judicial consideration precede administrative execution.

The function of judicial review is to assure that the administrator's action is authorized (within his delegated authority) and not an abuse of discretion (a reasonable choice supported by available evidence). It assures that, when challenged, the administrative action has not encroached excessively on private rights. Review is generally provided for by statute or by common law precedents. If the administrative sanction involves a significant personal or property interest, the right of review may also have a constitutional (due process) foundation. It is a procedure for public accountability of the administrative process and in the process legitimates the application of administrative sanctions.

On the other hand, the function of judicial review is not to insure the correctness of the administrative decision. That is a matter that the legislature has delegated to the administrator, not to the reviewing court. Rather, judicial review tests whether the agency (a) has exceeded its constitutional or statutory authority, (b) has properly interpreted the applicable law, (c) has conducted a fair proceeding, and (d) has not acted capriciously and unreasonably.

STAGES IN THE ADMINISTRATIVE PROCESS

The Administrative Procedures Act

The Administrative Procedures Act (5 U.S.C. Sec. 551 *et seq*.) grew out of the New Deal experiments with the use of administrative agencies to handle social problems. It was passed in 1946 and welcomed as a major instrument in maintaining fairness. The Act pro-

vides an important context for guaranteeing due process in administrative procedures.

The Act spells out the conditions under which the public can
participate in the administrative process, either through participation
in rule making, in formal hearings, or in adjudication. The remainder
of this chapter will focus on the rule making procedures social workers are most likely to encounter. Social welfare administrators, for
example, are frequent witnesses to numerous instances where clients
are adversely affected by regulations, and the rule making process
provides a major opportunity for intervention to change this regulatory environment.

The Rule-making Process

Rule-making involves developing regulations for future implementation. The agency issues three types:

- *Procedural rules,* which identify an agency's organization, describe its method of operation, and spell out the requirements of
  its practice for rule making and adjudicative hearings. . . . These
  housekeeping rules are usually authorized by the agency's enabling act and are binding on the agency.
- *Interpretative rules,* which are issued by an agency to guide both
  its staff and regulated parties as to how the agency will interpret
  its statutory mandate. They . . . are issued only after interested
  persons are given notice and an opportunity to be heard.
- *Substantive rules,* which are, in effect, administrative statutes. In
  issuing a substantive rule, the administrator exercises lawmaking
  power delegated to him by the legislature. Notice and hearings
  must usually precede issuance of the rule. (Robinson & Gellhorn,
  1972).

The rule-making process then unfolds in two stages. The *first stage*
deals with the proposed rules, which must be published prior to
implementation in order to allow sufficient time for public comment.
This event fulfills the requirement for notice to the public before the
rule is made final, and is accomplished by publishing the proposed
rule. (Federal regulations are published in the *Federal Register;* state
regulations are published in comparable documents.) The comments
from interested parties generally address their perceptions about how
the rules will affect them. The comment period is limited to a speci-

fied time (e.g. thirty days). Comments can be offered in writing, or in some cases at a public hearing. The *second stage* deals with the compilation and analysis of public responses following the comment period. The agency then announces its final rules or regulations, which proceed through a similar notice and comment period. The process culminates in the publication of the final regulations and the date on which they will take effect.

The following example, which details the events surrounding the issuance of the so-called "Baby Doe" regulations, illustrates the rule-making process.

THE BABY DOE REGULATIONS

The case involves an infant born in Bloomington, Indiana on April 9, 1982, who was born with two congenital problems. The child's parents refused to consent to the surgery needed to correct one of the problems and the child was subsequently denied all nutrition and fluids. The state's circuit court and its Supreme Court sanctioned the decision, and the child died on April 15, 1982. Although the case was not the first of its kind, it was the most celebrated, leaving in its wake a heightened public awareness and an announcement from the U.S. Department of Health and Human Services that it would propose regulations to address the problem. A synopsis of the most salient events from April 30, 1982 to July 5, 1983, found in 49 Fed. Reg. 1622 (1984), is provided below.

On April 30, 1982, President Reagan instructed the Secretary of Health and Human Services:

to notify health care providers of the applicability of section 504 of the Rehabilitation Act of 1973 to the treatment of handicapped patients. That law forbids recipients of federal funds from withholding from handicapped citizens, simply because they are handicapped, any benefit or service that would ordinarily be provided to persons without handicaps. Regulations under this law specifically prohibit hospitals and other providers of health services receiving federal assistance from discriminating against the handicapped. . . . Our nation's commitment to equal protection of the law will have little meaning if we deny such protection to those who have not been blessed with the same physical or mental gifts we too often take for granted. I support federal laws prohibiting discrimination against the handicapped, and remain determined that such laws will be vigorously enforced.

The President's instructions followed reports of the death, in Bloomington, Indiana, of an infant with Down's syndrome, from whom available
surgical treatment to repair a detached esophagus was withheld.

On May 18, 1982, HHS issued to approximately 7,000 hospitals a notice
stating:

> Under section 504 it is unlawful for a recipient of federal assistance to
> withhold from a handicapped infant nutritional sustenance or medical
> or surgical treatment required to correct a life-threatening condition
> if: (1) the withholding is based on the fact that the infant is hand-
> icapped; (2) the handicap does not render the treatment of nutritional
> sustenance medically contraindicated.

Soon after this notice, the HHS Office for Civil Rights (OCR) established expedited investigative procedures to deal with any case of a
suspected discriminatory withholding of life-sustaining nourishment or
medical treatment from a handicapped infant.

On March 7, 1983, HHS issued, with a scheduled effective date of
March 22, 1983, an interim final rule requiring recipient hospitals to post
"in a conspicuous place" in pertinent wards a notice advising of the
applicability of section 504 and the availability of a telephone "hotline" to
report suspected violations of the law.

On April 14, 1983, the Honorable Gerhard Gesell, United States District Judge for the District of Columbia, declared the interim final rule
invalid on the grounds that it was "arbitrary and capricious" and that there
was inadequate justification for waiving a public comment period prior to
issuance of the regulation. *American Academy of Pediatrics v. Heckler*,
561 F.Supp. 395 (D.D.C. 1983). Judge Gesell declined to order the
Department to discontinue use of the hotline.

On July 5, 1983, HHS issued a proposed rule in which the notice
requirement was revised; provisions were added concerning state child
protective service agencies; an appendix of standards and examples was
added; and a 60-day comment period was provided. 48 FR 30846.

The Department received 16,739 comments, of which 16,331 (97.5%)
supported the proposed rule, and 408 (2.5%) opposed it. [Other aggregate
descriptions omitted here.]

In addition to the written comments received, a number of meetings
were held after issuance of the proposed rule with representatives of
interested groups. The principal HHS officials involved in these meetings
were the Under Secretary and the Surgeon General. Minutes of these
meetings were kept and have been included in the public comment
file.

Every comment was read and analyzed. Readers determined whether
the commenter was in favor of or opposed to the proposed rule and
identified particular points made by the commenter. The decisions made
by the Department in connection with the rule are based not on the
volume of comments advancing any point, but on thorough consideration
of the merits of the comments submitted.

The above activity notwithstanding, Congress soon entered the scene. Searching for a broader legal "hook" than section 504, the House, in February, 1984, debated a bill to amend the Child Abuse Prevention and Treatment Act (Pub.L. 93–247, 42 U.S.C. 5101, *et seq.*). The amendment would broaden the definition of child abuse to include instances similar to the Bloomington, Indiana Baby Doe. The new amendment also required that states implement a reporting system that would alert state authorities when handicapped infants were being deprived of nutrition or treatment. Not surprisingly, this requirement was a condition for continued receipt of federal funds. The House passed the bill by a 231 to 182 vote. It then went to the Senate, which produced an amended version that was subsequently accepted by the House and enacted as Pub.L. 98-457.

Pub.L. 98-457 emerged from this show of Congressional concern. Known as the Amendments to Child Abuse Prevention and Treatment Act, it promised to be the final word on the topic. The new Act redefined the term "withholding of medically-indicated treatment" to mean:

> The failure to respond to the infant's life-threatening conditions by providing treatment (including appropriate nutrition, hydration, and medication) which, in the treating physician's or physicians' reasonable medical judgment, will be most likely to be effective in ameliorating or correcting all such conditions, except that the term does not include the failure to provide treatment (other than appropriate nutrition, hydration, or medication) to an infant when, in the treating physician's or physicians' reasonable medical judgment, (A) the infant is chronically and irreversibly comatose; (B) the provision of such treatment would (i) merely prolong dying, (ii) not be effective in ameliorating or correcting all of the infant's life-threatening conditions, or (iii) otherwise be futile in terms of the survival of the infant; or (C) the provision of such treatment would be virtually futile in terms of the survival of the infant and the treatment itself under such circumstances would be inhumane. (Pub.L. 98-457)

As a condition of receiving state grants under the Act, states must establish programs or procedures:

> [F]or the purpose of responding to the reporting of medical neglect (including instances of withholding of medically indicated treatment from disabled infants with life-threatening conditions), procedures or programs, or both (within the State child protective service system), to provide for (i) coordination and consultation with individuals designed by and within appropriate health care facilities, (ii) prompt notification

by individuals designated by and within appropriate health care facilities cases of suspected medical neglect . . . and (iii) authority, under State law, for the State child protective service system to pursue any legal remedies, including the authority to initiate legal proceedings in a court of competent jurisdiction, as may be necessary to prevent withholding of medically-indicated treatment from disabled infants with life-threatening conditions. (Pub.L. 98–457)

The Department of Health and Human Services, on December 10, 1984, announced proposed rules and interim model guidelines to implement Pub.L. 98–457. Pursuant to the notice and comment provisions, affected parties were given until February 1985 to comment on them. The response was comparable to the earlier announcements for the Sec. 504 rules—over 116,000 comments were received and analyzed. The overwhelming majority of those supplying comments generally supported the rule. Moreover, many respondents agreed that all disabled infants should receive appropriate nutrition regardless of their condition and endorsed the Department's position that life and death decisions should not be based on subjective assessments of "quality of life." There were also some commenters that disapproved of the proposed rules, either because they objected to any form of governmental intervention or because they thought the rule's language beyond Congress's intent. The final rules, along with accompanying interpretative guidelines, were published on April 15, 1985. As Nicholson (1985) describes below, the final rule tries to reconcile the contradictions in the proposed rule and thereby provide clearer guidance for the future.

The Final Rule*

The Department reiterated that reasonable medical judgment does not sanction decisions based on subjective opinions regarding the future "quality of life" of a disabled infant. The final rule deleted the examples of specific diagnoses used in the proposed rule to elaborate on the meaning of key terms, in order to avoid what some commenters called a "cookbook approach" to practicing medicine. The term "imminent" was deleted altogether, both from the final rule and accompanying appendix, but the interpretive guidelines "continue to make clear that treatment may not be withheld solely due to a distant prognosis of death." The Department also

---

*From E. Bruce Nicholson, Final Federal "Baby Doe" Rule Released. *Mental and Physical Disability Law Reporter, 9*(3) pp. 228–229. © 1985 American Bar Association, Washington, DC, (202) 331–2240. Reprinted by permission.

adopted the recommendations of many commenters that specific provisions in the final rule address child protective services (CPS) agency procedures to: (1) obtain access to medical records, (2) when necessary, obtain a court order or an independent medical examination, and (3) require CPS agencies to contact health care facilities to identify designated hospital liaisons.

At section 1340.15, the final rule mandates that, in order to qualify for basic state grants under the federal Child Abuse Amendments, states must have programs and/or procedures in place, by October 9, 1985 (within their child protective service system to respond to reports of medical neglect). Medical neglect is defined as instances of the withholding of medically indicated treatment from disabled infants with life-threatening conditions. Moreover, regardless of an infant's condition, appropriate nutrition, hydration and medication must be provided.

Section 1340.15 (b) defines the "witholding of medically indicated treatment" to mean the failure to respond to the infant's life-threatening conditions by providing treatment which, in the treating physician's or physicians' reasonable medical judgment, will be most likely to be effective in ameliorating or correcting all such conditions. The term explicitly excludes from coverage the failure to provide treatment to an infant when, in the treating physician's (physicians') reasonable medical judgment any of the following circumstances apply: (i) the infant is chronically and irreversible comatose; (ii) the provision of such treatment would prolong dying, not be effective in ameliorating or correcting all of the infant's life-threatening conditions or otherwise be futile in terms of the survival of the infant; or (iii) the provision of such treatment would be virtually futile in terms of the survival of the infant, and the treatment itself under such circumstances would be inhumane.

Sections 1340.15(b)(3)(i) and (b)(3)(ii) of the final rule retain the definitions of "infant" and "reasonable medical judgment" used in the proposed rules, but all other definitions have been deleted. Interpretive, but not binding, definitions of "life-threatening condition," "treatment," "merely prolong dying," "not be effective in ameliorating or correcting all of the infant's life threatening conditions," "virtually futile," and "the treatment itself under such circumstances would be inhumane" are now found in the interpretive appendix. The definition of "infant" in the proposed rule encompassed three categories of infants over one year of age: infants who have been continuously hospitalized since birth; those who were born extremely prematurely; or those who have a long term disability. The final rule states that "infants" may include those three categories of children for who the definition of "medically indicated treatment" should be applied. In addition, while protection for children over one year of age under general medical neglect standards is not affected by this rule, the standards of the more precise definition of "medically indicated treatment" should be consulted thoroughly in an evaluation of suspected medical neglect.

The term "reasonable medical judgment" is defined identically in the proposed and final rules in section 1340.15(b)(3)(ii)—"a medical judgment that would be made by a reasonable prudent physician, knowledgeable about the case and the treatment possibilities with respect to the medical conditions involved."

CPS Requirements: The proposed rule would have imposed three procedural requirements on state child protective services systems: coordination and consultation with designated persons in health care facilities, notification to those individuals of cases of suspected medical neglect, and the authority to initiate legal proceedings in courts to protect affected infants. The final rule retains those requirements and adds several more.

First, it requires child protective service systems to adopt procedures specifying that they will contact promptly each health care facility to obtain the name, title, and phone number of the designated person serving as liaison and, at least annually, verify this information for accuracy.

Also, the child protective services agencies must have programs and/or procedures to obtain, in a manner consistent with state law,

. . . (i) access to medical records and/or other pertinent information when such access is necessary to assure an appropriate investigation of a report of medical neglect (including instances of withholding of medically indicated treatment from disabled infants with life threatening conditions; and (ii) a court order for an independent examination in accordance with processes established under State law, when necessary to assure an appropriate resolution of a report of medical neglect. . . .

Section 1340.15(c)(4). Supplementary information regarding these requirements is provided in the preamble to the final rule.

Adoption of procedural requirements for access to medical records and medical examinations is consistent with existing federal child abuse and neglect regulations under The Child Abuse Prevention and Treatment Act. States must have procedures for adequate investigations and the provision of protective services.

Appendix: Interpretive Guidelines

The appendix includes nonbinding rules of law that are supposed to enhance effective implementation by setting out the department's interpretations of several key terms.

The term "life-threatening condition" in both the proposed rule and appendix means a condition that significantly increases the risk of complications that may threaten the life of the infant. The Department stresses the use of the physician's "reasonable medical judgment" in making interpretations of what is life-threatening.

The term "treatment" is defined as it was in the proposed rule—in the context of adequate evaluation. The role of "reasonable medical judgment is stressed in defining the breadth of the term "treatment." The guidelines indicate that a reasonably prudent physician faced with a particular condition about which he or she needs additional information and knowledge on treatment possibilities, would seek further evaluation with an appropriate specialist or at specialized facilities.

The term "merely prolong dying," as defined in the proposed rule, section 1340.15(b)(3)(v), *"refers to situations where death is imminent and treatment will do not more than postpone the act of dying"* (emphasis added).

The word "imminent" was specifically rejected during the course of the lengthy legislative negotiations, but was included in the proposed rules. The word "imminent" is deleted from the final rules and interpretive guidelines. The guidelines explain that the Department continues to interpret Congressional intent as not permitting the "merely prolong dying" provision to apply where many years of life will result from the provision of treatment, or where the prognosis is not for death in the near future, but rather in the more distant future. This distinction addresses the concern of the many comments of medical organizations over the exercise of "reasonable medical judgment" by physicians in decisions to provide life-sustaining treatment for infants who will die within a matter of weeks and for those infants whose prognosis is many years of life with the provision of treatment.

The definition of the term "not be effective in ameliorating or correcting all of the infant's life-threatening conditions" is unchanged in the interpretive guidelines. Specific diagnostic examples of this term, included in the proposed rule, were omitted from the appendix, which instead simply stresses the role of "reasonable medical judgment." This discussion fails to address the situation in which treatment could only serve to make a condition more tolerable, such as providing treatment to relieve severe pain, even if the final prognosis is death.

The term "virtually futile" was defined in section 1340.15(b)(vii) of the proposed rule to mean that "treatment is highly unlikely to prevent imminent death." As with definition of "merely prolong dying," the department deleted "imminent" from this definition in the appendix, and now interprets it "to mean that the treatment is highly unlikely to prevent death in the near future."

The phrase "the treatment itself under such circumstances would be inhumane," as in the proposed rule, is interpreted to mean that treatment is not medically indicated where it "involves significant medical contraindications and/or significant pain and suffering for the infant that clearly outweigh the very slight potential benefit of the treatment for an infant highly unlikely to survive." This interpretation stresses the effect of the process of treatment itself rather than an evaluation of its results. The Department notes parenthetically that the use of the term "inhumane" in this context does not suggest that the humaneness of treatment is not a legitimate consideration in other contexts.

JUDICIAL INTERPRETATION OF REGULATIONS

We observed in the last chapter that courts interpret legislation, and do so in the light of legislative intent. They also interpret regulations. Though inclined to defer to the presumed superior expertise of administrative agencies, the court will interpret agency regulations in the light of the enabling legislation. An example is provided in a Baby Doe-related case, *American Academy of Pediatrics v. Heckler*, 561 F.Supp. 395 (D.D.C. (1983)). The case involved the validity of an "interim final regulation" published by the Secretary of Health and Human Services on March 7, 1983. The plaintiffs charged that the regulation, which concerned the care and treatment of newborn infants in about 6,400 hospitals that receive federal funds, was published without providing for the usual period for public comment. They contended, therefore, that the regulation was arbitrary and capricious, that no justification existed for dispensing with public comment as required by the Administrative Procedures Act (APA), and that the Secretary lacked statutory authority to act.

The regulation, which was promulgated under the authority of Section 504 of the Rehabilitation Act of 1973 and issued as a "interim final rule", became effective on March 22, 1983. It required hospitals and other medical institutions receiving federal financial assistance to post permanently in a conspicuous place in each relevant ward and nursery a sign stating "Any person having knowledge that a handicapped infant is being discriminatorily denied food or customary medical care should immediately contact [the] Handicapped Infant Hotline. . . ."

The court ruled against the Department and found the rule invalid as an arbitrary and capricious act. It reasoned that

> The Administrative Procedures Act . . . was designed to curb bureaucratic actions taken without consultation and notice to persons affected. Broad delegations of rule-making authority from the Congress were intended to be tempered by assuring a degree of due process for those to be governed by the rule. . . . Thus the Act has been generally construed to curtail rule making without comment. . . . [G]round may have existed for undertaking a regulatory approach to the problem . . . [but this rule] is invalid as arbitrary and capricious agency action under the [APA].

SOCIAL WORK ADVOCACY
AND THE ADMINISTRATIVE PROCESS

Finally, we examine how our understanding of the above stages can be used in social work advocacy strategies. The previous description of the rule-making process clearly implies that there are certain conditions under which the rules could be modified. And an understanding of both the system's operation and its capacity for responsiveness is important for social workers. The discussion below highlights social work advocacy techniques and their role in the rule-making process.

Techniques for Participation in Administrative Hearings

Effective social work advocacy in the regulatory process will, as a practical matter, depend on the worker's ability to (1) analyze the regulations, (2) properly organize written comments and testimony for hearings, and (3) engage in pre- and post-notice activities to maximize their influence on the regulatory process.

How to Analyze Regulations: The purpose and intent of a regulation cannot always be discerned by simply reading it. As discussed earlier, regulations are issued pursuant to a broad statutory authority. You must, therefore, have a clear understanding of this authority before you can argue reliably whether a regulation is within the scope of the statute upon which it is based.

Statsky's (1975) advice on this point is especially compelling:

> ". . . because a regulation exists, you cannot assume that it is valid. Simply because the agency is giving an official interpretation of its regulations (in connection with the facts of your case), you cannot assume that that interpretation is correct, even though the same agency that passed the regulation is the agency that is now interpreting it."

His analytical framework is comprised of four questions, which are all aimed at making sense of the particular regulation in the light of the relevant statutory authority:

1. Is there some statute in existence that gives the agency authority to pass regulations on the *general subject matter* of the regulation before you?

2. Is there a statute that is the authority for the *particular* regulation before you?
3. Is the *agency's interpretation* of its own regulation consistent with the statute upon which it is based?
4. Is *your interpretation* of the regulation consistent with the statute upon which it is based? (Statsky, 1975)

The above materials offer ample opportunities for discovering how you might go about applying Statsky's framework. Essentially, your major task will be to reconcile your interpretation of the regulations with the agency's. Your effectiveness as an advocate may well turn on your competency in such regulatory analysis.

Organizing Written Comments and Testimony for Hearings: The comment period following the notice of proposed or final rules presents an opportunity for social work intervention. Social service administrators and supervisors are in an ideal position to witness regulation's potential impact on the services they deliver, and the comment period can be used to influence the scope of the rules that are ultimately implemented. A carefully drafted written response to the agency or an intelligently structured verbal presentation at a public hearing can be very influential. A related and perhaps obvious strategy is to engage in coalition-building to expand the number of individuals who send comments to the agency or offer testimony at a public hearing.

Offering testimony at a public hearing differs from written comments to the agency in that the hearing is a more formal setting, and thus requires a more structured response. Therefore, pay particular attention to techniques that enhance your verbal presentation, such as: making sure you identify yourself and your agency, your agency's interest in the regulations, citing your perception of the regulations' impact on your service delivery and on your clients, identifying your agency's unique expertise, if any, that "qualifies" you to address the subject matter of the regulations, recognizing the legitimacy of alternative views, while also being prepared to refute them through documentation, and stating your agency's longstanding experience with the regulatory topic.

Activities Before and After the Notice and Comment Period: Certain pre- and post-notice activities help provide a link with the analysis of regulations and the responses offered during the comment period. The activities essentially stress mutual education, information-sharing, and constituency-building, and are designed to enhance communication between the administrative agency and the social worker. The accomplishment of effective client advocacy is the essential objective around which the activities are built.

The assumption underlying this strategy is that both sides have something to gain from a mutual exchange of information and concerns about a regulation's impact on service delivery. Although both parties approach this exchange from different perspectives, they might each gain something from it. The commonality of interests can be used to facilitate negotiation on the points on which they differ.

Techniques for getting involved prior to publication of the regulations are varied, and include activities such as: educating yourself about the administrative agency's structure, decision hierarchy, jurisdiction, and policy statements; familiarizing yourself with agency staff, particularly those who seem receptive to your position; sharing your views with agency staff to educate them as to your interests and to inform them of the extent to which your views are representative of other service providers; identifying within the agency individuals who have expert knowledge in the substantive areas with which you are concerned; and researching the agency's position on your particular topic to predict potential agency decisions and to identify interest groups who seem to dominate agency decision making.

Activities following participation in the hearings can be as narrow or as comprehensive as the circumstances warrant. In the light of the above, certain activities seem *de minimus:* maintaining communications between you, other affected service providers, and sympathetic agency staff to keep abreast of developments; monitoring the relevant regulations and their subsequent hearings to spot actual or potential implementation problems; sharing relevant new information with agency staff; mobilizing support among other service providers to encourage their stake in the outcome; identifying actual or potential problems with regulatory enforcement to make the agency aware of such breakdowns and to prepare a foundation for any future legal challenge; and standing ready to organize service-provider pressure against a proposed or final regulation.

7 Institutional Interdependence in the Development of Social Policy

The previous chapters presented the processes by which courts, legislatures, and administrative agencies resolve problems. We noted each institution's unique functions, yet we also witnessed their interdependence. This chapter will briefly explore this interplay by examining Pennsylvania's attempts to create and implement law dealing with the civil commitment of the mentally ill.

THE RISE AND DEMISE OF PENNSYLVANIA'S MENTAL HEALTH/MENTAL RETARDATION ACT

Defining the Goals of the Mental Health/Mental Retardation Act of 1966

Pennsylvania's Mental Health/Mental Retardation Act of 1966 (MH/MR) established the present framework for the state's mental health delivery system and attempted to respond comprehensively to the needs of the mentally ill. It assigned state and county responsibilities, and provided for general procedures for admission, commitment, transfer, and discharge of patients. The focus here, however, is much narrower; we will only examine the statutory provisions for involuntary commitment.

Article IV of the MH/MR outlined, among other things, the requirements for involuntary commitment. This provision encountered the most legal resistance because its requirements could be met simply by a finding that someone was "mentally disabled and in need of care." The legislature was aware of the potential problems that follow from such a broad standard, as the following legislative journal excerpt attests:

> Mr. MAHADY. Mr. President . . . [Senate Bill No. 8, which was ultimately enacted as the MH/MR Act, contains] . . . the widest definition of mental disability I have ever seen in the law. . . . The definition includes "any other mental condition which so lessens the capability of a person to use customary self-control, judgment and discretion in the conduct of his affairs and social relations." In other words, if I do not manage my business and I have a lot of money and I have a lot of heirs, they can say that I come under this Act. The [state] Supreme Court says that the managing of one's business is not a question of whether he is sane or not sane and they have decided that on numerous occasions, as has the [state] Superior Court, which they have sustained. . . . [W]e are all in favor of mental health and we believe in the principles behind this bill but, in so doing, we should not go haywire and make everyone, including the fifty members of this Body, subject to the "booby hatch" on the motion of any close friend [33 Pennsylvania Legislative Journal 73 (1966)].

As expected, the standard's vague scope would undermine the Act's implementation, an unfortunate development because the legislature was very committed to caring for the mentally ill and the mentally retarded; enough so to provide adequate funding. They were ready ". . . to make it possible for every disabled person to receive the kind of treatment he needs, when and where he needs it. . . . [and] make those services available to every citizen in every community, which are now available only to a lucky few, in the more progressive communities" (34 Pennsylvania Legislative Journal 77 (1966).

In sum, the legislature's desire to serve the mentally ill and mentally retarded and to devise a scheme to separate the potentially dangerous mentally ill from the rest of the community was understandable, as was the broad standard applied to both. However, the two goals proved difficult to reconcile. The impact on the involuntarily committed would expose some of the more complicated problems associated with integrating legal rights and service delivery.

Judicial Responses to the MH/MR Legislative Goals

The MH/MR Act, as illustrated above, was handicapped from the start. The involuntary commitment provisions, in particular, could not withstand judicial scrutiny. For example, a series of court decisions between 1971 and 1976 nullified most of these provisions because they provided, in effect, for summary admission to state hospitals (a condition caused by the fact that the state had a minimal burden of proof to carry to support its assertion that someone was "mentally disabled and in need of care"). The gap thus created posed a significant challenge for the Pennsylvania legislature. (The judicial responses are numerous, so the description below identifies only those that effect the provisions under discussion.)

The judicial attacks on Pennsylvania's civil commitment legislation were actually a continuation of court challenges begun in *Lessard v. Schmidt*, 349 F.Supp. 1072 (E.D. Wis. 1972), which extended the procedural due process protections articulated in *In Re Gault*, 387 U.S. 1 (1967), to the mentally ill in danger of civil commitment. The *Lessard* decision stated the constitution required proof beyond a reasonable doubt of "imminent danger of bodily harm to oneself or others." This new standard, albeit vague, changed the burden the state had to carry. Subsequent Pennsylvania decisions continued the trend. For example, *Dixon v. Commonwealth*, 325 F.Supp. 966 (M.D. Pa. 1971) invalidated the provisions of section 404 of the MH/MR Act as applied to committed convicts; *Bartley v. Kremen*, 402 F.Supp. 1039 (E.D. Pa. 1975) invalidated section 402 and 403 as applied to minors admitted by guardians or parents; *Finken v. Roop*, 339 A.2d 764 (1975) invalidated the basic "mentally disabled and in need of care" standard; and *Eubanks v. Clark*, 434 F.Supp. 1022 (E.D. Pa. 1977) required that patient transfers to more restrictive facilities must be preceded by the type of hearing required in *Dixon*.

FILLING THE GAP: THE 1976 MENTAL HEALTH PROCEDURES ACT (MHPA)

Defining Legislative Goals for the 1976 MHPA

The MHPA (Act of July 9, 1976, No. 143, 1976 P.L. 817) conforms with the requirements specified in *Dixon v. Commonwealth* because each branch is aware of the other's developments, and each acknowledges these in their particular deliberations. In this instance, the Pennsylvania legislature was aware of the 1966 MH/MR Act, its service delivery structure, its deficiencies, and its reception by the court. They thus "heard" the judicial attacks and service delivery complaints about the earlier act and moved to reform it.

Regarding involuntary commitment and treatment, for example, the MHPA allowed the following: emergency examination and treatment (72 hour limit); extended emergency treatment (not to exceed 20 days); court-ordered treatment for emergency and non-emergency patients (not to exceed 90 days); and additional periods of court-ordered treatment (not to exceed 180 days).

To eliminate the vagueness of the 1966 MH/MR Act, the MHPA specified three criteria to replace the MH/MR's "mentally ill and in need of treatment" standard for involuntary commitment: (1) dangerous behavior as a result of mental illness in the last 30 days: (2) mental illness: and (3) reasonable probability that (without intervention) the dangerous behavior will be repeated. Therefore, persons may be subject to involuntary examination and treatment when, as a result of mental illness, their capacity to exercise self-control, judgment and discretion in the conduct of their affairs and social relationships or care of their personal needs is so lessened that they pose a clear and present danger of harm to self or others.

Generally, danger of harm to others is shown by establishing that within the past 30 days the person has inflicted, attempted to inflict serious bodily harm to another, or made threats of harm and committed acts in furtherance of the threat.

Danger to self is shown by establishing that within the past 30 days:

1. the person has acted in such manner as to evidence that he would be unable, without care, supervision and the continued assistance of others, to satisfy his need for nourishment, personal or medical care, shelter, or self-protection and safety; and that there is reasonable probability that death, serious bodily injury, or serious physical debilitation would ensue within 30 days unless adequate treatment were afforded under this act; or

2. the person has attempted suicide and that there is the reasonable probability of suicide unless adequate treatment is afforded under this act. For the purposes of this subsection, a clear and present danger may be demonstrated by the proof that the person has made threats to commit suicide and has committed acts which are in furtherance of the threat to commit suicide; or

3. the person has substantially mutilated himself or attempted to mutilate himself substantially and that there is the reasonable probability of mutilation unless adequate treatment is afforded under this

act. For the purposes of this subsection, a clear and present danger shall be established by proof that the person has made threats to commit mutilation and has committed acts which are in furtherance of the threat to commit mutilation.

The provisions of the MH/MR Act that permitted transfer to a more restrictive setting without a hearing were invalidated by *Eubanks v. Clarke,* and modified by the MHPA. The MHPA provides that whenever a transfer constitutes a "greater restraint", it shall not take place unless a judge or mental health review officer "finds it to be necessary and appropriate". Consistent with *Eubanks,* the MHPA also declared "the policy of the Commonwealth" to be the imposition of "the least restrictions consistent with adequate treatment."

The Act also contained provisions for enhancing the quality of the mental health delivery system, such as the use of mental health review officers and the use of statistical data to improve patient tracking and provide a greater link between hospitals and state offices.

Refining the 1976 MHPA Legislative Goals: The 1978 Amendment

About a year after its enactment, the MHPA was amended to address several weaknesses that surfaced during its initial implementation. As the following legislative debate attests, there were some major reservations about the MHPA's effectiveness. Notwithstanding, the amendment was enacted on November 26, 1978.

[The following debate unfolds in two stages. In the first stage, Senator Coopersmith seeks to revert to a prior printer's version of the bill, which contained slightly different language. The first vote, then, is on whether to use the current or prior printer's version of the bill. The second vote is on the amendment itself.]

Senator COOPERSMITH. Mr. President, if I may explain, the amendment which was put in at the previous Session, two weeks ago, amended, on page 6, the definition of determining clear and present danger to read: "Clear and present danger to others shall be shown by establishing that within the past 30 days the person has inflicted, (or) attempted to inflict," and then to this amendment was added, "or is likely to inflict serious bodily harm on another . . ."

The problem with the amendment is that the definition originally refers to what has happened in the past thirty days; it uses the past tense and then this new clause was added, "or is likely to inflict." The problem with that is there is no time limit—it is placed in the wrong part of the paragraph—because you cannot say that someone within the past thirty days was likely to inflict, you go by what has actually happened. . . . If you look at the language there is no time limit on it. Theoretically, if a psychiatrist would say that anybody, during the course of his lifetime, was likely to inflict some kind of harm on another, he could be committed. I do not believe anyone in this Chamber wants to do that. For that reason I urge my colleagues to vote that we revert to the prior printer's number.

Senator DWYER. Mr. President, I oppose the motion to revert to the prior printer's number. I believe the language of the bill is much clearer than has been explained by the previous speaker.

I would like to explain a few of the reasons for this particular amendment. . . . It is a particularly important problem to many people who have mental illness and to their families. I will tell you [a story which indicates] why this amendment was introduced, why I think it is necessary and why I think it is an improvement to the Mental Health Procedures Act of 1976.

Several months ago I received a call from a constituent, an elderly man, and he stated to me that he and his wife were both in their seventies. He reported that they had a son about thirty-five years old living with them. The son had been a healthy person but had been involved in an automobile accident. As a result of the accident he had sustained brain damage and he had been in a State mental institution. He had been discharged from that State mental institution and placed in the custody of his aged parents. This went on successfully for quite some time but the father and mother ascertained that the son was starting to deteriorate as far as his mental condition was concerned.

They went to the Crawford County Mental Health Director who told them that under the [MHPA] of 1976 there was nothing he could do. The father called me, he called several other local officials and we worked with the staff here in Harrisburg, both the majority and minority staff; we worked with the department trying to help this particular family. The father called two or three more times saying that his son's situation was deteriorating. The Crawford County Mental Health Director had stated that the son could receive treatment if the father would file a complaint and, after a five-day period, the son would be served with a notice at their home, at which time he would receive the involuntary treatment. The father said, "If my son receives this notice while he is living in our home, he will snap and I fear for the life of my wife and myself". This went on then for a period of several weeks. One day, in the paper, sure enough the father had been right. The father had been severely beaten by the son and the son was in a Crawford County jail.

If an amendment had been in the [MHPA] at that particular time, the Crawford County Mental Health Administrator would have had the flexibility, as an expert, to determine whether or not the father was right when he said the son needed the treatment that would have prevented the father from being assaulted and the son winding up in jail. . . .

As I said, with my amendment, at least my interpretation of it, if a member of the family finds that someone is likely to inflict serious bodily harm, they could go to the mental health authorities, the experts we designate to handle the programs, present the situation and those mental health authorities would then have the flexibility to use their expertise to decide whether or not a person should be treated.

This amendment provides a double protection that actually helps those people the 1976 [MHPA] is trying to treat.

[The debate continued on the merits of reverting to the prior printer's number. Ultimately, the senate voted 33 to 12 against reverting to the prior printer number. Following this vote, they went on to consider the bill for a third time. Excerpts from their discussions on this third consideration follows.]

Senator HESS. Mr. President, I rise to discuss certain aspects of Senate Bill 1105 before us today. . . .

Just a little over a year ago we were faced with the monumental task of drafting a new [MHPA] because many portions of the previous [MH/ MR act] were declared unconstitutional by the courts of the commonwealth. . . .

In 1976 we took the first step, that of enacting a new procedure. In the course of the past year we have tried hard to research, to study and to understand the individual segments of the administrative process in order to be sure that what we did in 1976 was in the best interests of the citizens. We could find through experience those areas of weakness and the areas which are functioning at their maximum potential.

Some of the concerns we were faced with during this period were brought to us by individual constituents, as well as community organizations that were propelled into the governmental forefront to advocate reforms because unfortunate and unusual events brought to light certain gaps in the system that needed correction.

We have tried in this legislation to fill in those gaps and to provide a coordinated process by which individuals can best be served in their need to receive mental health care. However, at this time, I must add that we cannot hold the hand of the examining psychiatrist, nor can we tell each county administrator case by case what to do, nor should we tell mental health review officers or judges exactly what they should and should not consider. But, it is left to us to formulate a tight and well-geared system by which the needs of the mentally ill can be met. There has been a clear lack of application in some instances and a lack of coordination between different parts of the delivery system. I think that Senate Bill No. 1105 goes a long way, but not all the way, in providing this well-coordinated end.

One area I hope to watch and monitor is the effectiveness and the depth of the definition of "clear and present danger." I feel there is a need to

*address the problem of "immediate potential to carry out a threat against
another," yet, I realize this is hard to define legally—but I want us to
continue to try.* (Emphasis added.)

[The debate ended with some remarks from Senator Dwyer, who
noted his support for the bill. The senate then voted 46 to 0 to enact
the bill.] (Pennsylvania Legislative Journal 53 (1978))

As the above debate illustrates, the legislature tried both to enact a
better law and to alert future legislatures to potential gaps in this
new—and refined law. Their success on this score, however, will be
decided against the background of the following judicial and policy
guidelines.

AFTERMATH OF THE MHPA: FUTURE POLICY ISSUES

Judicial Questions

Although the MHPA addressed the constitutional deficiencies in the
MH/MR Act, it too may be modified in the light of judicial decisions
announced since its enactment. The *Lessard* standard, which specified "proof beyond a reasonable doubt", has been superseded by
other U.S. Supreme Court decisions, such as *Donaldson v. O'Connor,* 422 U.S. 563 (1975) and *Addington v. Texas,* 441 U.S. 418
(1979). The new decisions suggest that the best standard is one that
balances individual rights, public interest, and available resources.

Agency Attempts to Implement the MHPA: The 1985 Guidelines

A 1982 study evaluated Pennsylvania's implementation of its Mental
Health Procedures Act. The study focused on the Act's implementation, and drew on analyses of commitment records, of county mental
health program and service data, and of attitudes of various system
participants about the commitment process. Given its compre-
hensiveness, the study produced a variety of recommendations
dealing with all aspects of the MHPA and its implementation. In
response to the study, the state's Office of Mental Health prepared,
among other things, some guidelines for assessing and documenting
the "dangerousness" standard under the Act. Though neither exhaustive nor the final word on the topic, they go a long way towards
providing some guidance for mental health professionals.

PENNSYLVANIA OFFICE OF MENTAL HEALTH GUIDELINES FOR ASSESSING AND DOCUMENTING THE DANGEROUSNESS OF MENTALLY ILL ADULTS

Assessing the Reasonable Probability that the Dangerous Conduct Will be Repeated—Involuntary Commitment Process

State mental hospital staff should consider the following factors when considering involuntary emergency examination and treatment, filing petitions, presenting court testimony related to involuntary commitments, and in other situations requiring assessment of dangerousness as a result of mental illness.

Danger to Others

It is more likely that dangerous conduct to others as a result of mental illness will be repeated when there is a:

1. History of violent conduct as a result of mental illness.
2. History of arrest(s) and/or convictions for violent crimes.
3. History of at least one inpatient mental hospitalization associated with dangerous conduct, whether that hospitalization was voluntary or involuntary.
4. History of dangerous conduct that was unprovoked and not directly related to a stressful situation.

Danger to Self

It is more likely that dangerous conduct to self as a result of mental illness will be repeated when there is:

1. A history of threats or attempts to commit suicide.
2. A diagnosis of a mental disorder in which suicidal behavior is a frequent symptom (for example, psychotic depression).
3. A history of threatening to, attempting to, or actually inflicting bodily harm upon oneself through a violent act.
4. A diagnosis of a mental disorder in which self-mutilating acts are a common symptom (for example, impulse disorders, certain psychoses and depressions).
5. An inability to provide for such basic needs as food and shelter as a result of mental illness especially when severe confusion and/or extreme environmental conditions contribute to a life-threatening condition of self-neglect.

In sum, the above guidelines will be as good as the specificity and consistency with which they are implemented. They may actually inform the decision-making by mental health professionals by, at least, limiting the conditions under which they exercise their professional discretion. The final test, however, will emerge from a court and its interpretation of the extent to which even these very specifically-drawn guidelines protect a patient's legal rights. The court will gauge professional conduct using many of the same criteria included in the above decisions—or even announce new ones. But given the specificity of the guidelines, one would hope the court would appreciate the agency's attempt to deal fairly with individuals.

CONCLUSION

We have thus come full circle in dealing with concerns that preoccupied the Pennsylvania legislature for over ten years. The policies instigated by the MH/MR and MHPA reflected the legislature's multiple (and unclear) goals, as well as their good intentions. Subsequent judicial opinions and legislation tried to refine these goals; and the administrative agency, caught in the middle, tried to respond to legal developments and their programmatic consequences. The agency has perhaps the most difficult job, because it must reconcile the judicially-mandated changes and legislative refinements with the very practical needs and complaints of both service recipients and providers.

Conclusion to Part I

The preceding chapters have introduced selected concepts about law, legal processes, and institutional interdependence drawn from an expansive body of knowledge. The intent was to present the concepts most relevant for social work professionals. The reader seeking additional exposure to this content can build on the foundation by delving into the nuances of judicial, legislative and administrative processes and the intracacies of the law and society connection. (S)he might want to learn more about, for example, the judicial decision making process, the judicial reformation of the common law, the interpretation of statutes by a court, the use of statutes as precedent, and the indirect influence of legislation on judicial law making. Among the recommended sources are Jones, Kernochan and Murphy (1980), Mishkin and Morris (1965), Mermin (1982), Aldisert (1976), Brennan (1986), and Horowitz and Karst (1969). Further investigation of the legislative process can focus on, for example, techniques for legislative drafting, the operation of the legislature (e.g. committee structure, leadership, seniority, etc.), the appropriation process, the scope of legislative power, the supervision of legislative procedure by courts, and the canons of statutory construction. Several noteworthy sources include Davies (1975), Hetzel (1980), Hurst (1982), and Ripley (1983). For the reader seeking additional insight into the administrative process, several topics come to mind: adjudicative procedures, the use and abuse of discretion, administrative organization, constitutional limitations on administrative decision making, enforcement procedures, the fair hearing process, and the overlap of legislative and administrative processes. Key sources include Robinson and

Gellhorn (1972), Davis (1971), Dodd and Schott (1979), Freedman (1981), and Mashaw (1983). Finally, the reader might want to dig further into the law and society connection, particularly the social functions of law. This exploration would emphasize the various ways law interacts with the social environment and effects social behavior. Sources here are varied, including Greenberg (1977), Abel (1982), Chambers (1985), Congressional Quarterly, Inc. (1982), Abel (1985), Levine and Howe (1985), Meeker, Dombrink and Schuman (1985), Benditt (1982), Joe and Rogers (1985), Dreyfuss and Lawrence (1979), Auerbach (1983), Jenkins (1980), Handler and Trubeck (1985), Simon (1985), Houseman (1985), Pearce (1985), Menkel-Meadow (1985), Janes (1985), and Woods (1985).

II | Skills Dimension

8 Legal Research Resources and Techniques

As the impact of the legal system on human services steadily increases, the need for workers at all levels to become more familiar with legal processes and standards has grown in proportion. A neglected but potentially important element in educating social workers about the law is the basic skill of legal research. This is the ability to find texts of statutes, regulations, and leading court opinions and to use the wealth of available interpretive aids.

Although the idea of legal research may seem intimidating initially, you will be surprised by how soon you will feel comfortable with legal documents. And the newly-developed competence will be its own reward. This chapter will examine selected legal research resources and some basic guidelines for applying legal research techniques to practice-based legal issues.

RESOURCES FOR FINDING THE LAW

For social work professionals, legal research will typically involve searching for the legislative and regulatory context for their agency's services. This process will provide valuable information about the federal and state rules governing service delivery. But this is only the beginning. Legislation and regulations are interpreted by courts, and these interpretations have practical consequences. The practitioner doing legal research, therefore, must also find and analyze relevant judicial opinions to ensure he/she has the most recent statutory or regulatory interpretation. "Looseleaf services", such as the *Family*

Law Reporter, provide further support of the primary search, by allowing the researcher to discover the most recent law. And to make sure the law is still authoritative, the researcher can turn to Shepard's citator. All these documents can be found in the law library, although some, such as the *Index to Legal Periodicals* and the *Federal Register*, also can be found in a college or public library.

The important thing to understand (and this can help expedite your research) is that the legal resources fall into three general categories: (1) primary sources (original legal documents for federal and state statutes, regulations, and judicial decisions); (2) "finding tools" (indexes, digests, "looseleaf services", citators, and similar devices that help you locate and update statutes, regulations, and judicial decisions); and (3) secondary sources (sources that help you better understand the primary sources and assist your search for and use of them).

The categories are a way of helping you organize the various legal resources. Though assigned to discrete groups, some of the resources fall into two categories. For example, "looseleaf services" and citators are both finding tools and secondary sources: they help you find and update primary sources and, consequently, support your understanding of primary sources.

Primary Sources

Statutes and Regulations

Federal Bills: Before a statute is enacted as law, it arrives at Congress as a bill. The best official source for the text of these bills while they proceed through Congress is the *Congressional Record*, which records Congress' daily activities. The text will typically cover the bill's essentials, such as bill number, sponsor, and title. The full version of the bill is often published as part of the official committee hearings on the bill.

A related and unofficial source for finding the text of these bills and their legislative history is the *United States Code Congressional and Administrative News (U.S.S.C.A.N.)*. Published by West Publishing Company, the *U.S.S.C.A.N.* refers you to the congressional committees that considered the bill and reprints of final committee reports.

The two above paragraphs refer to "official" versus "unofficial" sources. The difference between these two terms is based on the publisher of the legal document. An official source refers to a document published by the government. The distinction is primarily relevant for purposes of citation. An official source refers to a legal document published by the government. The official source is generally preferred for citation purposes, but an unofficial source is used when no official source is available. Often both official and unofficial sources are cited together, a technique that assists the researcher's search for legal documents. The unofficial version is published by a commercial publisher, and is generally the preferred source because it is more frequently updated and it can refer the researcher to valuable collateral sources.

Federal Statutes: Federal bills that have been enacted as statutes can be found in two official sources. First, there is the *U.S. Statutes at Large,* which arranges the laws chronologically (in the order they became law). The second is the *United States Code (U.S.C.),* which arranges federal statutes by topic or subject (as opposed to the chronological arrangement of the *U.S. Statutes at Large).* The *U.S.C.* is arranged under fifty titles.

Two related and unofficial sources are the *United States Code Annotated (U.S.C.A.)* and the *United States Code Service.* (The *U.S.C.A.* is organized mostly by the West Key Number System, which is described below.) These annotated versions offer brief excerpts from court decisions that have interpreted a particular section of the *U.S.C.* They provide access to these decisions through the: (1) popular names index (a listing of federal legislation as popularly known); (2) individual subject index for a particular title; or (3) general subject index. Consequently, they are very useful sources for federal law.

Both sources can be updated. For the *U.S.C.A.,* there are the "pocket parts" (an update found inside the back cover of each volume), "supplementary pamphlets" and "special pamphlets". Further updates of the *U.S.C.A.* and its pamphlets are provided by the *U.S.S.C.A.N.* and its supplementary pamphlets. The *United States Code Service* works like the *U.S.C.A.,* but refers to Lawyer's Co-operative materials rather than West.

Federal Regulations: The official source is the *Federal Register,* which provides a uniform system for announcing federal regulations (proposed and final) and legal notices. It also contains helpful supplementary information, such as the name of the federal public law under which each regulation was issued.

After their issuance, federal regulations are arranged topically and published in the *Code of Federal Regulations (C.F.R.)*. The *C.F.R.* is a compilation of the regulations issued in conjunction with federal statutes. It is divided into titles that encompass broad topical areas (only some of which correspond to the *U.S.C.*). Changes in the *C.F.R.* can be found in a monthly pamphlet called the *Cumulative List of C.F.R. Sections Affected,* which describes the *C.F.R.* sections modified by the new final or proposed regulations. A final check is provided by the *Cumulative List of Parts Affected,* which can be found in the most recent issue of the *Federal Register*.

State Statutes: The publications for state statutes are comparable to those on the federal level. There are both official and unofficial versions. The state's *Code* usually compiles state law under different topics. The unofficial publications are mostly modeled after the *U.S.C.A.*, and include references to judicial decisions and legislative history. They also contain references to relevant secondary sources such as legal periodicals and encyclopedias. There are usually indexes that provide access to the various state law titles, but you should be prepared to use "key words" to find the right volume. And once you have located the current volume, you can refer to the general subject index to get to various sections of the law. They can be updated with "pocket parts", "supplements", or with a "slip law" (a printed copy of a bill passed by the legislature that is distributed immediately once signed by the executive).

State Regulations: Many states have a system of reporting and codifying regulations that is comparable to the federal structure. You should first search for the state publication that announces the proposed or final rules and then try to discuss where they are compiled topically. Some hard work may be required to really get the most authoritative regulations, because states vary in the extent to which they publish and keep track of such things. Be prepared to contact the state agency to discover the most recent regulations or to find out their plans for announcing proposed or final rules.

Judicial Decisions

Federal Decisions: The official source for U.S. Supreme Court decisions is the *United States Reports*. There are no official versions for other federal courts, and any decisions that are published can be found in the West *National Reporter System* (described below).

There are two unofficial sources for Supreme Court decisions: the

Table 8.1 West National Reporter System

Regional Reporter	Coverage
Atlantic Reporter	CT, DE, ME, MD, NH, NJ, PA, RI, VT, and DC Municipal Court of Appeals
North Eastern Reporter	IL,.IN, MA, NY, OH
North Western Reporter	IA, MI, MN, NB, ND, SD, WI
Pacific Reporter	AK, AR, CA, CO, HI, NV, NM, OK, OR, UT, WA, WY
South Eastern Reporter	GA, NC, SC, VA, WV
South Western Reporter	AR, KY, MO, TN, TX
Southern Reporter	AL, FL, LA, MI

Federal Reporters	Coverage
Federal Reporter	U.S. Circuit Court, Commerce Court of the U.S., District Courts of the U.S., U.S. Court of Claims, U.S. Court of Appeals, U.S. Court of Customs and Patent Appeals, U.S. Emergency Court of Appeals
Federal Supplement	U.S. Court of Claims, U.S. District Courts, U.S. Customs Court
Federal Rules Decisions	U.S. District Courts involving Fed. Rules of Civil Procedure and Fed. Rules of Criminal Procedures
Supreme Court Reporter	U.S. Supreme Court

Lawyer's Cooperative *United States Supreme Court Reports* and West's *Supreme Court Reporter*. Both are annotated and used frequently. In addition to these sources, the most recent decisions are published weekly by two "looseleaf services": the *Commerce Clearing House Supreme Court Bulletin* and the *United States Law Week*.

State Decisions: The official sources of state court decisions report state opinions for the state's trial, appellate and supreme court. The unofficial source, which is reported as part of West's *National Reporter System,* publishes only the appellate and state supreme court decisions (see Table 8.1).

The *National Reporter System,* therefore, is a particularly useful source for state decisions. It is relatively easy to use and allows access to all state appellate decisions. We will take a brief look below at this system and its categorization scheme and search methods.

The *West Key Number Digest System* is the most widely used method for locating state and federal decisions. The digests are essentially subject indexes to case law. The West system divides the entire body of case law into seven main divisions, thirty subheadings, and over four hundred digest topics (and each topic is divided into numerous key numbers). Once you have located the key number that covers the point of law in which you are interested, it will give you access to all the cases that discuss that particular point.

Under the West system, there are three search methods that can be used with all West digests.

Descriptive Word Index: If you know the facts of a problem but not the name of the related case, you can find an appropriate key number through the descriptive word index. Use the subject you are searching for as the heading and then look under that to find the proper key number. A subsequent search under that number will describe other cases, if any, on point.

Table of Cases: If you know the case that deals with the issue you are researching, the table will indicate the topic and key numbers under which the variou points of law in the case have been classified. Through the key number, you will also find other relevant cases.

Words and Phrases: This table lists all words and phrases that have been judicially defined. It may provide another entry into the topic area in which you are interested.

The search through the *National Reporter System* is supplemented by the "advance sheets" (copies of decisions that will be subsequently printed in bound volumes) that accompany each reporter. They help you stay on top of the most recent decisions. To match a decision reported in the *National Reporter System* with one of the official versions (there may be instances where you will need to go back and forth between the two), you can use West's *National Blue Book*.

Finding Tools

There are numerous digests, looseleaf services, popular name tables, citators, etc., that help you locate specific statutes, regulations, or decisions. They also help you update what you find and stay on top of newly developing materials. Some have been referred to above (e.g. the "advance sheets," and the "supplementary pamphlets"). Think of them as keys to gaining access to the primary sources. For example, there is the *American Digest*, which is a comprehensive finding tool. Its major advantage is that it digests cases from all federal and state courts and indexes them according to points of law. On the other hand, it can be a little awkward to use. The *American Digest* is divided into units (the *Century Digest*, the *Decennial Digest*, and the *General Digest*), which cover designated time periods. The *Century Digest* covers cases between 1658 and 1897. The *Decennials* cover ten-year periods from 1897 to 1976 (e.g. the 8th *Decennial digest* covers cases between 1966 and 1976). More recent cases are found in the *General Digest*, which appears first as a monthly supplement to the *Decennials*.

Secondary Sources

Many of the secondary sources are particularly helpful for non-lawyers. Among the most useful are encyclopedias, periodicals, treatises, and looseleaf services. One, the *West Key Number Digest*, has already been discussed. We will discuss these below, along with several others that support the primary sources.

Shepard's Citation

This citator will help you find out what has happened to a statute, a case, a regulation, or other legal authority (e.g. law review article). The task is accomplished by referring you to all the places it (the statute, case, or regulation, etc.) has been mentioned (cited). This process has become known as "Shepardizing", and its importance cannot be overstated. Because law changes you need a strategy to get the most authoritative law, and Shepard's is the finding tool to do this. Thus, to be sure that the law you find is still "good law," you must "shepardize"; never formally use a statute, case, regulation, or other legal authority without "shepardizing".

To use the Shepard's, read the "how to use" information in the front of each citator you use. This section will tell you what to do and how to interpret the symbols. The process may be a little tedious initially, but speed will come with practice.

Legal Encyclopedias

These are arranged alphabetically by topic and work much like a general encyclopedia. They are particularly good to get a fast overview on a particular legal topic. The two most prominent are West's

Corpus Juris Secundum (tied to the West Key system) and Lawyer's Co-operative *American Jurisprudence*. Both have general indexes that should be used to gain access to your topic. After checking these indexes, be sure to check the "pocket part".

Legal Periodicals

These indexes refer to law review articles, typically but not exclusively published by law schools, which analyze an array of legal issues. The articles are located through the *Index to Legal Periodicals*, the *Current Law Index*, or the *Legal Resources Index*.

Treatises

Treatises are comprehensive treatments of a substantive topic, such as contracts or evidence.

Looseleaf Services

A looseleaf service deals with one area of law (e.g. family law), with one court or with a general legal topic. These services include important, and recent developments in statutory, regulatory, or case law. The *Commerce Clearing House* and the *Bureau of National Affairs* are two examples of such services (see Figure 8.1).

A UNIFORM SYSTEM OF CITATION

A citation is information about a legal document that helps you locate it in a law library. Because the law evolves, it is important that there be some uniform method for finding legal rules. Generally, a citation will describe the parties, the reporter or source where the information is located, the volume and edition of the reporter or source, the page number where the information is located, and the date. The citations are provided in both "official" and "unofficial" forms to help you locate the legal document in the form that best suits your research strategy. Table 8.2 illustrates a typical citation and its component parts. For a more complete description of the rules for citation (again, the rules provide for uniformity; it is important to know how to be precise, and the rules help accomplish this), see *A Uniform System of Citation*, Thirteenth Edition (1981).

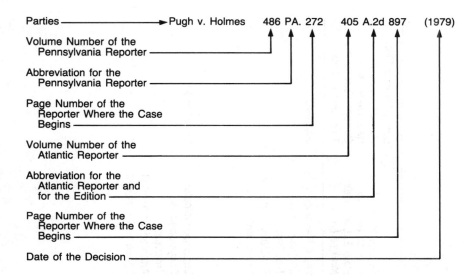

Parties ──────────────▶ Pugh v. Holmes   486 PA. 272   405 A.2d 897   (1979)

Volume Number of the
  Pennsylvania Reporter ─────────

Abbreviation for the
  Pennsylvania Reporter ─────

Page Number of the
  Reporter Where the Case
  Begins ──────────────

Volume Number of the
  Atlantic Reporter ──────

Abbreviation for the
  Atlantic Reporter and
  for the Edition ─────────

Page Number of the
  Reporter Where the Case
  Begins ────────────────

Date of the Decision ───────

FIGURE 8.1 Citation format

SUGGESTED LEGAL RESEARCH TECHNIQUES

Following is an outline of legal research techniques. Collectively, they comprise a strategy for educating oneself about a legal issue and for discovering the current law. They are not offered as the final word on the subject, and you will develop your own approach after practice. The attempt here is to introduce you to the idea that you can organize both the search and the use of legal documents. To test their utility, select a question that interests you and move through the process.

Step One: Beginning the Search

What is the issue or problem in which you are interested? Try to make this as specific as possible by thinking about the issue in terms of: (1) the parties involved (e.g. children and parents, worker and client, social problem, etc); (2) the procedures involved (e.g. arbitration, injunction, appeal, mediation); or (3) the substantive issue involved (e.g. child welfare, mental health, developmental disabilities). The issue should be narrowly drawn to best link it to your practice context.

Table 8.2 Sources For Selected Legal Documents

Kind of Law	Sets of Books That Contain the Full Text of This Kind of Law	Sets of Books That Can be Used to Locate This Kind of Law	Sets of Books That Can be Used to Help Explain This Kind of Law	Sets of Books That Can be Used to Help Determine the Current Validity of This Kind of Law
Opinions	Reports Reporters Legal Newspapers ALR Loose leaf services Slip opinion Advance sheets Westlaw, Lexis	Digests Annotations in ALR Shepard's Legal Periodicals Encyclopedias Treatises Loose leaf services Words and Phrases	Legal Periodicals Encyclopedias Treatises Annotations in ALR Loose leaf services	Shepard's
Statutes	Statutory Code Statutes Statutes at Large Session Laws Laws Compilations Consolidated Laws Slip Law Acts, Acts & Resolves Westlaw, Lexis	Index volumes of statutory code Loose leaf services Footnote references in encyclopedia, legal periodical, etc.	Legal periodicals Encyclopedias Treatises Annotations in ALR Loose leaf services	Shepard's

Constitutions	Statutory Code Separate volumes containing the constitution	Index volumes of the statutory code Loose leaf services Footnote references in encyclopedia, legal periodicals, etc.	Legal periodicals Encyclopedias Treatises Annotations in ALR Loose leaf services	Shepard's
Administrative Regulations	Administrative Codes Separate volumes or pamphlets containing the regulations of certain agencies Loose leaf services	Index volumes of the administrative code Loose leaf services Footnote references in encyclopedia, legal periodicals, etc.	Legal periodicals Treatises Annotations in ALR Loose leaf services	Shepard's (for some agencies only)
Administrative Decisions	Separate volumes of decisions of certain agencies Loose leaf services	Loose leaf services Index or digest volumes to the decisions Footnote references in other materials	Legal periodicals Treatises Annotations in ALR Loose leaf services	Shepard's (for some agencies only)
Ordinances	Municipal code Official journal Legal newspaper	Index volumes of municipal code Footnote references in other materials	Legal periodicals Treatises Annotations in ALR	Shepard's

Table 8.2 (continued)

Kind of Law	Sets of Books That Contain the Full Text of This Kind of Law	Sets of Books That Can be Used to Locate This Kind of Law	Sets of Books That Can be Used to Help Explain This Kind of Law	Sets of Books That Can be Used to Help Determine the Current Validity of This Kind of Law
Charters	Separate volumes containing the charter Municipal Code State Session laws Official journal Legal newspaper	Index volumes to the charter or municipal code Footnote references in other materials	Legal Periodicals Treatises Annotations in ALR	Shepard's
Executive Orders	Federal Register Code of Federal Regulations U.S. Code Congressional and Administrative News USC, USCA, USCS (for some orders only)	Index volumes to the sets of books listed in the second column Footnote references in other materials	Legal Periodicals Treatises Annotations in ALR	Shepard's Code of Federal Regulation Citations

Source: Reprinted by permission from Legal Research and Writing: Some Starting Points, Third Edition by William Statsky, Copyright © 1974, 1982, 1986 by West Publishing Company. All rights reserved. pp. 16–17.

Step Two: Preliminary Review of the Subject

This step allows you to educate yourself about the topic. It is especially helpful when exploring unfamiliar territory, but works just as well in areas where you are knowledgeable. The *Index to Legal Periodicals* is relevant here. A review of the articles on your subject will yield a selection of relevant articles and reviews of the law and analyses of controversial cases. The legal encyclopedia, such as *Corpus Juris Secundum*, is also a good introductory source. General texts on the topic, sometimes referred to as hornbooks, can also offer a solid yet sound introduction to an area of law. To initiate your search, consider the following:

- Obtain and use a legal dictionary. The dictionary will lead you to primary authority that defines the terms.
- Refer to the legal encyclopedias, such as *Corpus Juris Secundum*.
- Refer to treatises, as necessary, to obtain a comprehensive background on the research topic.
- Use the legal periodical literature to find relevant law review articles and to discover analyses of major cases.
- Locate agency reports available to the public. Again, they can provide useful background information.
- Check relevant legislative committee reports. They are not only good background but also excellent sources for legislative history. The *U.S.C.C.A.N.*, for example, can be very helpful.
- Reports and literature from special interest groups. These groups often produce studies that assess the impact of legal developments in their area (Statsky, 1982:75–76).

Step Three: Search for Statutes and Regulations

Generally, there will be both federal and state legislation on the issue you are investigating, although you will probably be more interested in state legislation and its relation to the services your agency delivers. Here, the *U.S.C.A.* and the annotation of the state code will be most informative. Your questions about the statute's meaning can be answered by a review of the legislative history, as contained in the *U.S.C.C.A.N.*, for example. There are numerous sources for history on federal laws, but states vary on the extent to which they develop such documentation.

Consider, for example, the following when constructing a legislative history.

For Federal Legislative History

- Review the historical information located at the end of the *U.S.C.* or *U.S.C.A.*
- Locate the Public Law number (Pub.L. #), which will help with identifying the legislative trial.
- Identify whether anyone else has compiled a legislative history on the topic you are researching.
- Be aware of the following texts and their purposes: *U.S.C.C.A.N.*, *CCH Congressional Index, Congressional Information Service (CIS), Digest of Public General Bills and Resolutions, Congressional Record Index, Senate and House Journals, and Congressional Quarterly.*
- Check with the legislative committees for leads. The staff can be very helpful; they often are aware of little-used sources.
- Check the legal periodicals (Statsky, 1982: pp. 129–130).

For State Legislative History *

- Locate the statute in the State Statutes Annotated or State Compiled Laws Annotated or their supplements.
- Locate the Public Act number or equivalent designation and the year in which the section was enacted or amended. This information is usually found under the section's history notations.
- To locate the text of the statute at any specific time in the past, go to the Public Acts of the last year the statute was amended prior to the time you are interested in. Only the current statute is given in the state's Statutes Annotated or Compiled Laws Annotated.
- To locate the legislative history of a statute or amendment, use the *Journals* of each house for the year of the act. Reference tables at the end of each *Journal* [or in some separate volume that acts as an index] will convert the Public Act number into the bill number. Once you have the bill number, check the reference table for that bill in both *Journals*. [The Journals will typically include a record of formal action and comments or remarks from

*From Otto J. Hetzel, Legislative law and process. p. 273. © 1980. The Michie Company, Charlottesville, VA. Reprinted by permission.

the floor. Also, you may find included a written statement that the legislator has included in the public record—even though he/she did not verbally present the statement.]

• Check the Bill and Joint Resolution of each *Journal* for any bills on the topic considered at the same session; the General Index tends to be very cursory.

• There are no regularly reported floor debates, committee hearings, or committee reports for most states. [Check with the particular state legislative committee in which you are interested to determine whether it makes available stenographic copies of committee hearings.]

• The Governor's messages to the legislature are printed in the *Journals* but only rarely will these be concerned with a particular bill. [The veto messages, for example, in connection with a particular bill may be found in this source.]

• Most often the only real source of legislative meaning in a state context is the words of the statute itself. [But this can be supplemented by your investigation of the above sources. There will be more work involved with state legislation, but diligence will generally pay off.]

The *Code of Federal Regulations,* the *Federal Register,* or their state counterparts contain the regulations that structure the implementation of legislation. You will need to refer to these to discover the structure for the services your agency delivers.

Consider, for example, whether you have touched the following bases:

• Contact the agency, if necessary, for their publications of regulations.

• Check the *C.F.R.* or its state counterpart.

• Locate material to discover any changes in the regulations.

• Refer to the *Federal Register* or its state counterpart (Statsky, 1982).

Step Four: Search for Judicial Opinions

The cases cited in the above annotations should be consulted first. Additional cases may be located by using the *West Key Number System*. The search may be facilitated if you consider the following:

- Use the West Digests.
- Refer to the legal periodicals. The law reviews are often good sources for cases on point.
- Use legal encyclopedias.
- Shepardize all or some of the cases you locate to discover others that have dealt with the case(s) you are researching (Statsky, 1982).

Step Five: Completing the Search

Make certain the most recent editions and supplements have been consulted. Also, check the relevant digests for "advance sheets" to ensure you have located the most recent law on your topic.

Step Six: Verifying the Search

To discover whether the statutes and cases you have found are still good law, it will be necessary to resort to the *Shepard's Citator*. This process, known as "sheparding", is also a good way to locate other cases on point.

A CONCLUDING NOTE

Although the above information is, no doubt, foreign (perhaps too much so for social service professionals), it must be understood that legal research resources and techniques can be learned; they are neither secret, intuitive, nor the exclusive province of attorneys. Reference sources are readily available, including Cohen and Berring (1983) and Jacobstein and Mersky (1981). Their successful use will depend on practice, on discovering opportunities to find the documents that comprise the legal context for service delivery and for professional conduct. The adage "practice makes perfect" is most relevant here, as is the implication that the outcome justifies the means. The additional benefit, however, is the glimpse of legal development, the opportunity to discover that legal rules are not as static as they appear. This insight is particularly compelling for social services, because shifts in the allocation of scarce resources and societal attitudes toward helping those in need are manifest in the law's processes for problem-solving and change. And because these shifts occur without warning, it is important to have some way of tracking the changes and the conditions that prompted them. The tracking begins with finding the rules.

9 Presenting Court Testimony

Social workers assist the court in its truth-finding process by presenting information as a witness or as an expert witness. The task is accomplished by organizing case records to be placed in evidence in court. The settings vary (e.g. juvenile court and criminal court), but the role has certain common features that will be explored in this chapter. In addition, some fundamental evidence concepts and techniques associated with the social-worker-as-witness role, will be examined together with some practical guidelines for record-keeping.

EVIDENCE CONCEPTS AND PRINCIPLES

The complaining parties in a legal dispute (the plaintiff in civil cases; the state, in criminal proceedings) obtain a favorable judgment only if they can prove their claims. The proof consists of evidence presented at trial. Evidence

> may be defined as that which demonstrates, makes clear, or ascertains the truth of the very fact or point in issue. . . . [It] is the means from which an inference may logically be drawn as to the existence of a fact; that which makes evident or plain. . . . Although the term "evidence" is sometimes used synonymously with "facts", the terms are not really synonymous, for "evidence" is limited to that which may properly be considered by the court or submitted to the jury for its consideration. . . . "Competent evidence" means evidence that tends to establish the fact in issue and does not rest on mere surmise or guess. (31 Corpus Juris Secundum Evidence Sec. 2)

Evidence may be presented through witnesses, records, documents, or concrete objects.

Evidence law consists of rules and standards that regulate the introduction of proof at trial. These rules are the framework within which the material facts are proved. They specify how any proof (whether testimony, writings, physical objects, photographs, etc.), will be admitted or excluded at trial. The law of evidence is enormous, so no attempt will be made here to cover it all. Rather, this section will examine some of the fundamental and evidence concepts most relevant to social work. They are all "terms of art", i.e., they express concepts that are best understood within a particular context. Here, the judicial decision-making process for getting at the truth is the context.

Standards of Proof for Evidence

The standard of proof will vary, depending on whether the suit is civil or criminal, and even among civil disputes, the level can vary. The "standard of proof" concept refers to the standard to be used to assess whether the evidence presented will allow the court to conclude that it actually proves the truthfulness of the assertions made by the complaining party and thus entitles them to their requested legal remedy. In short, it is how convincing the evidence must be to support a contention.

Criminal proceedings, which are instigated by the state (on the people's behalf) to determine whether someone has violated the penal code, require evidence that allows the court to conclude *beyond a reasonable doubt* that the defendant is guilty as charged. The state has to show that, based on the evidence it presents, there will be no reasonable doubt in the court's mind that the defendant has done what he/she is accused of. It will be ". . . entirely convinced; satisfied to a moral certainty . . . [and that] the facts proven must, by virtue of their probative force, establish guilt" (Black, 1968). The standard is "high" because our society wants to be nothing less than certain when it takes away a person's liberty. And the "beyond a reasonable doubt standard", in conjunction with several equally stringent procedural safeguards, helps ensure this certainty.

Civil proceedings, which settle non-criminal disputes, use a relatively less demanding standard of proof. The standards for these proceedings are as follows:

1. proof by *clear and convincing evidence:* Generally this phrase and its numerous variations mean proof beyond a well-founded doubt. Some cases give it a less rigorous, but somewhat uncertain meaning, *viz.,* more than a preponderance but less than is required in a criminal case. . . . The degree of proof which will produce in the mind of the court a firm belief or conviction; proof sufficient to convince ordinarily prudent-minded people. (Black, 1968.)

The phrase expresses "a standard frequently imposed in civil cases where the wisdom of experience has demonstrated the need for greater certainty . . ." (31 C.J.S. Evidence Sec. 1023).

2. proof by a *preponderance of the evidence:* Greater weight of evidence, or evidence which is more credible and convincing to the mind. . . . that which best accords with reason and probability. . . . The word "preponderance" means something more than "weight"; it denotes a superiority of weight, or outweighing. The words are not synonymous, but substantially different. There is generally a "weight" of evidence on each side in case of contested facts. But juries cannot properly act upon the weight of evidence, in favor of the one having the *onus,* unless it overbears, in some degree, the weight upon the other side. . . . It rests with that evidence which, when fairly considered, produces the stronger impression, and . . . is more convincing as to its truth when weighed against the evidence in opposition thereto (Black, 1968). In other words, it is ". . . evidence which is of a greater weight or more convincing that that which is offered in opposition." (32 C.J.S. Evidence Sec. 1018)

Best Evidence: "Best evidence" or "primary evidence" is that which is the most natural and satisfactory proof of the fact under investigation. . . . While in some circumstances "best evidence" may mean that evidence which is more specific and definite as opposed to that which is merely general and indefinite or descriptive, "best evidence" is variously defined as that . . . proof, which is indicated by the nature of the fact under investigation, as the most natural and satisfactory . . . (32A C.J.S. Evidence Sec. 776).

Material Evidence: Evidence is *material* when it relates to a substantive legal issue in the dispute. This concept communicates the idea of relevancy (in the usual, not legal sense). How do you know what legal issues are part of the dispute? Look at the complaint or the petition, which specifies the legal issues on which the parties disagree. These are the issues for which competent evidence must be presented. Evidence introduced to prove a point other than these can be excluded as immaterial.

Relevant Evidence: Evidence is relevant when it tends to show that the material facts (as defined above) are more true than untrue.

The concept speaks to whether or not the evidence is proof of an issue. It also expresses a link to materiality. Assuming the evidence proves a material issue, the next question is whether it proves that *specific* material issue. For example, evidence that shows that a parent neglected his/her child on a prior occasion is material (as defined above) because it addresses the present question of neglect. However, that fact alone does not prove the parent's negligence on this particular occasion. Thus, such evidence, albeit material, would be excluded because it is not relevant.

Evidence Classifications: Evidence can be (1) direct or (2) circumstantial.

Direct evidence. This is evidence presented by a witness who has actual knowledge of the fact it is offered to prove. A conclusion can be drawn directly from the witness's statement. For example, on the question of physical abuse, the testimony of a neighbor that he/she saw the parent repeatedly strike the child would be direct evidence.

Circumstantial evidence. This is evidence presented by a witness that allows certain inferences about the truthfulness of the facts it is offered to show. For example, on the question of physical abuse, the testimony of a neighbor that he/she saw a crying child emerge from the house with (apparent) welts on the arm would be circumstantial evidence.

Hearsay evidence. A witness's testimony can be excluded as hearsay when he/she offers a statement uttered out-of-court by some other party as proof that what he/she is saying is true.

Evidence is hearsay when its probative force depends on the competency of *some person other than the witness*. A clear example of hearsay evidence appears where a witness [A] testifies to the declaration [statement] of another person [B] for the purpose of proving the facts asserted by the witness [A]. . . . the general rule is that, subject to certain exceptions, hearsay evidence is inadmissible, or incompetent [as defined above]; the courts will not receive the testimony of a witness as to what some other person said, or told him, as evidence of the existence of the facts asserted [by the witness]. (31A C.J.S. Evidence Sec. 193)

Hearsay evidence is generally excluded.

The rule against its use is derived from a legal tradition that requires evidence to be direct, accurate and verifiable. Out-of-court statements offered by a witness cannot meet these criteria, because there is no "opportunity to test by cross-examination the veracity and accuracy of the statement offered" (31A C.J.S. Evidence Sec. 193). A hearsay "statement" can be (1) an oral statement (he/she said ". . ."); (2) a written document; or (3) so-called "assertive conduct," i.e., conduct that communicates an idea (e.g. the witness testifies that "the child pointed to the alleged assailant").

Given the court's truth-finding function, the hearsay rule has some intuitive appeal:

> . . . an unsworn statement of a person not called as a witness . . . is not recognized as having a sufficient probative effect to [allow us to believe] that the fact is as stated; and the rule is particularly applicable when such [out-of-court persons] can be summoned and sworn as a witness. The right of a party to test by cross-examination the veracity and accuracy of the person making the statement offered in evidence has been said to be the principal reason for the hearsay rule . . . (31A C.J.S. Evidence Sec. 193).

But there are exceptions to the hearsay rule. "Such exceptions are based on necessity, public policy, practical common sense, and the trustworthiness which experience has taught, or the circumstances indicate. . . ." (31A C.J.S. Evidence Sec. 193). Caulfield (1985) provides below an example of the rule, as well as some insight into its exceptions.

The Hearsay Rule*

Example of hearsay. The witness, a classmate of an allegedly neglected seven-year-old, testifies:

> Kathy came to school on March 10, and during recess I heard her tell the teacher this story: that her parents had gone away four days earlier and left her and her younger brother alone. Kathy also said that they ran out of food after two days and hadn't eaten since then. I guess the parents came home; but, on April 2, I heard Kathy tell the teacher that the same thing had happened again.

This evidence is inadmissible as evidence to prove the truth of the statements made in the testimony: that the parents in fact, twice left the two young children unattended and without food for long periods of time. This hearsay evidence is unreliable as proof because the witness might not have heard Kathy correctly or might be embellishing the story, or there might be a reasonable explanation, or maybe Kathy just made up the apparent abandonment to explain being late to school.

The witness's testimony could be admitted as proof of other facts; for instance, that Kathy was in school and not truant on March 10 and April 2, or that the schoolteacher had noticed a reportable case of child neglect. Kathy is not on the witness stand; her classmate is repeating Kathy's statement secondhand. (See Table 9.1)

Exceptions to the Hearsay Rule

Prior recollection recorded. Sometimes a witness can no longer recall an event at the time of trial but made notes about the incident at the time it occurred. Such notes may be admitted into evidence (i.e., read aloud at trial) as an exception to the hearsay rule, if the witness testifies that:

1. He or she at one time had firsthand knowledge of the event.
2. Now does not remember.
3. The notes were made when his or her memory of the event was fresh.
4. The notes were accurate when made.

Admissions. Admissions are statements made by a party to the action, and a party is a person with an interest at risk in the legal proceedings.

If a parent confesses to you that he or she abused the child, you can repeat the statement in court, even if no criminal prosecution is involved. The parent's admission is allowed as evidence to prove the fact that the parent committed the act, and the admission can be used in any subsequent hearing.

To be admissable testimony, such an admission must be made by a party to the action. A noncustodian of the child may be the abuser without being a party to the court action. Even if the noncustodian abuser makes a statement of admission out of court, the communication cannot be repeated secondhand in court because it does not concern a party.

Admission by silence. A party, by being silent, can agree with a statement made by another in his/her presence so long as it is shown that the party heard the statement, understood it, and could have objected to it but did not. Being silent shows agreement with what the other person says; in effect, it makes the statement one's own.

For example, you may testify that, in a conversation with both parents of an allegedly abused child, the mother stated that the father "would often get very mad at the child and whip her with his belt for things like not having the table set, being slow to take a bath, and especially for talking back. Sometimes he would hit the kid 20 times before he stopped." This testimony is admissible against the father as an adopted admission since he was in the same room and, under the circumstances, could be expected to deny the statement if it were untrue. The testimony could not be admitted if the father:

1. Was not present.
2. Did not hear the statement.
3. Had previously consulted an attorney who advised him to say nothing.

Excited utterance. An excited utterance is a spontaneous remark describing a startling event or condition said while the person was under stress of excitement caused by the event or condition.

Courts consider excited utterances reliable because the person making the remark does so in reaction to the "stress of excitement" and, having no time to reflect, cannot fabricate or embellish. Statements not made immediately after an event do not qualify, nor do statements in the form of a narrative or explanation of past events. For example, a statement made at the dinner table by a husband to a wife, that he had injured his head at work earlier that day cannot be repeated in court by the wife under the excited utterance rule. The husband's statement is inadmissible as hearsay because it was not made to the wife immediately after he had the accident.

To be an excited utterance, a remark must have all the following characteristics:

1. It must be made at the same time as the exciting event that produced it or so shortly thereafter that the person making it is still subject to the excitement caused by the event.
2. It must relate to the excitement caused by the event.
3. The person making the remark must have personal knowledge of the event. The person must have actually sensed, seen, heard, smelled, or felt the event he or she is describing.

Official records. Public records are excepted from the hearsay rule. Therefore, they are allowed as evidence because the character of public records makes them reliable. There is no motive for public officials to create false records because they are independent of the people or events about which they create records.

Public records include:

- Collections of data, such as birth and death records, and a child abuse registry.
- Daily operating records, such as hospital bills or agency payroll files.
- Investigative records, such as a social worker's contact file or a fire department investigation report.

Most states have statutes governing the admissability of official records and certificates. The statutes explicitly state the kinds of records that will be allowed as evidence under exceptions to the hearsay rule. [pp. 43–56]

See last section of this chapter for more on the topic of record keeping.

Table 9.1 Examples of Hearsay Rule Exceptions in Testimony

Secondhand Information	Admissible	Hearsay Rule Exception	Comments
Parent admitted abusing child to social worker.	Yes	Admission	Only if parent is a party to the action.
Mother exclaims spontaneously to doctor who is beginning to treat her abused child: "Oh my God. Have I killed my poor baby?"	Yes	Excited utterance	Even if mother is not a party.
Neighbor told you he saw baby sitter leave child in hallway for four hours in the evening. You testify.	No		No guarantee of truthfulness or completeness of neighbor's statement unless neighbor testifies.
Certified copy of child's birth certificate.	Yes	Official records	
Hospital records show child brought in four times within six months with severe head injuries.	Yes	Regularly kept business records	
Parent tells doctor treating child for severe head injuries that child "falls from her crib all the time."	Yes	Statement for medical treatment or diagnosis; Admission	
Definition of terms from Encyclopedia of Social Work	Yes	Learned writing	Not as substantive evidence.

WITNESSES

Generally, witnesses fall into two categories: (1) lay and (2) expert. The two are distinguished by the type of testimony they offer at trial. Witnesses typically testify to their knowledge of firsthand observations, to what they actually saw or heard. The expert witness, however, is an exception to this general rule.

Lay Witnesses

Actual concrete observations are the province of lay witnesses. They are limited to the facts they observe, so they can only testify about what they saw, heard, or otherwise experienced firsthand. Their role is a conveyer of facts. Consequently, they must refrain from drawing any conclusions from the facts they observe. Such inferences, no matter how obvious, will be disallowed by the court. (Exception: even a lay witness can draw a conclusion about a subject known by the average person, such as the indicators of drunkeness or the approximate speed of cars.)

Their limited role reflects the division of labor, so to speak, on which our trial system is based. Under this scheme, the jury or judge draws inferences from the facts presented by witnesses. Thus, the witness merely presents the evidence for the fact-finder's consideration. To the extent these roles remain separate, our judicial system can realize its truth-finding function.

Lay witnesses, unlike experts, possess no special knowledge or skill; they need none to offer "mere" firsthand experiences. This characteristic should not suggest they occupy a second-class status in relation to experts. Rather, the point is that their contribution to the process is more *limited* than the expert's, who can testify about both firsthand experiences and about the consequences that follow from these observations.

Expert Witness

The court's truth-finding process often requires it to incorporate information beyond its expertise. Lay witnesses may accurately represent relevant facts but these alone may not be enough, and the court may require informed opinions about the conclusions that may be drawn from the facts presented to it. Enter the expert witness, whose opinions, which are based on relatively superior knowledge, experience or skill, may help the court discover the truth.

Who is an expert? The meaning is narrower than generally understood. Experts need not be the best in their fields. The judge determines whether someone will be allowed to testify as an expert. The decision is based on the court's finding that the subject for testimony is beyond the average lay person's knowledge. The judge then evaluates the expert's credentials to determine whether he/she has the requisite specialized knowledge, education or experience. These qualifying requirements must be met before anyone— whether called by one of the parties or appointed by the court—is designated an expert. Once qualified, experts must testify that their opinion is based on a "reasonable degree of certainty."

Essentially, anyone who meets the court's expert–witness require-ments can qualify as an expert witness. (Indeed, one person can be an expert witness in one situation; a lay witness in another.) The court will first decide whether expert opinion is needed, and if so, whether the required information is within the expert's area of expertise. In some instances, even if the expert has been qualified, the judge may disallow the opinion testimony if he/she decides that the state of knowledge within a field is so unreliable or new that an opinion with a "reasonable degree of certainty" cannot be offered even by an expert.

The following examples, supplied by Caulfield (1985), may further clarify the practical distinctions between the two.

EXAMPLE 1

NONEXPERT A:	"A lot of times, I've seen the mother put away a whole six-pack of beer and then go off to the store for some more."
NONEXPERT B:	"I see the mother every afternoon when school gets out, and she's always drunk."
EXPERT:	"The mother drinks quite heavily and seems to have a strong dependency on alcohol. She frequently drinks to the point of unconsciousness. However, with a proper treatment program, such as AA, to teach her how to stop her drinking, I believe Mrs. C. would be capable of assuming her parental duties."

The expert in the last example was qualified in the areas of alcohol abuse and treatment or as a medical expert. Expert testimony is valuable here because the expert can draw conclusions about alcohol dependency, its extent, and correctability.

Usually a lay witness cannot give opinion testimony. "Drunkeness," however, is a conclusion that any lay person can draw, under a widely recognized exception to the opinion rule. Two other topics about which a lay witness can give an opinion are "craziness" and the speed of a moving vehicle.

Although one's reputation is really composed of the opinions of others, it is not excluded from evidence under either opinion or hearsay rules. Only a member of the neighborhood or community of the person in question may testify as to his or her reputation. Therefore, evidence of reputation in the community is given by a lay witness rather than by an expert.

A witness who testifies about a person's reputation is termed a "character witness." Reputation testimony does not include the character witness's personal opinion; only what the witness has heard in the community about a person's character or reputation is admissible. A person may not testify about his or her own reputation.

EXAMPLE 2

EXPERT: "I examined the x-rays of this child taken by the x-ray technician. They showed that the long bones of both arms were broken and that two of the bones that were broken this time had suffered prior fractures—on three different occasions each. In addition, there were hairline fractures of three ribs incurred recent to the examination, and hairline fractures of six other ribs that were in various stages of healing. It is difficult to state how long ago those injuries occurred. The recent three fractures were of the type caused by repeated beating with a blunt instrument, such as a stick."

Neither of the above statements can be offered by a lay witness; only an expert can give this kind of testimony. [And this example], involving conclusions based on medical information collected by others, can only be given by an expert physician who has training in interpreting x-rays.

Although a statement may be perfectly acceptable as expert testimony, it may not carry much weight with the judge. [43–56]

Read the following transcript, which describes the examination and cross-examination of a social worker in a child custody dispute. Evaluate her testimony in the light of the above. Then read the excerpt from the judicial opinion of the case on which the transcripts were based.

COURT TRANSCRIPT FOR IN RE CUSTODY OF J.S.S.
298 PA. Superior Ct. 428 (1982)
IX

THE COURT: Just to put on the record, this is in re: Custody of Jeremy S., a minor.

The parties are stipulating and agreeing that the report prepared by Pinebrook Services for Children and Youth for the Court in assisting the Court in deciding this matter shall be and become a part of the court record. Okay? All right. Anything else?

MR. FONZONE: No.

THE COURT: If you want to, you're the moving party.

MR. FONZONE: Just cross-examine.

Miss R., having been duly sworn, was examined and testified as follows:

THE COURT: It's Mrs., isn't it?

THE WITNESS: Miss.

THE COURT: Miss R., on behalf of this Court and through your employer, Pinebrook Services, you prepared an investigation and submitted a report to this Court relative to the minor child involved in these proceedings?

THE WITNESS: Yes, I did.

THE COURT: Now, in respect to that report, I believe copies have been sent to respective counsel, Attorney Fonzone and Attorney Keller; and in light of the posture of the case, they're allowed to question you in respect to your report. All right? So Attorney Fonzone was the moving party in this case, so we'll allow Attorney Fonzone to begin the questioning. All right, Mr. Fonzone. And the other attorney is Attorney Keller.

CROSS-EXAMINATION

By Mr. Fonzone:

Q: Ma'am, for the purposes of the record, could you state your name?

A: Miss R.

Q: And your age, ma'am?

A: Twenty-eight.

Q: And your formal education?

A: I have a B.A. in social science and a minor in psychology. I also received my social work certification from the Independent Colleges of the Lehigh Valley Consortium.

Q: With respect to the degree, when did you receive that?

A: 1975.

Q: And what have you been doing since '75?

A: I was employed at the Lutheran Home in Topton for five years as a diagnostic case worker, and also since September I've been working with Pinebrook Services.

Q:	And the other degree you mentioned, the social worker degree, what is that, ma'am? How do you achieve that?
A:	You're required to take courses beyond my social science degree and my psychology degree, specifically in the social welfare field.
Q:	And how many courses have you taken beyond your degrees?
A:	I have approximately thirty credits towards my M.S.W.
Q:	That would be a master of social work?
A:	Right.
Q:	What did you do at the Topton Home, ma'am?
A:	Basically I started out as a child care worker for a few months, and then I moved on to case worker. At that point I did therapy with the children in the institution. I also did home studies and then I became the diagnostic caseworker, which is a specialization in doing home study psychosocials for children who are referred to us for the report.
Q:	When you say home studies, what does that mean?
A:	Okay. A child is referred to us because of something they've done or family problems. It is my job to go out to the home, study the home, analyze the dynamics of the family, get extensive family background on them and determine whether that home is suitable for that child to return to.
Q:	And how many occasions were you called to do that, ma'am?
A:	I averaged six every month.
Q:	For what period?
A:	For five years.
Q:	Seventy-two a year then for five years?
A:	Well, my math is not that good, but—
Q:	Approximately. Ma'am, prior to being called on to do the home study in this case, did you know any of the parties?
A:	No, I did not.
Q:	Any of the attorneys?
A:	No, I did not.
Q:	Never dealt with anyone before?
A:	No.
Q:	Do you have your report with you?
A:	Yes, I do.
Q:	Could I refer you to the—it's an unnumbered page, but the first page at the bottom, the paragraph beginning with "While showing."
A:	Under what topic are you—
Q:	The first page of your report. It's not numbered, but it's the first page. The next page is Page 2.

THE COURT: Do you have your typed copy?
THE WITNESS: No, I don't.

By Mr. Fonzone:

Q: Could I see what you have? You just have notes. Could I
        see your notes?
A: Yes.
Q: This is all written by you. The first page of the report you
        have in front of you now, ma'am, begins with "While."
A: Yes.
Q: Are you saying that Alverta made a statement to you
        about what you have in that paragraph?
A: Yes, I am.
Q: And did you make a note of what she said at that time?
A: Yes, I did. When we were going through the home and
        looking at the rooms, she indicated to me that Jean had a
        single bed and was sleeping in the same room as two of
        her children, and indicated that she was no longer in-
        terested in men.
Q: And that's how you translate that into what you've type
        written?
A: And also that Barbara had a boy friend and she was the
        only female in the home that had a room to herself and a
        double bed.
Q: And did she tell you all of this at one time?
A: In the course of the conversation while touring the house,
        yes.
Q: And how long was that conversation?
A: While touring the house. I would say it took us approx-
        imately fifteen minutes to tour the house.
Q: And do you recall specifically when she told you those
        two separate facts?
A: We went to the two bedrooms, one right after the other,
        so it would have been in that period of time.
Q: And she told you basically what?
A: That Jean had a single bed and was sleeping in the room
        with two of her children because she was no longer in-
        terested in men, and indicated that Barbara had a double
        bed and she was seeing someone.
Q: And did she tell you that's why she had a double bed?
A: I can't say that she actually said that's why she had a
        double bed, no.
Q: But you agree that your typewritten statement would
        indicate that?
A: She alluded to the fact, yes, and that's what's in my
        report.

Q:	Well, there's no allusion at all in your typewritten statement. You say, "Barbara, for example, has private room and double bed because she is presently dating someone."
A:	Yes.
Q:	And is your recollection clear then that it was that matter of factly said to you, or is that a conclusion you arrived at?
A:	She did present the two facts one right after the other.
Q:	And your fertile imagination put them together?
MR. KELLER:	Objection.
THE COURT:	The objection is overruled.

By Mr. Fonzone:

Q:	You may answer.
A:	Well, since she stated the two facts one right after the other, yes, I put them together.
Q:	Now, with respect to the financial set up in the home, Alverta told you that all the working people contribute to the home?
A:	Yes.
Q:	Have you done anything to check the veracity of any statements made in your report? For example, if someone told you they ran away for a particular reason, did you ever attempt to find out why they ran away or do any work at all in that respect?
A:	I'm not sure I understand your question.
Q:	Well, you gained information that one person was placed in the Wiley House.
A:	Yes.
Q:	Did you ever check with the Wiley House as to why that person was placed there?
A:	No, I did not.
Q:	And I see in the early part of your report you have fifteen people residing at Alverta's house.
A:	Yes.
Q:	Would your conclusion change any if you knew there were less people residing there today?
A:	I would have to know how many, what the arrangements, the sleeping arrangements, were at this point.
Q:	With respect to Harold, what is your impression as to how often he's at that home?
A:	From what was indicated to me, it's sporadic.
Q:	Judy S., Tammy S. and Joanne and Danny S. no longer reside at that home, so four people have left.
MR. KELLER:	Objection, Your Honor. There's nothing on the record about that. Is that a question?

By Mr. Fonzone:

Q: Well, take that as a fact, hypothetical if you like.
MR. KELLER: Well, I object.
THE COURT: It's not on the record, but we have to have a little latitude
                here. The objection will be overruled, assuming that
                were a fact.

By Mr. Fonzone:

Q: Do you have those names?
A: Yes.
Q: Now, would the fact that they've left influence the opin-
                ion you've rendered in your report?
A: Certainly there would be less people living in the home,
                but I still feel that the home is overcrowded.
Q: And is that the objection you have to the home, that it's
                overcrowded?
A: Because of the amount of adults and the way the home is
                set up with no one being specifically responsible for the
                discipline of each child, that everyone takes turn, this
                certainly is going to affect the identity, any child's iden-
                tity growing up in such a home.
Q: And is that a second objection that you have?
A: Yes.
Q: Do you have any other objections to the home?
A: There was some question about the sexual practices,
                which you have, you know, discussed previously. But
                there are many—there are very many relationship prob-
                lems with all of Mrs. S's children, many of her daughters
                had illegitimate children, her sons have had difficulty in
                their marriages. As far as the dynamics of the family go,
                there seem to be relationship problems.
Q: That would be true of Sandra also?
A: She's also a product of that environment, yes.
Q: And she's had two illegitimate children?
A: Yes.
Q: She's living with a man she's not married to?
Q: Yes.
Q: Now, with respect to Mr. M., are you aware that he had a
                stepbrother?
A: No, I'm not.
Q: And were you aware that he hasn't worked for—I forget
                the precise facts, but twelve or fifteen years?
A: Yes, he did tell me he had been unemployed.
Q: Although you make the observation that although he's
                presently unemployed, he does odd jobs and has applied
                for several jobs?

A: Yes.

Q: What do you gather out of that? Is that a positive influence or why is it important that he's applied for other jobs?

A: That he is making an attempt at this point to find employment.

Q: Well, then you didn't do any investigative work as to the actual length of time he had not been employed?

A: Yes, I did. And although I can't find it right here in my notes, he did indicate to me that he had been a private chauffeur, which was his last permanent employment.

Q: Did he tell you when he did that?

A: That's what I'm looking for now. He told me four years ago he was self-employed as a private chauffeur.

Q: Did he tell you how long he did that?

A: No, he did not.

Q: And I suspect you had no reason or no opportunity to check on whether he actually was a private chauffeur?

A: Right.

Q: Now, on your last page, Page 4 of the Sandra home study, you say her affect was consistently appropriate. What does that mean?

A: The affect meaning a person's facial expressions, their mannerisms during questioning, composure.

Q: And what does that mean then, consistently appropriate?

A: It means when discussing a difficult area, a topic that may have been painful for her, she became upset as one would expect, but yet she was able to smile during more casual moments.

Q: Is that in opposition to something you found with Alverta?

A: Mrs. S. was much more guarded during the interview and was not as open with me as Sandra was.

Q: Did you have the opportunity to interview Sandra's son?

A: No, I did not.

Q: Don't you think that would be crucial, as he'll be a member of that household?

A: We did discuss that and—

Q: You discussed that with Sandra?

A: Exactly. And we had a lot of difficulty arranging times when I could meet with him.

Q: Why was that? This is a seventeen-year-old boy in high school.

A: With his working schedule, school schedule and my schedule.

Q: Well, don't you think it's relevant to your study?

A: Yes and no. He is, as you say, seventeen, and may not be in the household much longer. Mrs. —

Q: Why would you say that, Miss R? Why would you say he may not be in the household much longer?

A: The fact that he's seventeen, and usually people when they're eighteen leave the household. And Miss Shook indicated to me that she did not feel he would be there much past that.

Q: What do you base the fact that when people turn eighteen they leave the household on?

A: They're of legal age, they're out of school, they go out on their own.

Q: Is there a study that says that?

A: I can't quote studies to you, no.

Q: So it's an assumption you made based on a feeling you have?

A: And from what Miss S. indicated to me.

Q: Well, what did he indicate to you? Did she tell you he was living with her or he wasn't?

A: Oh, he's living there now, or at the time of my study.

Q: Are you certain of that?

A: I saw his room, his belongings.

Q: But you didn't see him, you didn't talk to him?

A: No.

Q: And the only reason you don't think it's so crucial to talk to him is because you think he may be leaving?

A: Well, whether he is or he isn't, he wouldn't have the child or responsibility, Miss S. will.

Q: Well, she's not going to have that during the day, is she?

A: She has plans for a day care center for him.

Q: But she's not going to have that during the day, the day care center is going to.

A: Exactly.

Q: When the child comes home, who's to say who's going to be at home, the boy or the mother?

A: Well, certainly she is the person who will be the legal guardian for him.

Q: Yes.

A: So she will I assume have the responsibility of child-rearing. She did not indicate otherwise to me.

Q: Well, did you ask?

A: Certainly.

Q: Did you ask her if she intends to have her son sit with the child?

A: Did I ask that specific question?

Q: Yes.

A: No.

Q: How many rooms did Sandra have in her apartment?

A: Five rooms and a bath.

Q: And how many rooms were in Alverta's home?

A: Nine and a bath.

Q: Did the nine include the attic?

A: Yes.

Q: And did it include the basement?

A: No.

Q: There is a full basement, though, isn't there?

A: Yes.

Q: And how much area do they have around the home?

A: Which home?

Q: Let's start with Alverta.

A: She has a large yard.

Q: And how about Sandra?

A: A small yard.

Q: Had you ever in your 360 home studies dealt with a home that was like Alverta's home?

A: Certainly every home is unique.

Q: What was unique about her home?

A: In comparison to my others?

Q: Yes.

A: The family dynamics, the size of the household, the way it was set up.

Q: I take it there's nothing directly wrong with having a large group of people?

A: No.

Q: When you talk about dynamics, what do you mean?

A: The interactions between the people. Certainly this is a very matriarchal household.

Q: Some societies are that way.

A: Certainly. I'm not passing judgment on that. I'm just stating a fact. I've never been in a household where everyone turned in their pay check to the head of the household and then it was divided up from there.

Q: Did anyone within that household tell you they didn't like the way it was being run?

A: The residents there at the time? No, no one voiced an objection.

Q: And there are certainly children who are no longer there in addition to Sandra. Did you have an opportunity to talk to any of them?

A: None of them were present.

Q: You're not aware of any of them?

A: Aware of them?

Q:	Yes.
A:	Mrs. S. did indicate to me that she had children out of the household, yes.
Q:	And you had their names and addresses?
A:	No, I do not.
Q:	Could you have gotten those?
A:	I'm sure Mrs. S. would have provided them for me.
Q:	Would you like to have them to talk to those people to get their impressions?

THE COURT:	This is of which people?
MR. FONZONE:	These are the other children not living within the home. In addition to Sandra there are others. And I believe some of them have testified before you, Judge. At least two daughters did.
THE WITNESS:	The study as I was required to do it was of the two households, not of anyone else's household.

By Mr. Fonzone:

Q:	I think you've indicated that none of the people within the household of Alverta expressed any discomfort or any objections to the way things were being run.
A:	The only person who voiced objection was Sandra.
Q:	Who was not in the household. And the three other daughters not within the household, you didn't speak to any of them?
A:	Right.
Q:	Would it be important to speak to them?
A:	I feel that I got a good understanding of what was going on with just the people I spoke to.
Q:	So it's not important to you then to speak to these other three?
A:	No.
Q:	Were you able to eliminate the animosity between Sandra and Alverta in arriving at your conclusions?
A:	Certainly it was there. As I indicated in the report, Mrs. S. preferred to tell unflattering stories about Sandra rather than present her own story.
Q:	But you wouldn't say that Sandra told you unflattering stories about Alverta?
A:	Certainly she did.
Q:	As a matter of fact, you put some of them in here, about legal papers and funeral?
A:	Yes.
Q:	Do you know who paid for the funeral?
A:	To my knowledge, it was an insurance company.

Q: If it were not for the insurance company, do you know who paid that?

A: It was pending when I spoke with Sandra.

Q: So you didn't ask Alverta who paid for the—

A: I did call Attorney Keller and asked him if he had a copy of the bill.

Q: And what did he tell you?

A: And it was his impression also, or from what I recall what he told me, was that the insurance company had paid and the rest was—the balance was due.

Q: You didn't want to see the receipted bill saying Alverta paid for it, the balance? Would that make any difference?

A: Certainly it verifies her story.

THE COURT: Is this the funeral of the daughter?

MR. FONZONE: The granddaughter of Alverta.

THE COURT: Sandra's daughter. What was her name? Debra?

THE WITNESS: Debra.

MR. FONZONE: Yes, Your Honor.

By Mr. Fonzone:

Q: Did you have the impression that this whole thing is about money?

A: That's what Mrs. S. indicated to me, that she felt Sandra was looking for the money.

Q: What is your impression? I didn't ask for what Alverta told you.

A: I don't feel that money is the motive here.

Q: And I take it from what you told us there's very little that would change your impression that you put in your report?

A: That's correct.

Q: Did you have an opportunity to speak to Jeremy?

A: Jeremy's an infant.

Q: Right. Did you spend any time—

A: Well, while I was there he was sleeping.

Q: Now, based on your experience, and the Court is going to be faced with a decision, if custody were changed, how should that be accomplished? Overnight, gradually?

A: I would prefer to see it gradually.

Q: And what do you mean by that?

A: Starting out with visits. I don't know at this point how often Sandra had contact with Jeremy. Certainly it would be a very difficult thing for any child to be changed from one household to another if they're not familiar with that person.

Q: And would you continue visitation with the grandmother once custody were completely changed?

A: I would have no objections.

MR. FONZONE: I have no other questions.
                Your Honor, the bill itself I haven't marked. I'd like to hold onto it.

THE COURT: Yes. The Court has had an opportunity to see it I think.

CROSS-EXAMINATION

By Mr. Keller:

Q: Miss R, you described your job classification as diagnostic home study. Do you also do family counseling?

A: Yes, I do.

Q: And would that involve dealing with families that are having domestic or other problems?

A: Yes.

Q: How long have you done that?

A: I received my training from Philadelphia Child Guidance Clinic last summer, the summer of 1980.

Q: Had you done counseling over the years prior to that?

A: As far as the children in our care involving the parents so that they would be able to have the child return home, yes.

Q: And have you had occasion to make evaluations for court regarding minor children?

A: Yes, I do.

Q: In what respect?

A: As I mentioned before, as a diagnostic case-worker, I do a complete study of the family and go into court and make recommendations whether that family is suitable to have the children return home.

Q: In what context would that be in? Would that cover a wide variety of situations?

A: Yes. Oftentimes the child has committed a delinquent act, is having school problems or there's something going on in the family that's in question.

Q: Now, can you tell me what day you went to Alverta's house?

A: December 1st, 1980.

Q: I think in response to Mr. Fonzone's questioning, you agreed that Sandra was a product of that same environment that exists at Alverta's house at this point, that she was a product of that environment. Is that correct?

A: Yes.

Q: Do you see any difference, however, in the present life-
       style between the two households?

A: Well, I think what Attorney Fonzone was pointing out
       was that Miss S. also had two illegitimate children, which
       is true; but that happened while she was under her moth-
       er's roof. She has not had any children since she's moved
       out.

Q: In discussing that issue with Sandra, were you able to
       gather any facts or impressions regarding her attitude and
       her present feelings about her upbringing and the en-
       vironment that she came from?

A: Certainly she had a lot of negative feelings about it which
       prompted her to move out. I see that she has made a life
       for herself and has been successful in supporting herself
       and her children since she moved out.

Q: Based on what you've observed and your discussions with
       the parties, could you characterize Sandra's attempt to be
       on her own as a positive motivation on her part?

A: She felt that her children were being affected by the
       lifestyle that she was living while with her mother, and
       feeling that that was negative moved out and faced some
       hard times, certainly, to start a new life and become the
       dominant and significant person in their lives as opposed
       to having the child-rearing shared by several adults.

Q: And on Page 4 of your home study regarding Alverta, the
       heading is "Impressions, continued." Do you see that?

A: Yes.

Q: In that paragraph, you state that "A child growing up in
       this environment might well experience problems in es-
       tablishing a secure sense of identity." Could you elabo-
       rate and give us some specific examples of what types of
       problems a child could face growing up in this specific
       environment?

A: Okay. First off and the most obvious, if everyone is
       sharing the responsibility of discipline and child rearing,
       there may be a loss of identity as far as who the true
       parents are, who is that significant person in the child's
       life. As can be expected, many adults are going to have
       different viewpoints on how to raise a child and there's
       going to be—it can be expected that there's going to be a
       lot of inconsistency in that. And oftentimes when a child
       is faced with so many inconsistencies, you're talking
       about some character disorders that may develop from
       that, maybe a lack of a sense of a true right and wrong,
       because what may be right and wrong in one adult's eyes
       may not be the same in another's.

Q: And would these problems also be affected by the other

	factors which you list in that same paragraph, which are the situation of open sexuality, little privacy and crowded conditions?
A:	Certainly.
Q:	On page 3 of your home study regarding Alverta, the paragraph entitled "Future plans," it would be fair to say, I take it, from what you say—You're saying there that Alverta informed you that she has no plans to alter her present living situation.
A:	Correct.
Q:	Now, did you observe a living quarters in the cellar of this household?
A:	Yes, I did.
Q:	And what is the nature of the cellar? Is it finished or unfinished?
A:	Unfinished.
Q:	What are the walls? What is the—
A:	It's a cellar.
Q:	Would these be cement walls?
A:	Yes. and she did—
Q:	So there's nothing on the walls except cement?
A:	Exactly.
Q:	And what is the floor?
A:	The floor was cement, but they had made an attempt to make it more livable by placing the rugs down under the living area.
Q:	What did the ceiling look like? Were there exposed pipes?
A:	I did not go completely into the basement. I was at the cellar stairs. I could not see whether there were exposed pipes or not.
Q:	Did you notice where the boiler was, where the—
A:	No, I did not see the boiler.
Q:	So you don't know where it is in relation to the sleeping quarters?
A:	In relation to the sleeping, no.
Q:	And were you informed who sleeps in the basement?
A:	Yes, I was. Judy and her two daughters, Tammy and Joanne.
Q:	And how old would Tammy and Joanne be?
A:	Tammy is seven and Joanne is six.
Q:	And are there any facilities whatsoever in that cellar that you know of, any facilities other than a bed?
MR FONZONE:	I'm going to object, Your Honor. She didn't see the cellar, it's pretty clear.
THE COURT:	Were you down in the cellar or just—
THE WITNESS:	We had toured the house. I went to the cellar stairs,

looked down and saw the beds and the rug and the floor and walls. But I cannot address myself to what the rest of the cellar looked like, just where their living quarters were.

THE COURT: I see. Well, if you can answer the question, the objection will be overruled.

By Mr. Keller:

Q: Did you note whether there were any bathroom facilities in the cellar?
A: The only bathroom that Mrs. S. indicated to me was on the second floor.
Q: The only bathroom in the household is on the second floor?
A: Yes.
Q: So we have one bathroom for all of these people?
A: Correct.
Q: And did you observe a cot in the hallway somewhere where somebody was sleeping?
A: On the landing before going up to the attic stairs, yes.
Q: Was that a child sleeping on that?
A: Yes, it was.
Q: Who was that?
A: Dean, age eleven.
MR. KELLER: Thank you.

RECROSS-EXAMINATION

By Mr. Fonzone:

Q: You learned that the lady that was in the basement had no place to go and Alverta let her go there?
A: Yes.
Q: And you since heard from me that she's not there any longer?
A: Correct.
MR. KELLER: I object.
THE COURT: Well, the objection will be sustained.

By Mr. Fonzone:

Q: I doubt that that has anything to do with your opinion, as to whether she is or is not down in the basement?
A: No, the rest of the house in my opinion was overcrowded.
Q: Jeremy himself had a room of his own?
A: Yes, he did.

Q:	And he's the individual that you're concerned with?
A:	Right.
Q:	And as far as the number of rooms in the home, there's nine plus the basement? That's what you told us before.
A:	Okay.
Q:	And the home that she's in has five; is that right?
A:	Yes.
Q:	And your opinion with respect to what is a suitable home is not influenced by the greatest area of living space?
A:	Certainly that's taken into consideration, but of course, all factors must be.
Q:	What is the most important factor?
A:	The environment that the child's going to be growing up in.
Q:	So if they had a home that was twice as large, you would still find it objectionable?
A:	Yes, I would.
MR. FONZONE:	I have no other questions.
THE COURT:	All right. You may step down. Thank you Miss R. The Court thanks you very much.
	Gentlemen, anything you want to state on the record at this time?
MR. KELLER:	I have nothing.
MR. FONZONE:	No, Judge.
THE COURT:	All right. We'll have a decision coming down as soon as possible.

(Proceedings concluded.)

The court reached a decision in the case connected with the above transcript that cast doubt on the worthiness of the caseworker's testimony. Essentially, the judge was not convinced that the trial court record, which included the above testimony, contained sufficient evidence to support awarding custody of Jeremy S. to Sandra S. The case, *In Re Custody of J.S.S.*, 298 Pa. Superior Ct. 428 (1982), was an appeal from an order of the Court of Common Pleas awarding custody of Jeremy S. to Sandra S., who is his grandmother. The appellant, Alverta S., is the great-grandmother of the child. The child's mother was killed in a car crash in May 1980 when the child was less than one year old. In reaching its decision, the court noted that:

The judge below awarded custody to Sandra essentially (1) because he was "concerned with the large number of people residing with Alverta," (2) because he was "concerned with exposing the child to the open sexuality of the Alverta S. household," and (3) because of the lack of "any type of steady relationship among men and women" in Alverta's household as compared with Sandra's. . . .

To affirm the order of the lower court, we must be persuaded that its decision comports with the best interests of the child. . . . For the reasons given below, we find that Sandra did not meet this burden [of proving that the best interests of the child will be served by placement with her], that the record is inadequate, that the lower court's opinion did not sufficiently consider and analyze all the testimony, and that the lower court drew conclusions that are neither based on, or are controverted by, the testimony. . . .

The caseworker's report . . . lacks any basic information about the atmosphere of Sandra's household and how Jeremy would adapt to it, and it lacks any information about the relationship between Sandra and Jeremy. Instead it contains conclusions that were shown on cross-examination not to be based on fact. For example, with reference to her conclusion, adopted by the court, that the atmosphere in Alverta's household was one of open sexuality because women who entertained men had double beds, the testimony on cross-examination was as follows: [see above transcript]. . . . Despite this testimony, the trial court adopted the conclusion of "open sexuality" as well as the caseworker's unsubstantiated conclusion that the house was "overcrowded" with people with "undefined roles." . . . On remand more information should be made available to the court in the form of testimony, expert or otherwise, with regard to the relationship between Jeremy and the people in Alverta's household and between Jeremy and those in Sandra's household. . . .

In its opinion, the trial court discusses the physical arrangements of the two households, and finds that both are equally clean. He decides, however, that Alverta's house is overcrowded. This conclusion had been reached by the caseworker in her report. . . .

From the trial court's opinion, relying heavily on the caseworker's report and testimony and ignoring almost entirely the rest of the testimony at trial, we are not convinced that the trial court overcame the hurdle of his disapproval of Alverta's household in order to consider where Jeremy would be happier and more loved and better cared for. . . .

The order awarding custody of Jeremy S. to Sandra S. is reversed. The case is remanded for further proceedings consistent with this opinion.

TECHNIQUES FOR EFFECTIVELY PRESENTING TESTIMONY

The effective presentation of testimony requires an understanding of evidence principles and civil process, as well as an ability to apply this knowledge in a professional role. The following techniques, supplied by Caulfield (1985), should support the performance of social workers as witnesses. Some may seem obvious; others will underscore the technicalities associated with the witness role. Collectively, they are effective practical guidelines and thus should help put the entire witness experience in perspective.

HOW TO BE A GOOD WITNESS*

Preparing to Testify

1. Dress appropriately.
2. Prepare ahead of time. You know in advance when you will be called to testify. Use the time . . . to refresh your memory and recall details. . . . Review these events in your mind and go over your notes. Don't expect to use your notes extensively at trial, although they may be used if necessary to refresh your memory. A witness is expected to testify from memory.
3. Don't memorize your testimony. Review your expected testimony mentally. It is not a good idea to prepare a script; spontaneous responses are more believable and less likely to be shaken on cross-examination. . . .

How to Answer Questions

1. Be sincere, dignified, and warm. Trials are inappropriate settings in which to inject humor or comic relief. . . . Your projection of a humane attitude may assist the judge in evaluating your credibility in a positive manner. A concerned appearance on the stand usually makes a better impression than does a frozen or calculating one.
2. Speak clearly and distinctly. The judge, attorneys, and jury (if it is a jury trial) have to hear your response, as does the court reporter if a record is being made of the hearing. Therefore, speak clearly and distinctly in a voice that is probably louder than the one you use in ordinary conversation.
3. Use appropriate language. Use ordinary English words with which you are comfortable. Avoid slang, jargon, and words with unfamiliar meanings.
4. Answer the question that is asked. You must listen to each question so you know what information is appropriate. For example:

Q: You stated that you are a licensed social worker. Where did you take your training?

That means formal school in social work—not the elementary and high schools you attended or the degrees you received that do not relate to your professional skills.

---

*Reprinted with permission from: Child Abuse and the Law: A Legal Primer for Social Workers, by Barbara A. Caulfield. © 1985, by permission of the publisher, the National Committee for Prevention of Child Abuse, Chicago, IL.

Q: What did you and Mary Jones talk about during your first
                            interview?

Give the time, date, and place of the conversation; then tell the substance
of the conversation or topics discussed.

Ordinarily you will not have to mention discussing such things as the
weather or bus schedules or other items that have no bearing on the
professional contact. You might summarize these kinds of conversations
by saying you "chatted briefly" or "discussed other matters" so the examiner can explore them if he or she feels they may be relevant.

Be alert to the kind of responses desired. Direct examination usually
calls for narrative responses, whereas cross-examination normally asks for
a "yes" or "no" or some other very short answer.

A common error of the witness is double-thinking or overthinking the
question. To help you avoid this, pause before answering a question, and
try to keep from overextending the questioner's meaning.

Avoid offhanded responses and likewise, too technical ones in attempting to draw meaning from the question.

The English language does not change because it is spoken in a courtroom. For example, if the questioner asks: "Were you at the home of Mrs.
Smith on August 29, 1979?" This does not mean: Were you in the home?
or Did you remain in the home any significant length of time? It simply
asks if you were at that house—inside, outside, or on the street in front of
the house at any time that day.

5. Let the attorney develop your testimony. This applies to both direct
and cross-examination. For example:

Q: "Do you remember an interview with Mary Jones on
                            Monday, April 15, at 10:15 A.M.?" The best response is
                            "yes" or "no." In the next question, the examining attor-
                            ney may ask you to narrate the substance or circum-
                            stances of the interview. The purpose of the first question
                            may be to prepare a foundation before introducing the
                            significant part of your testimony. This is the trial attor-
                            ney's job; don't jump ahead.

6. If you don't know the answer to a question, say so. Don't guess. If
you cannot remember, it is better to say so than to speculate. You may
remember the answer later during your testimony; if so, the attorney
questioning you may re-ask the question. Do not rely, however, on the
use of "I don't remember" or "I don't know" to avoid answering difficult or
indelicate questions. If you are the eyewitness of child abuse, you will not
be an effective witness if you cannot remember details.

7. Don't make your testimony conform to other testimony you may
have heard. You are called to testify regarding what you observed or what
your opinion is. Different eyewitnesses can have different impressions of
the same event. You are not expected to agree with or parrot someone
else's testimony; the other person may be wrong. You can discuss dis-
crepancies with your attorney, but this is done outside the courtroom.

8. When answering questions, look at the person asking the questions or at the judge. You are testifying in order to impart information to the judge or jury who will use it to determine the outcome. If you always look over at your lawyer before answering another attorney's question, it will look as if you are waiting to be coached. You are an impartial witness; you are not supposed to "win" the case for the other side.

9. Tell the truth. Pure and simple. . . . The lawyer is there to argue the case; you are there to report facts impartially to the judge. If a truthful answer seems to hurt the lawyer who asked you to testify, this should not be your concern. You are there to tell the facts.

How to Survive Cross-Examination

Cross-examination is a necessary part of the judicial process; it is also an inherent part of the American system of justice, which is adversarial. In this system, each side is obligated to attempt to throw a different light on the testimony of a witness.

All lawyers in the American system are required to cross-examine witnesses. Such cross-examination is not used against you personally; it is practiced on all witnesses and the more important the witness, the more vigorous the cross-examination.

1. State only what you remember. The cross-examiner may attempt to suggest details to you that you do not remember and that you did not state on direct examination. Do not follow the cross-examiner's leading question into an answer. For example, the cross-examiner may present a question in such a way that it seems eminently logical. If that is not what you remember, however, do not agree with the cross-examiner. Your weakness to the power of suggestion may cause you to change your answers without realizing it. For example:

Q: "You saw blood flowing from the arm of Jane Smith after she was hit by the hammer, didn't you?"
       The witness thinks, Well, I saw Jane hit with the hammer. I don't remember the blood . . . but there must have been some. I'll say yes.
A: "Yes."

This witness in this example may, in fact, have been too far away to see the blood, and that is why the witness did not remember seeing any. This distance perception problem will be argued by the cross-examiner as impeaching the witness's believability. Or it may be that the skin was not broken because the force was not great enough. In this case, the witness will be impeached because a doctor will testify to the fact of no blood loss.

2. Be very careful of what you say and how you say it. Even a friendly cross-examiner looks for inconsistencies by which to trip you whenever possible. Remember:

- Listen to the question.
- Make sure you understand what is being asked. If you don't understand the question, ask the questioner to rephrase it, or say you don't understand what information is being asked for. This situation can easily arise on cross-examination since leading questions (that is, questions suggesting the answer) are permitted. Leading questions are usually prohibited on direct examination of the witness.
- Don't volunteer information that is not asked for. Volunteering provides the cross-examiner with additional opportunities to try to confuse you.
- Don't explain why you know something unless you are asked.
- The attorney offering your testimony has a chance to ask additional questions after cross-examination to clear up any problems.

3. If a question has two parts requiring different answers, answer it in two parts. Many times, cross-examiners ask compound questions. Do not answer a partially untrue question with a "yes." When responding to a compound question, divide the question into parts and then answer it. For example:

Q: "Is it not true that you drove to the Smith home on August 16, 1976, stormed inside, and immediately picked up their child, Mary Smith?"

A: "There are three parts to that question, and each part has a different answer. I did go to the Smith home, but I spoke with Mrs. Smith on the porch for 15 minutes. Then we spoke in the living room for another 15 minutes. After that, she allowed me to take custody of Mary."

Do not begin your answer with "yes," because the attorney may cut you short and not allow you to complete your response, thus giving an erroneous impression of your actions.

4. Answer positively rather than doubtfully. Qualifiers such as:
"I think . . ."
"To the best of my recollection . . ."
"I guess . . ."
weaken the impact of your testimony. Be forthright if you know the answer. If you don't know the answer, say so.

5. Admit your beliefs or sympathy honestly. Often, a witness will be asked a question regarding sympathy for one side or the other in the case. It would be absurd to deny an honest sympathy, and honest admission of favoritism will not discredit a witness. For example:

Q: "Do you have a feeling as to how you would like this case to come out?"

A: "Yes . . . I'm afraid I do."

Q: "You would like the State to get custody of little Mary and
                remove her from her mother, wouldn't you?"
A: "Yes, I feel that way. But I have answered all of your
                questions as honestly as I possibly could. I have told the
                truth."

This is very different from coloring answers because of favoritism. When
an attorney shows that a witness will change testimony because of feeling
about a case, the attorney is showing that the feelings of the witness are
affecting his or her testimony. This is bias that can damage credibility.

6. Don't get caught by a trick question. If you are asked, "Are you
being paid to testify?" remember that it is acceptable for experts to be paid
and that, in most jurisdictions, lay witnesses receive statutory per diem
and mileage allowances for the inconvenience. If you are being paid to
testify, say so and explain. For example: "I am being paid a fee of twenty
dollars." If the expert is being paid his or her normal consultation rate, the
expert should state this. Of course, if the answer is no, say "no." You may
be asked, "Have you discussed this case with anyone?" And since you
naturally have discussed the case with the attorney from your side, say so.
Also, name your supervisor and anyone else with whom you have discussed the case.

LIVING WITH UNCERTAINTY: SOME PRACTICAL GUIDELINES

Finally, there is the issue of confidential records, which are frequently kept as documentation of communications between workers and
clients. These documents, under certain circumstances, can be subpoenaed—a fact the worker should keep in mind. The increase in
reporting requirements has imposed an additional burden on social
workers to maintain appropriate records. Wilson (1980) provides a
very comprehensive discussion of the topic and supplies extensive
references to readings dealing with all aspects of record keeping.
Such developments, along with concerns about statutory privileges
and liability for malpractice (as discussed in the next chapter), portend a significant degree of uncertainty for even the most responsible
professional; Schrier (1980), Woody (1984), Gevers (1983), Everstine
(1980), Hunter and Grinell (1983), Oyen and Beckford (1982), Sloan
and Hall (1984).

Rose (1978) suggests the following guidelines for dealing with the
uncertainties of record-keeping. Though directed primarily at child
welfare agencies, these may apply to record-keeping in all social
service agencies.

First, it is imperative that agencies familiarize themselves with the specific privacy and disclosure requirements that may apply to them, e.g., disclosure requirements under the state's child abuse statute or freedom of information statute. . . .

Second, the new statutes and decisions suggest that agency information and disclosure practice must contain at least the following components:

1. policies with respect to the a) types of information that the agency will disclose, b) persons and institutions to which such disclosure will be made and for what purposes, and c) conditions under which disclosure will be made;
2. procedures by which various persons and institutions may gain access to records they are entitled to see;
3. procedures by which the contents of records may be contested and, where necessary, corrected or revised;
4. procedures for informing clients and others of their rights to access and/or nondisclosure;
5. procedures to prevent disclosure of individual information to all but authorized persons and institutions, including a) conditions to prevent redisclosure by the initial recipients of such information, and b) methods to keep track of which persons have had access to such information.

. . . [Other] factors might guide the development of information and disclosure policies. Among these are:

1. the client's right to protection against undue intrusion on privacy through disclosure of records to persons who have no legitimate use of those records;
2. the public's right to be informed of matters of general interest, most particularly with respect to statistical data and general agency policies;
3. the special right of third parties to be informed of dangers to them stemming from their dealings with some [client] under agency care or control;
4. the right of the client to have access to records about himself, particularly where such records may follow him through his education or career, or when the client has some independent need for the materials . . .; and
5. a counterbalancing need to prevent harm to the client from direct disclosure of potentially upsetting materials. . . . [pp.. 61–62]

10 Privileged Communications and Worker–Client Relations

We have seen that sociai worker testimony offered as a lay or expert witness is a significant part of judicial fact finding. This testimony is presented within a legal structure designed to accomplish one goal: to search for the truth. No person can refuse to testify when called to do so. A court can subpoena (officially command) reluctant parties and thus compel them to testify. It can also command them to bring subpoenaed documents and records. Subpoenaed parties who fail to appear or to testify can be cited for contempt (a willful disobeying of a judge's command or official court order). In certain circumstances, administrative agencies also have this authority.

Thus, it may be surprising to discover that there are some situations where facts may be kept out of the truth-finding process. This chapter will address these situations and their relation to social work, specifically focusing on two dimensions of the social worker–client relationships: (1) the confidential communications privilege, and (2) the duty to warn.

CREATING THE COMMUNICATIONS PRIVILEGE

Privileged communications are communications that may be kept out of legal proceedings. The law requires that they be kept confidential and beyond the reach of the truth-finding process until public policy requires they be set aside:

> Where persons occupy toward each other certain confidential relations, the law, on the ground of public policy, will not compel, or even allow one

of them to violate the confidence reposed in him by the other, by testifying, without the consent of the other, as to communications made to him
by such other in the confidence which the relation has inspired. . . . This
rule of privileged communication is not a rule of substantive law, but a
mere rule of evidence, which does not affect the general competency of
any witness, but merely renders him incompetent [as defined in the
previous chapter] to testify to certain particular matters. . . . [S]tatutory
privileges are absolute in the sense that, even in matters involving public
justice, a court may not compel disclosure of confidential communications
thus privileged [this distinction between absolute and conditional privilege will be clarified below in *In Re Pittsburgh Action Against Rape*].
Privilege has been held to be a matter of statute and the general rule is
that there is no privilege in the absence of statute. (97 C.J.S. Witnesses
Sec. 252).

These privileges, which have been created by the legislature, are
necessary to protect communications between parties that share a
special relationship (Lutkis & Curtis, 1985; Sloan and Hall, 1984). For
example, husband–wife communications are protected from disclosure. Similarly, communications between doctors and patients,
priests and penitents, and lawyers and clients, for example, are
protected.

Not all relationships, however, are privileged. Legislatures vary
among the fifty states, so a protected relationship in one state may
not exist in another. For example, communications between news re-
porters and their sources are protected communications in Pennsylvania (42 Pa. Cons. Stat. Ann. Sec. 5942 (Purdon 1982)), but not
necessarily in all states. The social worker–client relationship is another illustration of varied state practices (Starobin, 1984; Savrin,
1985).

Because a privilege allows the exclusion of testimony from the
truth-finding process, only those communications that meet the following four requirements can expect to be protected from disclosure.
(Yet, as we will discuss later, even a valid privilege may be set aside
for public policy reasons.)

1. The communications must originate in a confidence that they
   will not be disclosed.
2. This element of confidentiality must be essential to the full and
   satisfactory maintenance of the relation between the parties.
3. The relation must be one which in the opinion of the community
   ought to be sedulously fostered.

4. The injury that would inure to the relation by the disclosure of the communications must be greater than the benefit thereby gained for the correct disposal of litigation (Wigmore, 1961).

Legislatures vary, so it is not surprising they do not have a uniform view on the relationships that require protection. For example, Pennsylvania's communications between sexual assault counselors and rape victims were only recently recognized as privileged. Before 1981, these communications did not, according to the Pennsylvania Supreme Court—and, presumably, the legislature—warrant absolute protection from disclosure. The relative merits of establishing this type of privilege and the factors that contributed to its creation can be seen in the following Pennsylvania judicial opinion. *In Re Pittsburgh Action Against Rape*, 494 Pa. 15 (1981), and in the subsequent legislative debate. The dissenting opinion is supplied below because it deals fully with the public policy that will be advanced by allowing an absolute privilege for communications between sexual assault counselors and rape victims. The majority opinion, which ruled against extending the privilege, is omitted. Justice Larsen's dissent, however, is sufficiently comprehensive to offer insight into both sides of the debate. (Also, note the excellent references cited in the opinion.) And although his dissent did not sway the majority, it sent a clear signal to the Pennsylvania legislature—one that was clearly received. Laurence (1984) provides an extended discussion of the issue and like Larsen, argues for the absolute privilege, and William (1984) proposes a model statute.

MATTER OF PITTSBURGH ACTION AGAINST RAPE
494 PA. 15 (1981)

LARSEN, Justice, dissenting.

The immediate facts of this case are simple. The resolution is not simple, involving as it does, important conflicting rights of the victim and the accused.

The issue is whether this Court should recognize a testimonial privilege for communications made between a rape victim and a rape crisis center counselor. To my knowledge, this issue is one of first impression, not only in this Commonwealth, but also in the American system of jurisprudence. I agree with the position advocated by Ann Pride, appellant and administrator of Pittsburgh Action Against Rape (PAAR), and Allegheny County District

Attorney Robert Colville, through their able counsel, Ms. Ann Begler and Deputy District Attorney Robert Eberhardt respectively, that the common law should be expanded to recognize an absolute testimonial privilege for all communications between rape victim and rape crisis center counselors, and accordingly voice my dissent. The facts are as follows:

Keith Glover was charged with rape, involuntary deviant sexual intercourse, indecent assault, simple assault, and terroristic threats. A jury trial was commenced on July 10, 1980 before the Honorable Ralph J. Cappy of the Court of Common Pleas of Allegheny County, Criminal Division. During cross-examination of the victim-complainant, defense counsel requested to examine the records of PAAR to ascertain whether or not she had made any prior statements to PAAR counselors which were inconsistent with her trial testimony.

Pursuant to that request, appellant Ann Pride was ordered to appear in court with the relevant records, which she did on July 11, 1980. With the consent of the victim, Judge Cappy conducted an in camera inspection and ruled, as a matter of fact, that no prior inconsistent statements appeared in the records. Nevertheless, at defense counsel's insistence that he was entitled to view the records, Judge Cappy ordered Ms. Pride to allow defense counsel to examine PAAR's files. Since the victim withheld her consent, Ms. Pride refused to comply with that order and was consequently held in contempt of court. Chief Justice Henry X. O'Brien granted a stay of the contempt order on July 14, 1980 and this Court subsequently exercised its plenary jurisdiction to decide the matter.

Initially, there can be no serious doubt that courts have the common law authority to judicially create testimonial privileges. Any lingering doubts were laid to rest by our recent decision of *In re B, Appeal of Roth,* in which we recognized a non-statutory, psychotherapeutic privilege for communications made between a psychotherapist and his client. While I certainly agree with the majority's sentiments that exceptions to the general rule requiring full disclosure of all relevant evidence should not be lightly established, nevertheless it is clear that access to information is not without appropriate limitations. Mr. Justice Roberts expressed appreciation for such common law limitations in his concurring opinion in *In re B* wherein he recognized the ability of the common law to create testimonial privileges barring access to certain information. . . .

Privileged communications take various forms and are protected from disclosure for different reasons of social policy. They may be classed into three categories: (1) those designed to protect the individual, often the accused (e.g., the privilege against self-incrimination or against having otherwise illegally-obtained evidence admitted); (2) those designed to protect the integrity of some system of government (e.g., "executive privilege"); and (3) those designed to encourage freedom from fear of disclosure in

persons partaking of certain relationships, the functions of which are deemed
extremely important to society and which are dependent for their effectiveness on full mutual disclosure between the parties to the relationship (e.g.,
attorney–client, priest–penitent, physician–patient). Fisher, The *Psychotherapeutic Professions* and the *Law of Privileged Communications*, 10,
Wayne L. Rev. 609, 610 (1964) (hereinafter Fisher); see also McCormick,
The Scope of Privilege in the Law of Evidence, 16 Texas L. Rev. 447 (1938)
(here-inafter McCormick).

Although we are here concerned with a privilege which would, if recognized, fall into the latter category, the majority opinion inexplicably focuses
upon cases falling into the first two categories. While all three classes of
privilege share a general aim . . . the specific underlying policies justifying
each class of privilege are significantly (and obviously) dissimilar, so as to
seriously diminish the precedential value of authority dealing with the first
two classes of privilege when considering a privilege ostensibly of the third
variety.

The only cases cited in the majority opinion dealing with privileges
justified by the relationship of trust between the parties, and the necessity
for complete mutual disclosure of information between them, are relegated
to a footnote and the importance of these cases is summarily dismissed with
the statement "(t)he fact that the function performed by PAAR personnel
resembles in some respects the function performed by a psychotherapist
does not of itself persuade us that PAAR personnel's communications with a
person seeking PAAR assistance should be absolutely privileged." . . . This
similarity in function, when adequately scrutinized, coupled with many
other considerations not addressed by the majority (discussed infra), are not
only persuasive reasons, but, I am convinced, compelling reasons for judicial
creation of an absolute rape victim–crisis counselor testimonial privilege.

While there have been a variety of historical justifications for many of the
privileges in the third class, it is generally conceded today that the sole
justification for such privileges is that the social utility of the particular
relationship is so great that it outweighs society's interest in having all
possible evidence disclosed in the litigation, Comment, *The Social Worker-
Client Relationship and Privileged Communications*, 1965 Wash. U.L.Q.
362, 365 (hereinafter Social Worker–Client Privilege), and that the relationship depends for its existence upon strict confidentiality between the parties. 8 J. Wigmore, Evidence 2291 at 549-53 (McNaughton rev. 1961)
(hereinafter Wigmore).

At present, there is one, and only one, justification — that the relationship
is rendered ineffective either because a person is deterred from entering
into it or because the person is frightened into nondisclosure during its
course, and, that the effect of such an absence of the privilege is undesirable
in light of the importance of the relationship to society. *Fisher, supra* at 611.

Thus, the two principal questions are whether the relationship is necessary to society and, if so, whether confidentiality is necessary to that relationship. Social Worker–Client Privilege, supra at 365.

These considerations have been succinctly set forth by Dean Wigmore in the form of four fundamental conditions:

1. The communication must originate in confidence that it will not be disclosed.
2. The element of confidentiality must be essential to the full and satisfactory maintenance of the relationship between the parties.
3. The relationship must be one which, in the opinion of the community, ought to be sedulously fostered.
4. The injury that would inure to the relationship by the disclosure of the communication must be greater than the benefit thereby gained for the correct disposal of litigation. Wigmore, supra at 2285.

These four conditions have found wide acceptance as prerequisites to creating a testimonial privilege of the third category. See, e.g., Social Worker–Client Privilege, supra at 365 and cases cited at 365, n. 19; Fisher, supra at 611; Comment, Under-privileged Communications: Extensions of the Psychotherapist–Patient Privilege to Patients of Psychiatric Social Workers, 61 Cal. L. Rev. 1050, 1056–57 and cases cited at 1057, n.36 (1973) (hereinafter Underprivileged Communications). . . .

As was previously noted, the four fundamental conditions of Dean Wigmore provide a convenient and widely accepted framework to analyze the necessity for a privilege. I shall apply each condition to the rape victim–rape crisis counselor relationship. The first is:

(1) The communication must originate in confidence that it will not be disclosed.

The privileges recognized in the third category (i.e., those designed to encourage full disclosure of confidential communications made between parties to a relationship viewed as extremely important to society in which full disclosure is essential to maximize the benefits of the relationship) all involve relationships in which one party confides information to the other with the understanding and expectation that the information will be kept confidential. Thus, the client confides fully in his attorney, secure in the knowledge that the information he discloses will be kept confidential; so too the penitent confides in his priest; so too the patient confides in his psychotherapist.

It is undisputed that communications between a rape victim and her rape crisis counselor are imparted in the utmost expectation of strict confidence. It is undisputed that in this case the victim was expressly advised that her

communications to the PAAR counselor were made with the expectation that
those communications would not be disclosed without her consent. PAAR is
"billed" in brochures and leaflets as providing "confidential treatment—the
victim has the exclusive right to decide who should be told." Moreover,
PAAR requires each staff person to sign a confidentiality statement which
provides that the PAAR member

> agree(s) to treat as confidential their identity of and all information
> about every person who comes to or telephones PAAR for service, as
> well as all . . . records. I am aware that this identity and information is
> confidential. I further agree to exercise great care in protecting PAAR's
> records from any scrutiny by unauthorized persons. Brief for Appellant,
> Exhibit C.

Perhaps the strongest proof that the communications originated in confidence is the fact that Ann Pride, the appellant herein and the administrator
of PAAR, was prepared to face jail rather than violate the mutual trust of the
relationship by breaching the assurances of confidentiality which PAAR gave
the victim.

The second, and most important, condition of Wigmore's test is:

> (2) The element of confidentiality must be essential to the full and
> satisfactory maintenance of the relationship between the parties.

As the majority noted, "the function performed by PAAR personnel resembles in some respects the function performed by a psychotherapist." . . .
This function is partially explained in the majority opinion:

> (PAAR) volunteers are extensively trained in rape-crisis counseling.
> They listen, offer support to those who call regardless of when crime
> occurred, and aid in providing the needed physical, psychological and
> social help. . . . Attention is placed on the condition of the victim, both
> physically and psychologically. Also, the counselor inquires of the treat-
> ment the victim has received from various individuals and agencies that
> she or he has encountered in dealing with her/his crisis legally or
> medically. The information is used to ascertain the victim's medical and
> psychological needs and to monitor the various institutional systems
> that the victim may encounter. In most cases, if not all, the forms are
> filled in after talking with the client to avoid the atmosphere of direct
> questioning. (quoting from PAAR's brief)

As I agree that the functions performed by rape crisis center counselors are
similar to those performed by psychotherapists (a similarity I will elaborate
on *infra*), the case law and scholarly authority dealing with the psychotherapeutic relationship are instructive.

Mr. Justice Louis Manderino described the nature of the psychotherapeutic process in *In re B*, . . . wherein he stated:

The nature of the psychotherapeutic process is such that disclosure to the
therapist of the patient's most intimate emotions, fears, and fantasies is
required. As pointed out in appellant's brief,

People usually enter psychotherapy because they have deepseated conflicts and impairment of functioning which limit their ability to work effectively and to enjoy fully satisfying relationships with other people. To alleviate these blocks and conflicts, the therapist asks the patient to abandon "rational thought" and to express thoughts and fears that may never have been revealed to anyone else. Indeed, these innermost thoughts are often so painful, embarrassing or shameful that the patient may never before have allowed himself to acknowledge them.

The patient in psychotherapy knows that such revelations will be expected if the process is to be beneficial. In laying bare one's entire self, however, the patient rightfully expects that such revelations will remain a matter of confidentiality exclusively between patient and therapist.

Confidentiality is not only expected in the psychotherapeutic relationship, it is *absolutely indispensable!* In recognizing the psychotherapeutic privilege, District Judge Wm. Matthew Byrne, Jr. speaking for the District Court of Hawaii, made the following observations:

This right to choose confidentiality is particularly crucial in the context of communications between patient and psychotherapist. . . . The possibility that the psychotherapist could be compelled to reveal those communications to anyone . . . can deter persons from seeking needed treatment and destroy treatment in progress. . . . Many courts and commentators have concluded that, because of the uniquely personal nature of mental and emotional therapy, accurate diagnosis and effective treatment require a patient's total willingness to reveal the most intimate personal matters, a willingness that can exist only under conditions of the strictest confidentiality. See Statement of the American Psychiatric Ass'n before the Subcommittee on Government Information and Individual Rights, April 9, 1979 (further citations omitted).

Mr. Justice Clark, of the California Supreme Court, has identified three interests that are promoted by the assurance of confidentiality in the patient–psychotherapist relationship:

"First, without assurances of confidentiality, those requiring treatment will be deterred from seeking assistance." . . .

Second, the guarantee of confidentiality is critical in eliciting the patient's total willingness to reveal all of his/her innermost fears, feelings and anxieties and his/her most treasured secrets—in other words, it is essential to achieve the maximum benefit from the therapy . . .

Third, "even if the patient fully discloses his thoughts, assurance that the confidential relationship will not be breached is necessary to maintain his trust in his psychiatrist—the very means by which treatment is effected. "The essence of much psychotherapy is the contribution of trust in the external world and ultimately in the self, modeled upon the trusting relationship established during therapy." (Dawidoff, *The Malpractice of Psychiatrists*, 1966 Duke L.J. 696, 704). . . .

In short, "(t)reatment of the mentally ill is too important, and the assurance of confidentiality too central to it, to risk jeopardizing the whole because of the relevance of some patient's statements to some legal proceedings." Goldstein and Katz, Psychiatrist–Patient Privilege: The GAP Proposal and the Connecticut Statute, 118 American Journal of Psychiatry 733, 735 (1962). Virtually every school of psychotherapy recognizes confidentiality as the *sine qua non* of effective therapy.

Given that confidentiality is absolutely essential to the psychotherapeutic relationship, it still must be demonstrated that it is equally essential to the rape victim–crisis counselor relationship. Robert Fisher has observed the "revolution" in the 20th Century in the behavioral sciences—this revolution has spawned a variety of new "professions" designed to promote mental health and treat mental distress . . . The approach he favors is to discard the shop-worn tendency of the legal system to identify relationships calling for privileged confidential communications (e.g., psychologist–patient, physician–patient) and to instead adjust our legal reasoning to facilitate new "professions" generated by the behavioral sciences revolution, which are the functional equivalent of recognized psychotherapeutic professions . . . It is the therapeutic *function* that the psychotherapeutic privilege is designed to protect—*not* a particular group of individuals; therefore, there is "little justification for extending privileged status to these (already recognized as privileged) groups but not to psychiatric social workers, when the job specifications of the latter also include administering therapy to psychologically disturbed people." Underprivileged Communications, supra at 1059.

Thus, Fisher would include, within the umbrella of the psychotherapeutic privilege, marriage counselors, school guidance counselors, and social case workers to the extent each is performing a psychotherapeutic function, which relies for its effectiveness upon the assurance of confidentiality . . . He defines this function as:

> that relationship which exists between two persons (or more, where marriage counseling or group therapy is involved) where one (or more) is seeking help in the solution of a mental problem caused by psychological and/or environmental pressures from another whose training and status are such as to warrant other persons confiding in him for the purpose of such help . . .

This functional approach was implicit in our decision in *In re B*.

Examining the nature of the relationship between rape victim and crisis counselor, it is apparent that relationship is the functional equivalent of the psychotherapeutic relationship and that the need for confidentiality is critical to that relationship. First, the information revealed to the counselor by the rape victim, often deeply embarrassed, guilt-ridden and stigmatized by society, is of an extremely sensitive nature. Such communications are likely to be among the most personal imaginable—the woman is traumatized not only by the violence of the assault but by the offensive intrusion into her human sexuality, compounded by the unique social reaction to the victim as influenced by the cultural myths of rape. These revelations are certainly of a much more personal nature than a client's discussions of business matters with his/her attorney or even of a patient's discussions of physical conditions with his/her physician.

Second, there have been many affidavits submitted in this case—from victims, from crisis counselors, from law enforcement officials and from members of the medical profession. All of them stress the critical importance of confidentiality to the rape victim/rape crisis counselor relationship . . .

A final factor necessitates the finding that communications made to rape crisis counselors should remain confidential. For a great number of women, especially the poor and much of the middle class, a rape crisis counselor is their only available psychotherapeutic assistance. If a woman of means is sexually assaulted, she may seek the effective but costly counsel of a psychiatrist or a psychologist, secure in the knowledge that all communications made to that psychotherapist will be held in the strictest confidence and will receive the full protection of the law. Those women who are less financially situated, however, do not have that alternative available to them and must, consequently, seek help where they can find it. The most accessible psychotherapeutic help for these women is the rape crisis counselor who in fact provides equivalent services. Withholding the privilege of confidentiality from the rape victim–rape crisis counselor relationship works an invidious discrimination against those unable to afford a psychologist or psychiatrist and will deprive these victims of their equal protection under the law. Underprivileged Communications, supra at 1059.

I find it indisputable that confidentiality is essential to therapy victim–rape crisis counselor relationship—both to encourage victims to seek treatment, which they might otherwise avoid and to facilitate realization of the maximum therapeutic benefit from that relationship.

Wigmore's third criterion assesses the importance of the relationship to society, to-wit:

(3) The relationship must be one which, in the opinion of the community ought to be sedulously fostered.

Indeed rape crisis centers are vital to the community and have been industriously encouraged. As the majority notes:

There is an undoubtable public interest in helping victims of rape to cope with inevitable disruption of emotional stability caused by the physical assaults they suffer. There is an equally compelling public interest in encouraging victims of violent crime to come forward. We would be closing our eyes to reality were we to discount the value of rape crisis centers in fostering these vital public interests.

The growth of the rape crisis centers has been rapid (there are currently twenty-seven such centers in Pennsylvania). In the Allegheny County area, an Interagency Task Force on Rape-Related Services has been created—the number and variety of participating organizations bespeaks the community concern. Membership includes the Allegheny County Coroner's Office; the Allegheny County Crime Lab; the Allegheny County Medical Society; the Allegheny County Police; the Center for Victims of Violent Crime; the Chiefs of Police of Allegheny County; the Criminal Division, Court of Common Pleas; the District Attorney's Office; Health Systems Agency of Southwestern Pennsylvania; the Hospital Council of Western Pennsylvania; Pittsburgh Action Against Rape; the Pittsburgh Police; People Concerned for the Unborn Child; and, the Urban League of Pittsburgh.

The number and variety of the various community organizations and individuals who have submitted amicus briefs, affidavits and letters to this Court also indicate the importance of rape crisis centers to the community. Such support includes law enforcement agencies and personnel, health organizations, members of the medical profession (nurses and doctors) and women's organizations such as various YWCAs. Media treatment too has been extremely supportive. . . .

Wigmore's final condition balances the competing victim-defendant interests:

> (4) The injury that would inure to the relationship by the disclosure of the communication must be greater than the benefit thereby gained for the correct disposal of litigation.

Every privilege carries with it an attendant loss of information available to the truth-seeking process. However, with each privilege, it has been determined that the concomitant benefit to the confidential relationship overrides the loss to the litigation.

Undoubtedly the interests of the defendant are great—the law must and does zealously insure that he receive a fair trial. The majority opinion has adequately enumerated those interests. I will therefore highlight the remaining factors in favor of nondisclosure. (Several others have already been advanced in the prior sections.)

First and foremost is the victim's right of privacy. Inherent in the expectations of confidentiality between a psychotherapist and his/her patient, or between a rape victim and her crisis counselor, is the constitutionally protected right of privacy. We concluded, in *In re B*, "in Pennsylvania, an individual's interest in preventing the disclosure of information revealed in the context of a psychotherapist-patient relationship . . . is constitutionally based." . . .

"A breach of this right of privacy occurs when the information is transmitted to another, whether or not that person (the recipient) promises not to further transmit the information to others. It is knowledge of private and personal matters by another that is offensive—not that the knowledge may or may not continue on a course of travel to yet another eager ear." . . . This breach is no less severe because an inspection of the confidential communication has been made *in camera*. Under the procedure required by the majority, the confidential disclosures would be made available to the trial court, and at that moment, the confidence is broken, the trust in the relationship is shattered. And, the more sensitive the nature of the communication, the greater the need for protection.

Moreover, even if the victim consents to letting the trial court view the crisis center records, what assurance does she have that it won't go beyond? If the court should determine that no information is available to the defense counsel, counsel will surely appeal the adverse ruling. As the inspection is *in camera* and without the participation of counsel, such an appeal would be almost automatic as counsel would have no other means of verifying the validity of the trial court's secret ruling. This appeal would necessitate transmittal of the records to the appellate court. Thus at least three more judges (a three judge panel of Superior Court) and their staff will have access to the confidential communications and will be required to review them. Further appeal is also quite possible and could result in review by seven members of this Court and their respective staffs, which includes secretaries and law clerks. . . .

For all of the foregoing, I am convinced that an absolute privilege should exist for confidential communications made in the rape victim–rape crisis counselor relationship. I would, therefore, reverse the trial court's order and remand for proceedings consistent with this opinion.

Since my position is, alas, only a dissent, I appeal to our legislature to take cognizance of the rape victim's plight and to act promptly and compassionately in legislatively enacting a rape victim–rape crisis counselor testimonial privilege.

PENNSYLVANIA LEGISLATIVE JOURNAL
OCTOBER 14, 1981

Statement Submitted for the Record

Mr. Alden submitted the following statement for the Legislative Journal:

Mr. Speaker, I rise today in support of SB 532. The original SB 532 is actually HB 1160 which we amended in committee. The bill provides absolute privilege for a rape crisis counselor regarding any information acquired in the course of counseling a rape victim. It provides that all communications between a rape counselor and the rape victim shall be confidential. . . .

In January, in a 5-to-1 decision, the [Pennsylvania] State Supreme Court ruled that conversations between a counselor and a rape victim are not confidential, that the rapist's defense counsel may use portions of a victim's statement to a counselor to attack her credibility in a trial.

There are several compelling reasons to reverse the court's ruling and to provide complete confidentiality for rape victims and counselors. One is to protect the victim from the devastating effects of a rape. As Supreme Court Justice Larsen eloquently pointed out in his dissenting opinion to the court's majority decision, a rape or other sexual assault triggers intense personal and unsettling reactions in the victim, including bodily violation, shock, fear, disgust, anger, guilt and shame. Recognition of these reactions, known as the rape-trauma syndrome, and the professional attention only recently provided to rape victims may be severely limited unless confidentiality is guaranteed. There must be a full and satisfactory relationship between victim and counselor, a relationship that should be fostered by community opinion. No such relationship is possible when the threat of a breach of privacy exists.

This bill would also preclude the discrimination against sexual assault victims that may occur as a result of the court's decision. Women who can afford private psychiatric help may do so with no fear of disclosure. Those not so well off who must seek help from rape crisis centers are not afforded the protection of confidentiality. That is a double and an unfair standard.

Third is the detrimental effect the court's decision has already had on rape crisis and counseling centers. . . . In developments immediately following the court decision . . . several rape victims have asked for all of their records back. Several have stopped all counseling sessions, not because they had completed treatment or did not desire to continue, but because of the fear that their private, personal conversations with their counselors would be revealed in open court. Anonymous calls to counseling centers have risen dramatically.

In short, the court decision has severely undermined the effectiveness of rape counseling centers. . . . I believe we have an overwhelming public interest in helping rape victims cope with their trauma. We also should encourage sexual assault victims to come forward to prosecute their assailants. To do so, we must protect their rights, including the right of confidentiality with these trained counselors. To do less would be to plunge the rape victim into the Dark Ages, from where she has only recently begun to emerge. . . .

As the above makes clear, Pennsylvania created the privilege for sexual assault counselors, some of whom may be social workers, but did not create it for social workers, per se. Thus, Pennsylvania social workers still cannot invoke this protection.

ASSERTING THE PRIVILEGE

A confidential communication privilege can be thought of as something that is "owned" or "held" by the party asserting that certain information be kept out of court. In social worker–client relationships, the client, as the "holder" of the privilege, makes the assertion. As Woody (1984) notes ". . . the recipient of services has the privilege, and it can be either waived [more on this in the next section] or invoked. . . . There may be "two types of holders" of a privilege, which is intended to encourage accurate communication of potentially self-damaging information. The primary holder is the one whose immediate interests are harmed if disclosure occurs. (S)he is the communicator. It is (s)he whom the laws seek to encourage. His/her assertion or express waiver of the privilege should thus always prevail over anyone else's wishes, including those of a secondary holder. A secondary holder is one who is allowed to assert the privilege in certain instances where the primary holder is unable to assert the privilege for himself. Stated differently, the human services professional is not at liberty to invoke the privileged communication—that must be done by the client."

The conception of a "holder" of a privilege implies a one-to-one relationship between client and worker. The privilege can remain intact, provided the communications remain with these two. But once the communications go beyond them, the privilege ceases to exist. (This is one of several exceptions to the privilege that will be examined in the next section of this chapter.)

What about clients whose treatment is based on group therapy or counseling? Can they expect the worker to keep their confidences? Are they prohibited from invoking the privilege because of their group participation? Generally, these clients cannot expect the group members to keep the discussions confidential. Consequently, a group member could be subpoenaed to testify about the communications made in his/her presence. (Indeed, it is likely that even the professional would be required to divulge communications between himself/herself and a group member because, under the circumstances, the court would find that there was no expectation that client–professional communications remain confidential.)

A January, 1984 Minnesota Superior Court opinion speaks directly to these situations. In *Minnesota v. Andring*, 10 FLR 1206 (1984), the court considered the difference between one-on-one and group therapy sessions in relation to the medical privilege. Specifically, the defendant, while out on bond for alleged sexual abuse of his stepdaughter and niece, entered a treatment program that involved participation in group therapy sessions. During the sessions, he discussed his sexual conduct. The state learned about the disclosures and tried to obtain the records of the session. Andring argued that the disclosures, even those made in a group setting, were protected by the Federal Comprehensive Alcohol Abuse and Alcoholism Prevention, Treatment, and Rehabilitation Act Amendments of 1974 and the regulations issued thereunder. The Act and regulations provide for confidentiality of records regarding patient identity, diagnosis, prognosis or treatment. The regulations also purport to preempt any state law, such as Minnesota's Maltreatment of Minors Reporting Act, which authorizes or compels any disclosures prohibited by the federal law. The court was thus asked to rule on the question: Do the federal alcohol treatment act and regulations preempt the state child abuse act? It concluded that this result could not have been the intent of Congress, and held that the federal act and regulations do not preempt state law. The holding was a narrow one, however, and allowed only a limited abrogation of the medical privilege. The court stated the following:

> What then does the state child abuse reporting act require? Does it totally abrogate the medical privilege, as the state argued to the trial court, or does it only permit evidentiary use of the objective information, which the act requires to be reported, as defendant contended?
>
> A minor maltreatment report, in order to be sufficient under the act, must "identify the child, the parent, guardian, or other person responsible for his care, the nature and extent of the child's injuries and the name and address of the reporter. . . ." The statute also provides that, despite a physician–patient or husband–wife privilege, "[n]o evidence regarding the child's injuries shall be excluded in any proceeding arising out of the alleged neglect or physical or sexual abuse." Minn. Stat. Sec. 626.556, Subdivision 8. Certainly, subdivision 8 was meant to allow evidentiary use of the information reported to authorities under the mandate of the reporting act. We do not, however, construe the reporting act so broadly as to require that defendant's record from the crisis unit [where he was being treated at the time of the disputed disclosures], which includes confidential statements made to professionals in one-on-one sessions and within group therapy sessions, be handed over, in its entirety, to prosecution authorities.
>
> The legislature may well have decided that the need to discover incidents of child abuse and neglect outweighs the policies behind the

medical privilege. Once abuse is discovered, however, the statute should not be construed, nor can the legislature have intended it to be construed, to permit total elimination of this important privilege. . . . We hold that the medical privilege is abrogated only to the extent that it would permit evidentiary use of the information required to be contained in the maltreatment report—the identity of the child, the identity of the parent, guardian, or other person responsible for the child's care, the nature and extent of the child's injuries, and the name and address of the reporter. . . .

We then reach the question certified to this court pursuant to Minn. R. Crim. P. 29.02, Subdivision 4 as to whether confidential group therapy sessions, which are an integral and necessary part of a patient's diagnosis and treatment, are to be included within the scope of the medical privilege. The troublesome aspect of this question lies in the fact that the third parties, other patients and participants in the therapy, are present at the time the information is disclosed. Does this presence destroy the privilege?. . . . [W]e conclude that the medical privilege must be construed to encompass statements made in group psychotherapy. The participants in group psychotherapy sessions are not casual third persons who are strangers to the psychiatrist/psychologist/nurse–patient relationship. Rather, every participant has such a relationship with the attending professional, and in the group setting, the participants actually become part of the diagnostic and therapeutic process for co-participants. . . .

An interpretation, which excluded group therapy from the scope of the psychotherapist–patient, would seriously limit the effectiveness of group psychotherapy as a therapeutic device. . . . Because the confidentiality of communications made during group therapy is essential in maintaining its effectiveness as a therapeutic tool, we answer the certified question in the affirmative. We hold that the scope of the physician–patient medical privilege extends to include confidential group psychotherapy sessions where such sessions are an integral and necessary part of a patient's diagnosis and treatment. We reverse the order of the trial court allowing disclosure of defendant's statements made during group therapy.

EXCEPTIONS TO THE PRIVILEGE

The court determines whether the requirements for privilege communications have been met. If not, the parties must testify. In a few instances, however, even a valid privilege may be set aside. These instances are rare but they do arise, and the court determines whether public policy considerations warrant such action.

Wilson (1979) provides below a comprehensive list of exceptions to the worker–client communications privilege. The following summary, paraphrased from her text *Confidentiality in Social Work,* is not exhaustive, but it addresses relevant social work issues. Research into your state law will reveal how these operate and whether there are additional ones.

The client waives privilege. The client is the "holder" of the privilege, so he/she can waive it, and the court will generally make the worker comply.
Client introduces privileged material into litigation. If the client offers the privileged information, he/she effectively waives any claim that such information be treated as privileged.
The social worker is called to testify in a criminal case. This situation would arise where a statute requires a professional to testify if the issue involves a criminal offense.
A client sues his/her counselor.
A client threatens a criminal act. This exception approximates the conditions in the celebrated *Tarasoff* opinion, which will be examined in the next section.
A patient threatens suicide. This exception raises many of the same concerns as the above, and is equally difficult to predict.
A client threatens to harm his therapist. Again, this exposes many of the same concerns expressed above.
Physicians must report certain medical conditions and treatments. For example, the reporting of venereal diseases.
Child abuse or neglect is suspected. The reporting requirements in many abuse or neglect statutes mandate the reporting of suspected violations, and provide penalties for failure to report.
A treating professional needs to collect fees for services rendered.
Information is shared in the presence of a third party. Where the third party is *not* a member of the group, as described above in *Minnesota v. Andring.*
Emergency action is needed to save a client's life. This raises issues similar to the suicidal–client exception.
Legal action is needed for protection of a minor.
A pre-sentence investigation report is prepared.
The treating professional is employed in an agency/institution. Typically, professionals in an agency setting will share information to expedite service delivery. Not all of them, however, can invoke the confidential communications privilege, and this can pose problems.

THE DUTY TO WARN: THE LEGACY OF TARASOFF

Perhaps the most celebrated exception to the privilege communication rule is the "duty to warn" when the client threatens a criminal act or to harm a third party. Under these circumstances, the safety of others supersedes confidentiality requirements. A 1976 case, *Tara-*

soff v. Regents of the University of California, 17 Cal.3d 425 (1976), is the hallmark case on the topic. In *Tarasoff*, the court held that the welfare of the community overrides worker–client confidentiality. A worker who acts otherwise is likely to be found liable for any injury caused by his/her failure to warn a third party.

In *Tarasoff*, the plaintiffs alleged that the defendants had a duty to warn them that Mr. Prosenjit Poddar had confided to them his intention to kill their daughter, Tatiana Tarasoff. No warning was provided by the defendants. Subsequently, Mr. Poddar realized his intentions and killed Ms. Tarasoff. The plaintiffs argued that they should have been warned of the danger so they could alert their daughter. The court agreed with the plaintiffs and concluded that they had a valid cause of action. In so concluding, it noted that:

> When a therapist determines, or pursuant to the standards of his profession should determine, that his patient presents a serious danger of violence to another, he incurs an obligation to use reasonable care to protect the intended victim against such danger. The discharge of this duty may require the therapist to take one or more of various steps, depending upon the nature of the case. Thus, it may call for him to warn the intended victim or others likely to appraise the victim of the danger, to notify the police, or to take whatever other steps are reasonably necessary under the circumstances.

This type of determination turns on the worker's ability to predict dangerousness. Yet, under *Tarasoff*, the worker must reach some conclusion on the matter or risk liability. The problem persists because, as Woody (1984) notes

> . . . this body of law is still evolving and should not be considered fixed. At this time the court's message seems clear: The safety and welfare of others must be protected, even if it is at the expense of the confidentiality. . . . Without doubt, the prediction of dangerousness is unsure. . . . [But] public policy maintains that the benefits of being deemed a professional entail a concommitant duty to predict. Failure to accomplish this charge is to leave one's professional functioning vulnerable to legal attack. [p. 392]

Recent discussions on the subject indicate that the law is anything but settled (Weil and Sanchez, 1983; Bernstein, 1984; Applebaum, 1985).

Post-*Tarasoff* developments are even more complicated. For example, *Hedlund v. Superior Court of Orange County*, (669 P.2d 41 (1984)), a California Superior Court *extended* the therapist's liability for patient violence originally announced in *Tarasoff*. Needless to say, the *Hedlund* ruling portends concern among helping professionals (George, 1985; Winslade & Ross, 1985). In *Hedlund,* Ms. LaNita Wilson, in seeking to establish a legal cause of action for professional malpractice, charged that the defendants had a duty to warn her about Mr. Stephen Wilson's intention to seriously harm her. She further argued that the defendants owed her and *other foreseeable victims* a duty to diagnose Stephen's condition and warn her. Having failed to so diagnose and warn, Stephen Wilson used a shotgun to seriously injure LaNita. The court agreed with LaNita and found in her favor. It also agreed with her argument that the defendants should be liable to foreseeable victims; in this instance her son, Darryl, who was seated next to her at the time of the shooting. LaNita threw herself over the boy and saved his life, but she was seriously injured in the process. Darryl also sued the defendants, charging that they should have known that Stephen's threats, if carried out, would be potentially harmful to anyone in proximity to LaNita. The court also agreed with Darryl and stated that he too had a valid cause of action against the defendants. In reaching its conclusion, the court relied on an earlier precedent and stated:

> Darryl was both foreseeable and identifiable as a person who might be injured if Stephen assaulted LaNita. The conclusion that a young child injured during a violent assault on his mother may state a cause of action under *Tarasoff* as a foreseeable and identifiable victim is compelled by [our earlier ruling in] *Dillon v. Legg* (1969) 68 Cal.2d 728, 69 Cal. Rptr. 72, 441 P.2d 947. In *Dillon,* a mother alleged that she was present when the defendant, driving negligently, ran over and killed her young child, and that she suffered emotional trauma [similar to that which Darryl suffered due to witnessing his father shoot his mother] and physical injury as a result. . . . In determining in such a case whether defendant should reasonably foresee the injury to plaintiff, or whether defendant owes a duty of due care, the courts will take into account such factors as the following: (1) Whether plaintiff was located near the scene of the accident as contrasted with one who was a distance away from it. (2) Whether the shock resulted from a direct emotional impact upon plaintiff from the sensory and contemporaneous observance of the accident, as contrasted with learning of the accident from others after its occurrence. (3) Whether plaintiff and the victim were closely related, as contrasted with an absence of any relationship or the presence of only a distant relationship. . . . It is equally foreseeable when a therapist negligently fails to warn a mother of a patient's threat of injury to her, and she is injured as a proximate result, that her young child will not be far distant and may be injured or, upon witnessing the accident, suffer emotional trauma. Nor is it unreasonable to recognize the existence of a duty to persons in close relationship to the

object of a patient's threat, for the therapist must consider the existence of such persons both in evaluating the seriousness of the danger posed by the patient and in determining the appropriate steps to be taken to protect the named victim. . . . The possibility of injury to Darryl if Stephen carried out his threat to harm LaNita was no less foreseeable than the harm to the mother in *Dillon v. Legg.* . . . We conclude, therefore, that in alleging his age and relationship to LaNita, and defendants' negligent failure to diagnose and/or warn LaNita of the danger posed by Stephen, Darryl has stated a cause of action.

Making Sense of the
Social Work and
Law Connection

11 Addressing Socio-Legal Problems: A Unifying Perspective for Social Workers

Many practical challenges confront professionals who deal with problems where social work and law overlap. The challenges can be seen on several levels. First, legislation remains a conspicuous legal structure for social welfare funding (Reamer, 1983). Second, practitioners encounter client problems that are becoming increasingly "legalized" (Cavanaugh & Sarat, 1980). Third, social service clients possess (even if they are unaware) an array of legal rights (Hannah et al., 1981). Finally, increasingly, professional conduct is being measured against legal requirements (Woody, 1984; Besharov, 1983). Collectively, these developments portend significant consequences for professionals working at the law–social services juncture.

The literature on this subject includes diverse viewpoints, including the benefits of interprofessional collaboration (Hoffman, 1983; Needleman, 1983; Weil, 1982; Constantino, 1981), the settings that require legal skills (Craige, 1982; Schroeder, 1982), the prerequisites for implementing legal mandates (Sosin, 1979; Moss, 1984), the prospects of teaching law and legal skills to social workers (Miller, 1980; Katkin, 1974), the inquiry into who should administer the social services (Gelman, 1981), the "due process" requirement as a constraint on social work practice (Stone, 1978), the social work advocacy ethic and its skill requirements (Albert, 1983; Epstein, 1981; Kutchins, 1980), the phenomenon of legal discretion and its implications for practitioner decision-making (Gaskins, 1981), the principle of confidentiality and its relation to practice (Wilson, 1979), the legal consequences for irresponsible professional conduct (Woody, 1984), and the issues that arise with particular target groups or in particular settings (Besharov, 1983; Hardin, 1983; Roberts, 1983; Gelman, 1982).

These contributions are descriptive and helpful as such, but the practitioner needs more. Although they describe certain interdisciplinary issues, they stop short of explicating a way to structure problem-solving. The omission is a serious one, because the law's role in relation to social policy and service delivery is likely to expand to encompass virtually every aspect of social work practice. Given the potential for growth in this area, then, the question arises: How can the social work professional address multi-dimensional problems? A unifying perspective, such as the one proposed in this chapter, would provide a mechanism that would bring into focus the interaction between the two fields and thereby enhance the professional's approach to these interdisciplinary problems. The perspective's practical worthiness, therefore, lies in its ability to inform professional conduct and to promote an awareness of disciplinary interdependence.

CONCEPTUALIZING SOCIO-LEGAL PROBLEMS IN SOCIAL WORK PRACTICE

Law fulfills many roles in society, and each shapes the scope of social problems that emerge ultimately in social work (Kutchins, 1980). "Conflict between relatives, friends, and neighbors," according to Cavanaugh and Sarat (1980),

> belongs to the province of family or community. As both lose their ability to impose order and develop normative consensus, disputes that once would never have been expressed in terms of legal breaches of legal duty are increasingly cast in precisely those terms. . . . Regulation by public processes, especially litigation, replaces regulation by parents, teachers, and clergy and the order provided by shared norms. [pp. 413–414]

Social workers figure prominently in this interchange between law and social processes. Their role is based on longstanding concerns about the conditions under which legal intervention into an individual's private affairs is appropriate. Consequently, they assume a mediating role (Schwartz, 1974) in an array of knotty issues, such as: judicial control of disputes as volatile as child abuse (Hardin, 1983;

Besharov, 1983), spouse abuse (Constantino, 1981), involuntary commitment (Reisner, 1985), and divorce (Bernard, et al., 1984; Saposnek, 1984; Markowitz & Engram, 1984); institutional reform litigation (Moss, 1984); juvenile and criminal justice settings (Roberts, 1983); and agency regulations and public participation in the regulatory process (Albert, 1983).

The concrete problems that unfold within this law and society context, as a practical matter, can be defined operationally as *socio-legal*. The definition is both practical and consistent with similar conceptualizations in the literature (Schroeder, 1982; Bradway, 1929). It also places social work in relation to law in a way that exposes the legal context within which social work problems unfold. More important, it underlines that the interdisciplinary dimensions of these types of problems are sufficiently entangled to require the professional to structure their problem-solving approach accordingly.

The operational definition is also connected to a very straightforward perception of client concerns in a socio-legal setting: clients bring problems to social workers and do not articulate the various dimensions of their troubles; By seeking assistance they expect to place themselves in a better position than they were in prior to social work intervention. Practitioners can meet this expectation, but only if they appreciate the complicated (i.e. interdisciplinary) nature of the problems they encounter.

A PERSPECTIVE FOR ADDRESSING
SOCIO-LEGAL PROBLEMS

The perspective is built around issues that surface when the professional encounters problems where social work and law interact. Though gleaned from the literature, these issues are supported by the author's survey of law-trained social workers and by discussions with professionals who routinely deal with socio-legal problems. Collectively, they suggest the conditions under which socio-legal problems are resolved and, implicitly, underscore the requisite knowledge and skills for effective problem solving.

In constructing the perspective, the author borrowed from a method suggested by Mullen (1978), and drew heavily on literature that specifically dealt with socio-legal issues in social work practice. Some may seem obvious, but the literature suggests they are all interrelated and important. Further, neither the literature nor the survey respondents indicated that any one is more important than another. Perhaps future research will not only validate their individual importance, *per se*, but also indicate their relative weight in the problem-solving process.

As the discussion below will show, then, the perspective is built around a recognition that socio-legal problems are addressed most effectively when the social work professional appreciates:

1. that there are legal boundaries for service delivery and for social worker–client relations;
2. that a problem may provide a legal basis for intervention and/or may suggest a strategy for law reform;
3. that interprofessional collaboration can be productive, if occasionally frustrating; and
4. that certain legal concepts and skills are essential supplements to an intervention strategy.

The Existence of Legal Boundaries

The legal context for social work practice takes several forms: the legislative structure for social welfare funding; the boundaries that simultaneously protect the client's legal rights and control official discretion; and the sanctions for professional misconduct.

First, we note that legislation articulates social policy choices, identifies rights and obligations, and allocates funding for program implementation. Under these circumstances, legislation specifies the limits of available program funds, provides the framework for services to be delivered, and outlines substantive rights, the broad purposes and goals of the legislation, and its intended beneficiaries.

For example, in the child welfare field, there is the legal context for balancing the tripartite interests of the parent, the state, and the child. The Child Abuse Prevention and Treatment and Adoption Act of 1978 and the Adoption Assistance and Child Welfare Act of 1980 are two illustrative federal statutes. There are numerous state counterparts. The context thus provided exposes a difficult practical dilemma: to respect parental rights while also communicating that these rights can be forfeited upon proof of abuse or neglect *AND*, in the process, to provide statutorily-mandated social services.

Second, the legal context helps protect a client's legal rights by imposing a structure, which typically includes regulations that stem from a specific piece of legislation, designed to guard against an administrative agency official's abuse of "discretionary power". Regulations are "promulgated" (issued) pursuant to their enabling legislation. They must be consistent with the legislation from which they stem and their implementation must follow from the legislation's intent. These regulations are, in effect, the context for the routine decision-making of those most frequently in contact with clients. [For a discussion of this regulatory process and the social worker's role in it, see Albert (1983)]. Administrative agency officials must make their decisions within the context of the regulations that govern the programs they administer. They have the authority to exercise their discretion in the interpretation of regulations in relation to enabling legislation. Although they do not enjoy total control (their decisions may not be "arbitrary" or "capricious") they generally have considerable leeway to determine how a particular regulation will be interpreted, given a particular set of facts. These safeguards are the result of the law's increasing reliance on administrative agencies (and the officials who control them) to implement the goals embodied in social legislation (Freedman, 1981; Handler, 1984; 1979).

Hoshino's (1974) discussion of the pursuit of administrative justice in the welfare state illustrates this structure.

> The social service state He observes, is characterized by mass bureaucratized professionalized administrative agencies. Because of their statutory authority, functional roles, command of highly specialized knowledge and skills, ability to ration or secure access to needed or desired services, and capacity to apply sanctions in overt and subtle ways, professionals in service delivery systems have enormous discretion, and therefore, power over the ordinary individual. Under these circumstances, how does the individual cope with large bureaucracies, especially if he is poor, or a minority group, or is socially, or legally vulnerable? [63–64]

Thus, he concludes, administrative agency officials still exercise considerable discretion despite the existence of these limits on their exercise of authority.

Drawing again on the child welfare field for an example, we note that the law may allow state intervention to remove a child from unfit parents, but the decision must also withstand constitutional scrutiny. In this instance, the Due Process clause of the Fourteenth Amendment demands that the state present certain proof before severing parental rights in the child. The concept of "due process of law" stems from a view of the relationship between the state and the individual, and articulates the conditions under which the state may deprive an individual of life, liberty, or property. It represents the notion that individuals have a constitutionally guaranteed right to fair treatment by government. The concept is made operational through the imposition of certain procedural requirements on the state; i.e., steps it must take before it can interfere in an individual's private affairs or deprive him/her of freedom or property. These procedural steps, perhaps best thought of as *requirements* for the state; *safeguards* for the individual, include: (1) timely notice; (2) opportunity for examining witnesses; (5) open or public proceeding; (6) impartial decision-maker; (7) decision based on the record; and (8) timely hearing. As a practical matter, social work professionals must recognize that their recommendations will also be evaluated against this standard, despite their clear convictions about parental incompetence. The United States Supreme Court articulated this standard in *Santosky v. Kramer*, 455 U.S. 745 (1982), when it announced that "before a state may sever completely and irrevocably the rights of parents in their natural child, due process requires that the state support its allegations by at least clear and convincing evidence."

Finally, Wilson's (1978) discussion of legal boundaries stresses the existence of sanctions awaiting professionals whose conduct exceeds legal limits. "The topic of confidentiality," she observes, "is becoming a primary area of concern for many of the helping professions. The consumer's increasing sensitivity to confidentiality and his desire to assert and protect basic privacy rights are giving rise to complex legal and ethical problems that were not imagined only a few years ago. [p. x]" A corollary concern is the confidential communications privilege. Essentially, the concept that certain communications are privileged against disclosure by a witness in a trial is a rule of evidence, based on the notion that, for public policy reasons, certain confidential relationships between parties give rise to communications, which the law will not compel one of the parties to divulge. Although not all states currently provide for such privileges, professional licensure of social workers may increase the likelihood that this protection will be extended to the officially licensed practitioner. When this occurs, no professional will be able to escape knowing the legal prerequisites for protecting client communications. The California Supreme Court, in *Regents of the University of California v. Tarasoff*, 17 Cal. 3d 425

(1976), underscored this point. In *Tarasoff*, a therapist was informed by his client that he intended to harm a third party. The therapist failed to warn this third party, who was subsequently killed by the client. The court, in holding that the welfare of the community overrides any claim of confidentiality between the therapist and patient, stated:

> when a therapist determines, or pursuant to the standards of his profession should determine, that his patient presents a serious danger of violence to another, he incurs an obligation to use reasonable care to protect the intended victim against such danger. The discharge of this duty may require the therapist to take one or more of various steps, depending on the nature of the case. Thus, it may call for him to warn the intended victim or others likely to appraise the victim of the danger, to notify the police, or to take whatever other steps are reasonably necessary under the circumstances.[1]

The exercise of discretion by child welfare workers provides another concrete example. The exercise of discretion carries with it the responsibility to decide correctly, and experience has shown that this is not the case always. Besharov (1983) states that social workers are often accused of exercising poor judgment in adequately protecting a child, in violating parental rights, in inappropriate foster care services, and in inadequate follow-up of children in foster care placements. But this is not to suggest that social workers are at fault at all times. The law is sometimes worded ambiguously, and they do their best under unclear legal mandates and overwhelming practical conditions. Legal ambiguities aside, however, the social worker must make certain judgments for which (s)he will be held accountable.

Addressing The Problem's Socio-Legal Scope

The interchange between law, social policy, and social problems, given the law's multiple social functions, exemplifies the debate over legal competency and effectiveness (Kidder, 1983; Jenkins, 1980; Nonet & Selznick, 1978). Social workers enter the fray by instigating an examination of the law's responsiveness to client needs and social issues.

---

[1]For an interesting discussion of the topic and its relation to social workers, see "New Privilege for Communications Made to a Rape Crisis Counselor." 55 *Temple Law Quarterly* 1124 (1982).

As a practical matter, however, identifying the problem's legal aspects is compounded because problem identification varies with the social caseworker, the clinical social worker, the agency administrator, the social planner, and the community organizer. This does not mean that each allows their particular methodological approach to limit their professional world view—at least it should not because they are all connected by a shared knowledge base, by professional values and ethics, and by the profession's stated commitment to social justice. The most recent definition of the purpose of social work emphasizes these common attributes. Nevertheless, professional training and experiences directly influence the practitioner's selection of intervention options, which, in turn, can shape their recognition of and response to any interdisciplinary aspects of client problems (Schwartz, 1974).

Lukton (1978), for example, discusses an apparently straightforward social work problem whose scope was broadened to recognize and take advantage of its underlying legal issues. Faculty at Adelphi University School of Social work collaborated with Nassau County Legal Services in a suit brought against a landlord on behalf of a group of families who charged that their rented premises were substandard. They argued that these dwellings violated the "implied warranty of habitability" and, consequently, had a negative impact on their emotional, mental, and familial conditions. The implied warranty of habitability helps ensure that the landlord will provide premises that contain all services essential to maintaining the tenant's health and safety. The warranty applies from the beginning of a residential lease and continues for its duration. For example, the Pennsylvania Supreme Court noted:

> In order to constitute a breach of the warranty, the defect must be of a nature or kind which will prevent the use of the dwelling for its intended purposes to provide premises fit for habitation by its dwellers. At a minimum, this means the premises must be safe and sanitary—of course, there is no obligation on the part of the landlord to supply a perfect or aesthetically pleasing dwelling. (*Pugh v. Holmes*, 486 Pa. 272, 289 (1979))

The plaintiffs hoped to establish a legal precedent that would clarify available tenant remedies when the landlord failed to fulfill obligations under the implied warranty. The Adelphi faculty gathered data to use as evidence and for their role as expert witness. They hoped their data would substantiate the tenant's claims of psychological harm caused by the substandard housing. For Lukton, the experience ". . . offered a unique opportunity to develop methods for intervening at a crucial point of articulation between the individual and the milieu." [p. 524]

The challenge, then, is to delve underneath the problem—to scratch beneath the surface—to expose its legal dimensions. As suggested above, the task may be difficult; but the worker who backs away from this challenge does so at the client's expense.

Interprofessional Cooperation and Conflict

There are numerous opportunities for friction between social workers and lawyers. The basis for these confrontations has remained essentially unchanged since Bradway's (1929) observations on the topic. Although conflict will continue, it is not unreasonable to expect the differences to yield to rational discussion. Indeed, the array of socio-legal settings suggests that a growing number of social work problems are cast in interdisciplinary terms. Given these types of settings, interprofessional collaboration will need to be the norm. Legal Services is a prominent example. Craige (1982) asserts,

> The legal difficulties of the poor are frequently symptomatic of longstanding economic, social, and personal problems. . . . Legal services attorneys share the [social work profession's historical] goal of enhancing the lives of poor people through . . . direct services . . . and through the modification of socio-legal forces in society. [p. 308]

The events depicted by Lukton (1978), Schottland (1968), and Stein and Golick (1974), for example, illustrate the potentially fruitful opportunities for social worker–lawyer alliances. Constantino's (1981) description of lawyer–social worker collaboration in dealing with battered women provides another example of the benefits to be gained from interprofessional partnerships. Bernstein (1980) describes the rich possibilities for interdisciplinary teams in child custody and divorce. Barton and Byrne (1975) assert that social worker–lawyer tensions could be reduced if they better understood each other's roles, values, purposes, methods, and the contributions each could make to support mutual interests. And Weil's (1982) study points to positive experiences between social workers and lawyers in the areas of child dependency and adoption.

Using Legal Concepts and Skills to Supplement Social Work

Socio-legal problems require an intervention scheme that integrates both social work and legal skills. Dickson's (1976) survey of legal skills, though not the final word on the subject, is a useful starting point. "Along with a general knowledge of law, legal systems, and procedures," he suggests, "the legal skills social workers need are investigation, interviewing, legal research, legal writing, and preparation of case materials, informal and formal advocacy, and an understanding of discretionary decision making."

Dickson also states that the reciprocity between social work and law requires an appreciation of some of the more abstract concepts of legal theory. He suggests that social workers must be aware of

> the extent to which cases and statutes control or influence rules, procedures, and behavior; the relationships among legal organizations and their impact on how laws are enforced; and locating and understanding decisions that affect careers of individuals who enter, go through, and leave legal systems. [pp. 170–177]

Jankovic and Green's (1981) research into child welfare worker training concluded that social work education is not fully responsive to a clearly identified need for specialized knowledge and skill in law. Their model for incorporating legal concepts into the curriculum would address:

> confidentiality, client consent to social work intervention, understanding legal rights of parents and children, evaluation and documentation of evidence in a case record, using legal authority for one's position as a base for practice, giving substantive, factual testimony in a court hearing, and legal duties implicit in professional practice. [p. 28]

Finally, Sosin (1979) stresses the value of mastering legal skills where social workers advocate for the implementation of legal mandates. He cites legislative analysis, and by implication, the understanding of legislative and administrative processes upon which such an analysis is based, as one of the legal skills needed to reconcile service delivery with legislative purposes and goals. The ability to decipher and interpret statutes, for example, can increase the advocate's ability to challenge attempts to ignore, evade, or subvert legislative purposes. He states that "social work expertise in substantive areas such as child welfare, mental health, or public welfare can be combined with skills in legislative process in order to help bring about needed social reform." [p. 265]

CONCLUSION

Essentially, the above perspective is an attempt to at once expose some of the unique interdisciplinary dimensions of socio-legal problems and elucidate a way of thinking about how these dimensions surface for the practitioner. We discussed several conditions that the literature and experience have identified as central to the resolution to these types of problems, but the reader is cautioned that these conditions are not offered as an absolute formula for problem solving. Rather, the intention is to express that they constitute a foundation for structuring the professional's approach to a particular type of practice situation; namely, where social work and law converge. And these instances, as this article has argued, are best addressed when the social worker is aware that certain influential questions arise concerning the existence of legal boundaries, the legal basis for intervention, the role and impact of social worker–lawyer partnerships, and the requisite legal knowledge and skills to support intervention. These questions are not exhaustive, and others will be presented in the course of practice. The important point is that they are threshhold concerns; ones that are sufficiently fundamental to initiate a search for an effective interdisciplinary resolution.

In the light of the law's expansive role in social policy formulation then, social work professionals will be pressed to respond to an increasing number of situations that contain both legal and service delivery aspects. The above perspective is offered to prod practitioners to think about these types of problems. The conditions described, therefore, are perhaps best viewed as introductory, and the reader is urged to evaluate their validity through application in practice.

12 Social Worker–Lawyer Partnerships

The rich possibilities of social worker–lawyer partnerships, though long extolled, are realized only to the extent that both groups recognize their interdependent roles. Both practice and the literature depict successful social worker–lawyer collaboration in a variety of settings. This chapter will examine the phenomenon from five perspectives: (1) the historical antecedents, with particular attention to the conditions that warranted interdisciplinary alliances; (2) some current models for social worker–lawyer unions; (3) research and issues on interdisciplinary collaboration; (4) divergent views on social change; and (5) conditions that augur increased future mergers.

HISTORICAL ANTECEDENTS

The progressive-era reforms initiated in response to the nascent industrial revolution offered the first opportunities for social worker–lawyer dialogue. Each profession appreciated the ensuing inhumanity, and each looked to the law to address industrialization's consequences (Davis, 1975). Both exhibited some degree of sympathy for social victims, although the discrepancy between the caring and the callous within the legal community was more pronounced (Auerbach, 1976). There were, however, still sufficient reform-minded attorneys to constitute (along with their colleagues in the embryonic social work profession) an effective movement for social change.

Progressive reformers sought to arrest the destructive forces that followed industrialization's wake. They challenged institutional in-

adequacy in areas, such as juvenile delinquency, worker safety, unemployment, and child labor. The feat was accomplished through
"protective legislation": enactments that specify broad remedial
schemes for the purpose of eradicating similarly far-reaching social
evils. Their overall achievements were impressive, and they forced
significant inroads into an array of early 20th century public problems
(Zimring, 1983).

These early reformers resorted to the legislature (versus the court)
because they considered it the best means to accomplish their aims.
Legislation's major advantage was its ability to produce a solution applicable to a wide range of people. The remedy would go beyond
the two disputing parties that bring their case to a judge; instead, it
would embrace, so to speak, a group of people, all of whom are affected by the "evil" the legislation is designed to exorcise. The legislative route also was relatively quicker, and did not require the time
investment demanded by the deliberative, case-by-case judicial process. The strategy implies a lot about the comparative competency of
legal institutions, of their ability to best solve a particular public
issue. Essentially, one is not inherently better than another, however, this is not really the issue. Rather, the main point is that the
forum selection (court versus legislature) reflects expectations about
what it can do best, as perceived by those who would use it to
advance their view of social justice.

They also preferred legislation to judicial action because they saw
the court as a mechanism for the enemies of reform, to be used by the
unscrupulous to thwart social progress. They thus used the court only
if they felt compelled to "fight fire with fire", so to speak. Although
this attitude would change later, especially against the background of
the 1960s, the prevailing wisdom trusted the "benevolence of the
state [i.e., legislation] against the procedures of lawyers" (Rothman,
1982).

This reform plan was informed by the collection of large amounts of
so-called social data, which was then used to make a "social diagnosis". Social ills, then, were to be cured by dosages of progressive
legislation. "The settlement house experience," according to Rothman, "provided the occasion for collecting an abundance of data. . . .
[I]n all, [they] assembled an array of information about the depths of
social problems affecting American society that make legislative intervention compelling" (Rothman, 1982).

Social workers, happily, were very visible during this reformist period. The most prominent assumed diverse roles and achieved noteworthy results. As one observer notes:

> More than anyone else, Florence Kelly devised the new technology of social reform. . . . [Her] National Consumers League battled against child labor, and against night work and excessive hours for women. The League's investigations turned facts to stir public conscience. Then the League's lawyers drafted bills, and the League's lobbyists sought to push them through legislatures. The League thus initiated the fight for minimum-wage laws and worked out a model statute, soon enacted in thirteen states and D.C. (Schlesinger, 1957, p. 24)

It soon became evident, however, that legislation could not be the sole reform strategy. The early social reformers remained skeptical about courts, yet also realized that legislation could be challenged, and these attacks had to be confronted head-on.

For example, when Florence Kelly's protective legislation for women workers was challenged [the case was *Muller v. State of Oregon*, 208 U.S. 412 (1908)], she enlisted Louis D. Brandeis to argue its constitutionality before the U.S. Supreme Court. Brandeis, a prominent Progressive and distinguished attorney, shared Kelly's belief that the law could be responsive to social needs. His advocacy before the nation's highest court was enormously successful, and ultimately signaled the legality of similar state statutes. Indeed, in his personal reform initiatives, he attempted to bridge the gap between social needs and legal rules, suggesting that the latter had to bend to accommodate the former. This was a relatively singular vision of social justice and legal responsiveness—one that found expression ultimately in the famous "Brandeis brief", an innovation in legal appellate advocacy and the first of several social-data based research tomes he compiled with the very able assistance of Josephine Goldmark of the National Consumers League—submitted in the *Muller* case. The brief, which essentially argued that the facts as well as the law were relevant to any determination of community welfare, and both comprised the social environment within which legal rules were shaped, embodied his belief in what he termed the "living law" (Urofsky, 1981).

But, overall, legislation did predominate, and the initiatives begun during the early part of the 20th century also formed the basis for similar efforts that culminated in the New Deal. The period's reformist ethos thus begun grew steadily and paved the way for subsequent attempts to influence public policy in the 1930s when "through Belle Moskavitz the social work ethos infected Alfred E. Smith; through Frances Perkins and others, Robert F. Wagner; through Eleanor Roosevelt, active in the Women's Trade Union and a friend of Florence Kelly's. . . ., Franklin D. Roosevelt" (Schlesinger, 1957, p. 25).

The New Deal prompted different responses from the social workers and lawyers. The social work community welcomed its emphasis on a governmental role in assisting the poor. The legal sector's reaction, however, was mixed. More traditional factions eschewed Roosevelt's program because it threatened their view of the legal order and of the administration of justice. Reform-minded elements, on the other hand, embraced New Deal goals and turned their energies to the poor, particularly to trying to meet this group's legal needs (Auerbach, 1976).

Both professions, however, recognized the emergence of an enlarged governmental role, which seemed to expand steadily through the '40s and culminated in the political economy of the New Frontier and the Great Society. This latter period coincided with the requisite social climate needed to inaugurate the Office of Economic Opportunity's legal services program (Auerbach, 1977). Its structure departed from the traditional scheme for legal services delivery, according to Carlin, in several significant ways.

> [By] the importance placed upon the establishment of neighborhood law offices to increase the accessibility of legal services to the poor; (1) the requirement that the poor be represented on the governing body of the legal services agency; (2) the adoption of a more aggressive stance in promoting the collective as well as individual interests of the poor; and (3) concern for insuring the independence of the legal services organization from those vested interests that might be threatened by more vigorous representation of the poor. (Carlin et al., 1966)

The existence of legal services thus provided myriad opportunities for social workers and lawyers to join together during this period to ameliorate social conditions repugnant to both fields. They collectively attacked the regulatory inconsistencies that obstructed poor people's efforts to obtain or retain welfare benefits, as well as legislative rules that institutionalized the subordinate legal status of the poor (landlord–tenant law, for example). They also mounted successful judicial challenges, using the "class action" device, on an array of problems affecting the socially disadvantaged (Morales, 1981).

In sum, the initial dialogue between social workers and lawyers emerged in response to industrialization and matured in conjunction with the government's assumption of an obligation for the poor. Interdisciplinary cooperation, based on legal challenges, which dramatically altered the relation between the poor and the state, institutionalized this obligation. Social services, consequently, have become increasingly cast in legal terms, thus blurring the distinction between legal rights and service delivery. The trend is likely to continue and will compel both disciplines to work through their mutual apprehensions about each other. They will have to recognize, as Bradway predicted over fifty years ago, that

> social workers [sh]ould look to the law and government as the form towards which much of their work is constantly drifting . . . [and] lawyers might be expected to anticipate, from social work and others, new additions to the law as soon as social and economic factors warrant. (Bradway, 1929, p. 19)

MODELS FOR INTERPROFESSIONAL COLLABORATION

As the above discussion illustrates, interprofessional collaboration has certain historical roots. How, then, and under what conditions can this partnership notion be made operational? What can it look like in practice? To begin to answer these questions, we shall examine briefly several models, which depict a range of practice situations where the interdisciplinary convergence is most prominent.

The models illustrate settings in which social workers and lawyers work together. No attempt is made to present an exhaustive list; it would not be possible, given the diversity of collaborative enterprises. Rather, the models depict instances where the two professions worked towards a goal that would enhance the quality of life for their shared concern—the client. They are distinguishable along two levels: public versus private sector, and service delivery focus (direct versus non-direct services). The dichotomy is presented to underscore the array of opportunities and to convey how they are manifested in practice.

Public Sector Direct Services

Child welfare offers one example where interprofessional collaboration is essential. State and federal statutes have thrown social workers into the fray over the conditions under which the state may intervene in private family matters to protect the child's rights. Here, the responsibility for protecting children from abuse and neglect fall to the state's law enforcement branch, usually the City Solicitor (locally) or the Attorney General (at the state level). These offices perform their functions in conjunction with the state or local social services protective services division. Legal rights thus are enforced simultaneously with the development of a treatment (case management) plan, which is developed with the expectation that it will be incorporated within the state's petition for an adjudication of neglect or dependency. All this occurs easily only if both professions recognize their shared interests (the child client), their common goal (protecting the child) and their mutually supportive role in making the legal system respond to their mutual concern.

A related example is provided by a Philadelphia program: The Child Advocacy Unit of the Defender Association. Its purpose is to provide independent legal counsel in instances where the court feels the child's and the parent's interests are incompatible. The unit not only represents the child in court but also negotiates with the systems it encounters during the time the agency has jurisdiction over the child. The staff consists of attorneys and social workers as well as psychologists, psychiatrists and pediatricians who are available as consultants. Each case is approached from an interdisciplinary perspective: the lawyer provides the legal knowledge and can argue the case in court; the social worker contributes his/her knowledge of child development, of intra-family dynamics, and of the social services system. The team discusses their assessment of the child and submits their recommendations to the court. The collaborative process allows them to become very familiar with each other's special expertise. The attorney develops an appreciation of child development theory and of the structure of social service delivery. The social worker is exposed to the statutory and regulatory context within which services are delivered, to judicial decision making and to the adversary process. Ultimately, both professions use this awareness to carry out their interdependent roles.

Another type of public-sector partnership is the model found in
Legal Services Programs. Legal services attorneys routinely deal with
socio-legal disputes generally associated with social work practice.
The major distinction is that they focus on clients' legal troubles, and
generally employ social workers to handle clients' non-legal problems. The arrangement recognizes that clients' legal problems dictate
any supportive social services they receive. The social worker thus is
the attorney's agent. For example, food stamps are obtained by social
workers as a result of the lawyer's finding that the client is entitled
to these benefits. Additionally, even where the social worker has
slightly more law-related responsibility (for example, where (s)he
represents clients before an administrative agency, such as the welfare department), (s)he acts under the attorney's guidance and supervision; no independent judgment of the case's merits is made by the
social worker.

Private Sector Direct Services

On the private side, one model for collaboration is provided by
Columbia University's Graduate School of Social Work. Their partnership with a local union involves the use of law students and
graduate social work students. The teams work independently,
although each deals with a separate aspect of the client problem. The
social work students handle the services end, while the law students
help clients articulate their legal grievances. The program's most
unique feature is the interdisciplinary seminar in which both student
groups discuss the issues that arise at the union. It is also a forum for
exploring the application of key legal concepts to different aspects of
the experience.

In Philadelphia, the work done by Women Organized Against Rape
(WOAR) in conjunction with the District Attorney's Office illustrates
another direction for collaborative ventures. The agency instigated a
close working relationship with the DAs Office to improve its response to rape victims. The partnership expanded to other areas and
ultimately resulted in the creation of a special child sexual abuse unit
in the DAs Office.

Finally, there is the model provided by the Juvenile Law Center of
Philadelphia, a nonprofit public interest law center committed to
assisting children and youth through a program of legal representation and community education. The Center focuses on children who

have problems with the major institutions of society—family, school, courts, and state—and who need legal representation. The Center's model is unique in its commitment to act as a "traditional" lawyer for each child, i.e., to listen to and really represent the child's needs. This model sharply contrasts with the more prevalent model of representation by the *guardian ad litem*.

The center's goal is to force the legal system and child welfare system to carry out their legal mandate in relation to the child. Cases in the Center are handled by an interdisciplinary team consisting of a lawyer and a social worker. Philosophy aside, the model is not without its problems. For example, it is difficult to use with young children.

Private Practice

This area promises to grow steadily. Social workers have begun to carve out a role in domestic relations, which is based on close working relationships with lawyers to resolve problems, such as child custody, divorce and child support. The most recurring format is the attorney–social worker team that works to help troubled couples mediate their dispute. The roles are clearly delineated to avoid having the social worker give legal advice. Yet, the arrangement preserves and underscores the social worker's unique strengths: helping the disputing parties work through their emotionally-charged disagreement to construct a mutually satisfactory legal settlement. This particular interdisciplinary arrangement is not without problems. For example, care must be taken to avoid the social worker's unauthorized practice of law. The potential benefits, however, make it a valuable model (Abrahams, 1982).

Public Sector Non-direct Services

Non-direct services, for our purposes, can be defined simply as social work intervention that emphasizes policy modification. The professional roles are diverse, but they all share a common orientation: social–environment change, especially through the alteration of adverse legislative goals.

Legal services, again, provide the main model. Historically, legal services, through its law reform unit, worked with advocacy groups to modify legislation in areas, such as welfare, housing, debtor–

creditor, and landlord–tenant (Handler, 1978). The practice usually required collaboration with social workers and other helping professionals, and was favorably received until the mid-1970s, when the prospects of suits brought against the government by publicly-funded lawyers chilled political conservatives. Debate on this score continues today, as indicated by the Reagan administration's dissatisfaction with such activities. But all may not be lost. Congress balked against the cutbacks and subsequently reinstated some funding, although it appears certain that the restored money will be used for direct services rather than law reform activities.

Private Sector Non-direct Services

Private agencies, especially those who assume an advocacy posture in relation to the client and his/her social environment, work with attorneys to promote social change through the courts or the legislature. For example, WOAR (see above), dissatisfied because communications between its rape crisis counselors and rape victims were not privileged from disclosure in court, joined with the Philadelphia-based Women's Law Project to argue the need for the protection. The collaboration eventually produced state legislation that created the privilege. (See Chapter 10 on privileged communications and worker–client relations for more details on related events and concepts.)

COLLABORATION RESEARCH: MAKING THE MODELS WORK

Several studies have uncovered an array of issues that threaten interdisciplinary enterprises (Weil, 1982; Sloane, 1965). They all stress that each practitioner brings to the setting certain assumptions about his/her role and certain predispositions toward the problem. But, as Weil (1982) suggests below, the situation is not hopeless.

Role Perceptions and Attitudes Toward Interprofessional Collaboration*

The University of Southern California study focused on issues of collaboration related to role perceptions, task allocation, and attitudes of social workers and lawyers about their own and the other profession. A purpo-

*From Marie Weil, Research in Issues Collaboration Between Social Workers and Lawyers. Social Service Review, 56.3 (September 1982), pp. 395–405. © 1982. The University of Chicago, Chicago, IL. Reprinted by permission.

sive sample was drawn from four subgroups: (1) social workers practicing in child dependency, (2) lawyers practicing in dependency court, (3) social workers in adoptions, and (4) lawyers practicing in adoptions court. The total sample of county counsels and panel attorneys consisted of four of twelve dependency county counsels, five of twenty dependency panel attorneys, the only adoptions county counsel, and ten of thirty-three adoptions panel attorneys responding to the survey. Lawyers in two subsamples thus had a one-third response rate, one subsample a one-quarter response rate, and one subsample consisted of only one possible respondent. A one-third response rate is typical for mailed questionnaires, but self-selection factors that influence the choice to respond or not are not known. A sample of ninety-two of 659 dependency social workers was drawn with a response of thirty-seven, a better than one-third response rate. All adoptions workers with court experience within the last year were sampled with twenty-four of thirty-eight responding, which provided close to three-quarters of the subsample as respondents. The participation of dependency social workers was determined by selecting two court dates and sampling all workers who were scheduled to appear on those days. The higher response rate among social workers may reflect greater interest or be related to the social work auspicies of the study.

The study used modified versions of the instruments developed by Brennan and Khinduka and the instrument measuring attitudes developed by Smith. In addition, two attitude measures were developed by the research team to assess perceptions of positions and attitudes about each profession. The four subgroups were compared with each other to determine similarities and differences in perceptions.

Perceptions of role function in court. Using the Brennan–Khinduka model, role functions were divided into the three major court phases: preadjudication, adjudication, and disposition. Respondents were asked to identify the person or persons who ideally should be and who actually are responsible for each of the identified functions. Responses from the Los Angeles sample indicated far more agreement regarding ideal assignment of functions than was the case in the Brennan–Khinduka study. All respondents strongly associated the responsibilities of the disposition phase to social workers. Both social workers and lawyers, again in contrast to the earlier study, indicated a desire to collaborate in court functions with the other profession. Each profession recommended transferring from social workers to lawyers some specific legal functions currently carried by social workers in the preadjudication phase. The congruence of assignment of roles and greater similarity between actual and ideal role assignments may reflect differences in organizational climate, as Smith cited, and was markedly different from the Brennan–Khinduka study.

Perceptions of own and other profession. Dependency social workers perceived their position more positively than did adoptions workers. Department of Public Social Services (DPSS) social workers perceived lawyers positively, while adoptions workers perceived lawyers negatively. Lawyers in both subgroups viewed their own position positively. Adoptions attorneys viewed their position as more "satisfying" than did dependency court attorneys. Substantial differences were noted in the attorneys' perceptions of their social work counterparts. Generally, dependency court lawyers viewed social workers more positively than did adoptions attorneys. Two-thirds of dependency lawyers viewed the social work position in their service areas as "stimulating," compared with one-third of adoptions lawyers. Less than one-third of adoptions lawyers and more than one-half of dependency lawyers viewed their social work counterparts' positions as "satisfying." Fifty percent of dependency lawyers perceived the social work position to be "creative," compared with ten percent of adoptions lawyers. The more positive self-view held by the dependency social workers may be related to greater clarity about role in court procedures than adoptions workers. The more positive view of dependency workers by dependency court lawyers may also reflect role clarity and the organizational climate in dependency court, which has supported collaborative work. The less positive view of their own role held by adoptions workers was an unexpected finding and may well relate to organizational climate and less preparation for court-related functions. In addition, the positive views dependency social workers and lawyers have of each other may be mutually reinforcing in interaction, as may be the negative views of those in adoptions. If perception of professional role affects performance, these findings merit further consideration.

Attribute ratings. Using a modified form of Smith's attitude measurement scale of paired adjectives, social workers and lawyers rated their own and the other profession on thirty-seven items grouped for analysis into clusters related to "intelligence," "effectiveness," "assertiveness," "concern for the others," and "practicality." As with Smith's results, ratings tended toward the positive end of the attitude scale. Social workers in adoption rated themselves lower than the three other groups rated themselves, while lawyers in dependency rated social workers considerably higher than the social workers rated themselves on "effectiveness." Overall, the law groups gave social workers highest ratings on "effectiveness" and lowest ratings on "concern for others." This seems to go against negative stereotypes, which attest that lawyers think social workers are "all heart and no brain." Lawyers gave the highest possible rating to themselves on assertiveness, a judgment that was not repudiated by the social workers. Social workers gave lowest ratings to lawyers on concern for others and highest ratings on effectiveness and assertiveness. Social workers gave a positive but lower range rating to themselves on effectiveness and the highest possible rating to themselves on concern for others. Obviously, some differences of opinion prevailed here.

The relatively low assessment on the concern for others cluster that social workers and lawyers assigned to each other may be related to each profession's parochial view that their own service exhibits more concern for client welfare. Stereotypical views that social workers do not concern themselves sufficiently with clients' rights may color lawyers' views, whereas a typical criticism of lawyers is that they evidence more concern with winning than for their clients' needs. Indeed, positive professional identification may have a counter-effect of lowering the appraisal of other fields. It is interesting that both social workers and lawyers questioned their own effectiveness. Inability to achieve desired goals within the complex adversary process and bureaucratic structure of the court may account for this assessment. Seeing the other's profession as more effective may reflect greater retention of feelings about cases, which were not settled in accordance with the lawyer's or social worker's judgment. Despite the variation in assessment, the prevailing views of their own and the other profession were positive for the sample.

Information on collaboration experience and training. One possible reason for the more positive views of the counterpart profession's practicing in the dependency area was the finding that 66% of the DPSS social workers reported that they had participated in a two-week special agency training program related to social work in the courts, court processes, and legal issues. Other groups reported minimal to no training, and the majority of all three of the other groups reported that their experience in collaboration came solely from experience on the job. It seems likely that the intensive training provided for the DPSS social workers aided them in clarifying roles, functions, and areas of collaboration. This may account for their more positive view of lawyers as well as the lawyers' more positive view of them, which may have resulted from the social workers' solid grounding in court processes. This finding was unexpected because such training had not been offered in the past few years. But, nonetheless, the DPSS's sample drew 66% who had had that intensive training experience. In general, the total Los Angeles sample was more positive than earlier respondents about the other profession. Yet they also expressed some problems related to lack of communication, lack of training in collaboration, and lack of clarity regarding professional identity.

Dependency court lawyers and social work counterparts demonstrated a better understanding and greater respect for each other's positions than did the adoptions group. The special training program for DPSS social workers was considered by respondents to have been very helpful in court-related work. No other group had received any specified inter-professional work role training. The need for role clarity and for collaborative planning relationships regarding shared court duties was clearly identified.

In comparison with the earlier studies cited, the Los Angeles sample showed more favorable attitudes toward collaboration. Lawyers indicated a willingness to share court functions with social workers and, in general, showed a high regard for social workers. With regard to organizational climate, it should be noted that the chief county counsel in Los Angeles dependency court has been very positively disposed to social workers and has been supportively involved with the DPSS court liaison unit that assists with cases. This relationship was not studied, but the positive results seem to indicate that some factors in the organizational climate of the Los Angeles court have eased relationships reported to be strained elsewhere. Although social workers in both adoptions and dependency had longer work experience related to the court, they felt that they were less effective in court than the less experienced lawyers. While DPSS workers saw their professional role in court as generally very positive, they also perceived it as "frustrating". . . . Blurring of roles and possible role confusion appeared to be more obvious in the area of adoption.

After examining the research data and noting the importance which dependency social workers assigned to the training they received in court functions, the research team concluded that intensive training in court functions, roles, and interprofessional collaboration should be provided to all social workers involved with the courts. Further, the research team thought that both social work and law schools should develop curriculum content related to interprofessional collaboration, with the goal of increasing knowledge and understanding of the counterpart profession's involvement in legal processes related to family problems.

DIVERGENT VIEWS ON LAW AS AN INSTRUMENT OF SOCIAL CHANGE

Perhaps the major issue that distinguishes the two disciplines is their discrete views on the use of law and legal institutions to promote social change. Their perspectives may seem comparable on the surface, but there are sufficient underlying tensions that, under the best circumstances, tend to undermine cooperation.

Each profession has a peculiar view of social justice and its role in bringing it about, and each incorporates this vision into the "baggage" that individual practitioners bring to specific situations. This is accomplished primarily by recognizing that although a practitioner may attend to his/her client's day-to-day problems, (s)he is also bound by the collateral expectation (usually implied in the Code of Ethics) that one may aspire to the profession's higher goals or principles to try to engage a drive toward the profession's ultimate aims.

For the social work profession, the principal underlying assumption is its longstanding commitment to advocacy. This ethic, generally endorsed in the Code of Ethics, encourages a certain activist stance in relation to meeting client needs. Intervention is built around the advocacy *role* (a posture, not incidentally, that exposes social workers to systems and techniques generally associated with lawyers).

The social-worker-as-advocate role emerged formally from NASWs

1968 Ad Hoc Committee on Advocacy's deliberations on the "advocate/champion" function (NASW Ad Hoc Committee, 1969). The 1960s social climate made it apparent that the profession had to reassert its historical relationship with the poor (Braeger, 1968). The Committee cast the social worker/advocate as one who "sees as his primary responsibility the tough-minded and partisan representation of . . . [client] interests, and this supersedes his fealty to others" (Brager, 1968).

The concern with advocacy persists today [Sosin & Caulum (1983)]. The ethic, however imprecisely articulated, influences the profession's views on the uses to which the law can be put to advance its vision of social justice (Kutchins, 1980). Social work practitioners thus frequently make the leap from normative assertions that the law *should* do something in relation to their client to absolute conclusions about the legal system's capacity to respond. Unfortunately, the leap is more often one of faith, because it fails to consider each legal institution's capacity to respond. In short, they may say that there "ought to be a law", but this ignores whence it should come or whether, ultimately, it will put their clients in a better position.

For lawyers, the major underlying assumption has two sides: concern for law reform and for effective client advocacy. This dual orientation reflects the legal profession's commitment to the highest principles for dispute resolution: to ensure the legal system promotes the expectation that justice will emerge from the application or modification of legal rules. Lawyers are not only concerned about the idea of reform; they must also inquire, necessarily, into the conditions under which it can come about. And this inquiry requires an assessment of institutional competency, an examination of which legal institution seems best prepared to cope with a particular social issue. The commitment to client advocacy is put into effect alongside the law reform ideal, and, sometimes, the two may collide. The attorney must reconcile both within the context of the Code of Professional Responsibility. Not surprisingly, this situation can produce an uncomfortable level of disagreement between the two disciplines, sufficient to short-circuit an otherwise promising partnership.

Thus, when the two professions collaborate, there is always the chance that their divergent world views will threaten the joint venture. The best route around this potentially destructive situation may lie in each discipline's willingness to appreciate the value premises each brings to their shared concerns. The task may not be easy; in fact, given each field's interpretation of its professional ethical obligations in a particular situation, one can reliably predict some level of tension. Notwithstanding, it seems just as likely that both practitioners can effectively move beyond these tensions if each recognizes that their different perspectives can nonetheless preserve, rather than obstruct, the opportunity for collaboration.

13 Continuing Socio-Legal Issues

This chapter will briefly explore five socio-legal topics: child welfare, education, developmental disabilities, criminal justice, and liability of nonprofit agencies. They are characterized as such because of the interaction between both social service and legal issues. Each examination will be limited to a review of selected legal issues that pose continuing practical problems. Reference will be made to prominent legal authorities, but there will be no attempt to present an exhaustive review of the law for each area. Such a presentation would be unproductive because the law changes, without notice and sometimes unpredictably, and the key to understanding the law in each is the reconciliation of existing principles with emerging rules. The reader is thus encouraged to apply his/her newly acquired knowledge of legal research resources and find the collateral statutory and case law in order to discover the evolving legal context for social work practice.

CHILD WELFARE: DISENTANGLING AND BALANCING THE RIGHTS OF PARENTS, CHILDREN AND THE STATE IN ABUSE AND NEGLECT CASES

Historically, the terms for parent–child relations have been dictated by parents. Parental authority, which was based on longstanding and unexamined assumptions about children and their parents, was an area in which the state rarely intruded. Parents, it was assumed, would act in their children's best interest.

Legal developments since 1963 (when child abuse reporting legislation was initially proposed), however, have changed the relationship between the child, the family, and the state. The spectre of abused and neglected children clearly demonstrated that some parents were unfit and that the state, therefore, needed to step in to protect the child. Unfortunately, the symptoms that prompted public outcry masked the more complicated problems with which the state was asked to become involved. The questions seem almost endless: Can abuse and neglect be adequately defined? Are there conditions under which relatively unorthodox parental conduct and beliefs can be mistakenly perceived as abuse or neglect? Is the state a more attractive alternative to parents, even under the worst situations? How do we know that the state can advance the best interests of the children within its custody? How do the competing interests get balanced? Will the state, unwittingly, undermine the integrity and privacy of the family? How can professionals make the best decisions about families, given the vagaries of the law? How much discretion should child welfare professionals have in applying the law?

There are, then, an array of legal issues that surface for the child welfare professional, including the issue of privacy, the balancing of individual rights versus the state's compelling interest to intervene, the right to family integrity, the parties due process rights, the constitutionality of the termination of parental rights, and the worker's opportunity for discretion in applying the law. Among these, four appear to predominate and suggest practical implications, so we will discuss them in more detail below: (1) the criteria for balancing child–parent–state interests, (2) due process rights regarding termination of parental rights (and due process as a general context for social work), (3) worker decision-making and exposure to liability, and (4) the conflict between legal requirements and service delivery. (For an overview of court procedures see Figure 13.1 below.)

Criteria for Balancing Tripartite Interests

That the law must seek to balance all parties' interests is clear; that it does it well is another matter. The law's aim, however, is unambiguous: To protect children from abuse and neglect *and* to do so without ignoring parental rights. For example, there is the Child Abuse Prevention and Treatment and Adoption Act of 1978, 42 U.S.C. Sec. 5101, and the Adoption Assistance and Child Welfare

Act of 1980, 42 U.S.C. Sec. 670. These federal statutes are mirrored in comparable state statutes. There is also federal case law, which addresses, for example, child abuse and termination of parental rights. The case law is particularly interesting because of the balance it tries to strike. The decisions reflect the law's willingness to respect parental rights to raise their children, yet they also signal that these rights can be forfeited upon a showing of abuse or neglect. The legal restraint, on the one hand, versus the opportunity for state intervention, on the other, converge to produce a very dynamic body of law.

Given the presumption of parental authority and familial autonomy, the state must have a good reason to assert parental incompetence and assume custody of the child(ren). That the state has the authority to act is one thing; that it is always correct when it acts is another. The legislative goals are sufficiently complicated to undermine a clear articulation of criteria for state intervention. Nonetheless, practitioners must act within the confines (however unclear) of the law. What criteria should guide their decision making? The easy answer is: the criteria suggested by the law. But we know that the easy cases are more the exception than the rule (not to mention that even the most careful legal analysis may not yield these "obvious" criteria). The practical complications arise in trying to strike this balance (Snyder, 1985; Urban, 1985).

Parental Due Process Rights

The law may require that all interests be balanced before allowing the state to intervene and remove the child from unfit parents, but the decision must also withstand constitutional scrutiny. The Due Process clause of the Fourteenth Amendment demands that the state present certain proof before it can sever irrevocably parental rights in the child. As a practical matter, the worker must recognize that his/her recommendations will also be evaluated against this standard, despite their clear convictions about parental incompetence.

The "right to due process" may be conceptualized as the framework for assessing the government's role in relation to the individual. The framework acts as a boundary for identifying the conditions that must be met when the state restrains or limits individual activity. Governmental non-intervention is the rule unless a sufficiently compelling reason exists for intervention. We will focus briefly on this doctrine as a context for social work.

FIGURE 13.1 Overview of court procedure

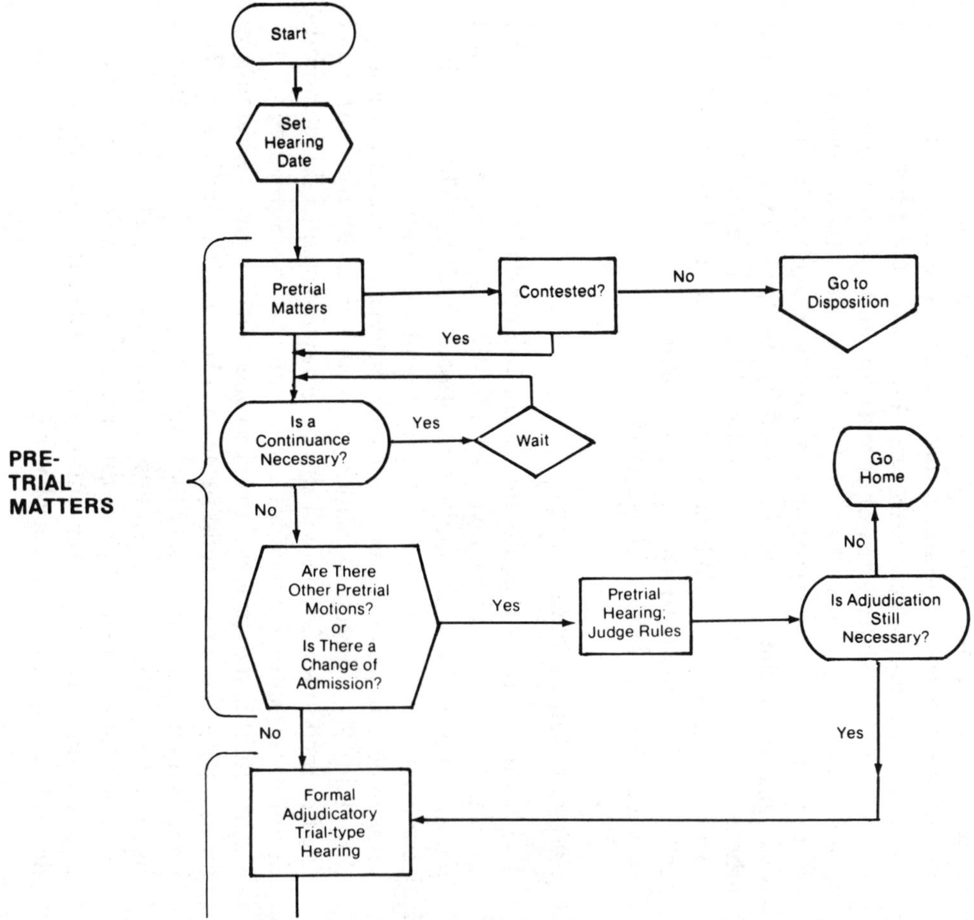

224

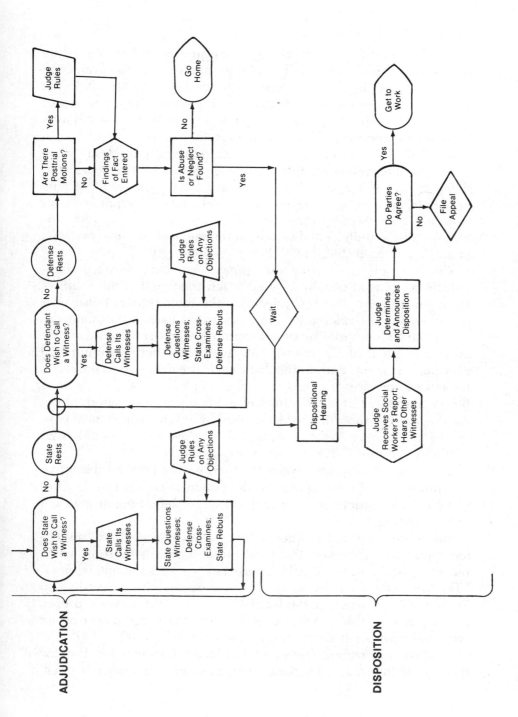

ADJUDICATION

DISPOSITION

225

Due Process Analysis

The U.S. Constitution provides for "due process of law" before an individual can be deprived of life, liberty, or property. The protection typically takes the form of procedures designed to structure the relationship between the individual and the state. The ultimate goal is to supply certain procedural safeguards to ensure that law enforcement is not arbitrary. "This has traditionally involved," according to Tribe (1978) "the elaboration of procedural safeguards designed to accord to the individual 'the right to be heard' before being condemned to suffer a grievous loss of any kind' as a result of governmental choices. . . . The extent to which one may require officials to submit to judicial or quasi-judicial review of conduct which disadvantages the individual depends on the range of personal interests qualifying as protected 'life,' 'liberty,' or 'property.' "

The principle underlying due process is straightforward: individuals are constitutionally entitled to fair treatment at the hands of their government. But the principle, like most constitutional doctrines, is not self-enforcing. Courts must evaluate government decisions and their goals to best determine whether they adversely affect an individual. This is not to suggest that every governmental decision is suspect. Rather, the doctrinal construct exists to provide a framework for assessing instances where an individual feels (s)he is the victim of governmental unfairness. As a practical matter, then, the due process concept must be applied by a court, which must pose questions, such as: What process is due? How much? Under what conditions (Bitner, 1985; Hershkowitz, 1985)?

Due process is typically conceptualized on two levels: substantive and procedural. In one sense the distinction is not critical, but because the two notions frequently dovetail, a brief statement on each will be supplied.

Substantive due process generally conveys the idea that law enforcement should be fair, that legal rules, especially those in which the state has a stake, should incorporate concerns about fairness. "The key issue for substantive due process analysis," according to Stone (1978) "is whether the legislation in question serves a proper public purpose, that is, whether it is within the police power of the state and whether it serves the public welfare." [p. 403]

In short, substantive due process is focused on whether the law seeks to accomplish a legitimate objective and, assuming it does, whether it does so in a way likely to advance the public welfare. Thus, if the law will achieve a legitimate purpose but infringes on individual rights (particularly so-called "fundamental rights"), then it is likely that a court will find the law unconstitutional for violating substantive due process. For example, the substantive due process doctrine was used, beginning in the mid-1960s, in cases dealing with the right to privacy. Topics in this category ranged from distribution of contraceptives to matrimonial relationships to abortion.

Procedural due process is concerned with the steps the state must take before it enforces a law that might deprive an individual of fundamental rights. The concept can be thought of as providing certain *protections* for the individual while imposing certain *requirements* on the state. Such procedures typically include: (1) timely notice; (2) the opportunity for presentation of evidence; (3) representation by counsel; (4) opportunity to confront and cross-examine; (5) open and public proceeding; (6) impartial decision maker; (7) decision based on a record and evidence presented; and (8) timely hearing. The net effect is to protect the individual against potentially arbitrary governmental decisions by restraining or limiting law enforcement.

Procedural due process, like its substantive counterpart, expresses the belief that an individual should be fairly treated by the government. "The essence of procedural due process," according to Stone (1978) "is to ensure that an individual not be deprived . . . without a fair appraisal of what he is likely to lose, and why, and without an opportunity to defend his interest. Thus, procedural due process calls for laws and regulations reasonably calculated to inform a person of . . . the right that is to be affected and to provide an opportunity to be heard."

The *Goldberg v. Kelly*, 397 U.S. 254 (1970), decision is a familiar example of due process protections provided for welfare recipients. At issue was whether these recipients were entitled to due process protections before the state could terminate their welfare benefits. Essentially, the court did not question the state's right to terminate benefits; instead it articulated the steps the state had to go through before it could halt them. The court reasoned that such benefits could be thought of as property, thus entitling the recipients to a hearing that incorporated the due process procedures (notice, hearing, representation by counsel, presentation of evidence, cross examination of witness, etc.).

Social work's most recent concern about the impact of due process has resulted from the extension of the due process model to decisions made by social workers in areas such as child welfare and mental health. Practitioners have increased the areas in which they make decisions but have done so, it has been alleged, at the expense of client rights.

Contemporary courts have demonstrated a willingness to circumscribe professional decisions. Indeed, the movement towards "judicializing" social service delivery underscores the court's reluctance to trust professional judgment. But, as Gaskins (1981) suggests, the judiciary is not necessarily the most competent institution in this regard. Courts are capable in some ways, but inadequate in others. Unfortunately, the past failures of professionals to safeguard client rights have forced courts to resort to the due process model as a check on professional judgment. They may be no better equipped than social work professionals, but they do have authority social workers lack.

This judicial response may seem an overreaction. But the individual rights at stake are too significant to dismiss the court as reactionary. Social workers in public welfare, in mental health, in corrections or juvenile justice, and other related settings are in a position to structure official intervention and affect client rights. Social welfare professionals can meet potential problems directly by being aware of the legal "baggage" clients bring to their encounters with the social welfare system and by monitoring their professional decision making to ensure they promote fairness.

To illustrate the application of the due process doctrine to decisions regarding parental rights in child welfare disputes, consider the following 1982 U.S. Supreme court decision, *Santosky v. Kramer*, 455 U.S. 745 (1982).

SANTOSKY v. KRAMER: COMMISSIONER, ULSTER COUNTY DEPARTMENT OF SOCIAL SERVICES
455 U.S. 745

Justice Blackmun delivered the opinion of the Court.

Under New York law, the State may terminate, over parental objection, the rights of parents in their natural child upon a finding that the child is "permanently neglected". . . . The New York Family Court Act . . . requires that only a "fair preponderance of the evidence" support the finding. Thus, in New York, the factual certainty required to extinguish the parent–child relationship is no greater than that necessary to award money damages in an ordinary civil action.

Today we hold that the Due Process Clause of the Fourteenth Amendment demands more than this. Before a State may sever irrevocably the rights of parents in their natural child, due process requires that the State support its allegations by at least clear and convincing evidence.

Petitioners John Santosky and Annie Santosky are the natural parents of Tina and John III. In November 1973, after incidents reflecting parental neglect, respondent Kramer, Commissioner of the Ulster County Department of Social Services, initiated a neglect proceeding under Fam. Ct. Act 1022 and removed Tina from her natural home. About 10 months later, he removed John III and placed him with foster parents. On the day John was taken, Annie Santosky gave birth to a third child, Jed. When Jed was only three days old, respondent transferred him to a foster home on the ground that immediate removal was necessary to avoid imminent danger to his life and health.

In October 1978, respondent petitioned the Ulster County Family Court to terminate petitioners' parental rights in the three children. Petitioners challenged the constitutionality of the "fair preponderance of the evidence" standard specified in Fam. Ct. Act 622. The Family Court Judge rejected this constitutional challenge, . . . and weighed the evidence under the statutory standard. While acknowledging that the Santoskys had maintained contact with their children, the judge found those visits "at best superficial and devoid of any real emotional content". . . . After deciding that the agency had made " 'diligent efforts' to encourage and strengthen the parental relationship," . . . he concluded that the Santoskys were incapable, even with public assistance, of planning for the future of their children. . . . The judge later held a dispositional hearing and ruled that the best interests of the three children required permanent termination of the Santoskys' custody.

[Petitioners appealed again through the appellate levels, but without success.] . . . We granted certiorari to consider petitioners' constitutional claim. . . .

The fundamental liberty interest of natural parents in the care, custody, and management of their child does not evaporate simply because they have not been model parents or have lost temporary custody of their child to the State. . . . [P]ersons faced with forced disolution of their parental rights have a more critical need for procedural protections than do those resisting state intervention into ongoing family affairs. When the State moves to destroy weakened familial bonds, it must provide the parents with fundamentally fair procedures.

. . . [T]he process due in parental rights termination proceedings turns on a balancing of the "three distinct factors" specified in *Mathews v. Eldridge:* . . . the private interests affected by the proceeding; the risk of error created by the State's chosen procedure; and the countervailing governmental interest supporting use of the challenged procedure. . . .

In parental rights termination proceedings, the private interest affected is commanding; the risk of error from using a preponderance standard is substantial; and the countervailing governmental interest favoring that standard is comparatively slight. Evaluation of the three *Eldridge* factors compels the conclusion that use of a "fair preponderance of the evidence" standard in such proceedings is inconsistent with due process.

"The extent to which procedural due process must be afforded the recipient is influenced by the extent to which he may be 'condemned to suffer grievous loss' ". . . . Whether the loss threatened by a particular type of proceeding is sufficiently grave to warrant more than average certainty on the part of the fact finder turns on both the nature of the private interest threatened and the permanency of the threatened loss. . . .

Thus, the first *Eldridge* factor (the private interest affected) weighs heavily against use of the preponderance standard at a state-initiated permanent neglect proceeding. We do not deny that the child and his foster parents are also deeply interested in the outcome of that contest. But at the fact-finding stage of the New York proceeding, the focus emphatically is not on them.

The fact-finding does not purport (and is not intended) to balance the child's interest in a normal family home against the parents' interest in raising the child. Nor does it purport to determine whether the natural parents or the foster parents would provide the better home. Rather, the fact-finding hearing pits the State directly against the parents. The State alleges that the natural parents are at fault. . . . The questions disputed and decided are what the State did—"made diligent efforts," . . . —and what the natural parents did not do—"maintain contact with or plan for the future of the child". . . . The State marshals an array of public resources to prove its case and disprove the parents' case. Victory by the State not only makes termination of parental rights possible; it entails a judicial determination that the parents are unfit to raise their own children.

At the fact finding, the State cannot presume that a child and his parents are adversaries. After the State has established parental unfitness at that initial proceeding, the court may assume at the *dispositional* stage that the interests of the child and the natural parents do diverge. . . . But until the State proves parental unfitness, the child and his parents share a vital interest in preventing erroneous termination of their natural relationship. Thus, at the fact finding, the interests of the child and his natural parents coincide to favor use of error-reducing procedures.

However substantial the foster parents' interests may be . . . they are not implicated directly in the fact-finding stage of a state-initiated permanent neglect proceeding against the natural parents. If authorized, the foster parents may pit their interests directly against those of the natural parents by initiating their own permanent neglect proceeding. . . .

Under *Mathews v. Eldridge*, we next must consider both the risk of erroneous deprivation of private interests resulting from use of a "fair preponderance" standard and the likelihood that a higher standard would reduce that risk. . . . Since the fact-finding phase of a permanent neglect proceeding is an adversary contest between the State and the natural parents, the relevant question is whether a preponderance standard fairly allocates the risk of an erroneous fact finding between these two parties. . . .

At such a proceeding, numerous factors combine to magnify the risk of erroneous fact finding. Permanent neglect proceedings employ imprecise substantive standards that leave determinations unusually open to the subjective values of the judge. . . . In appraising the nature and quality of a complex series of encounters among agency, the parents, and the child, the court possesses unusual discretion to underweigh probative facts that might favor the parent. Because parents subject to termination proceedings are often poor, uneducated, or members of minority groups . . . such proceedings are often vulnerable to judgments based on cultural or class bias.

The State's ability to assemble its case almost inevitably dwarfs the parents' ability to mount a defense. . . . Indeed, because the child is already in agency custody, the State even has the power to shape the historical events that form the basis for termination.

The disparity between the adversaries' litigation resources is matched by a striking asymmetry in their litigation options. Unlike criminal defendants, natural parents have no "double jeopardy" defense against repeated state termination efforts. If the State fails to win termination, as New York did here . . . it always can try once again to cut off the parents' rights after gathering more or better evidence. Yet even when the parents have attained the level of fitness required by the State, they have no similar means by which they can forestall future termination efforts.

Coupled with a "fair preponderance of the evidence" standard, these factors create a significant prospect of erroneous termination. A standard of proof that by its very terms demands consideration of the quantity, rather than the quality of the evidence, may misdirect the fact finder in the marginal case. . . . Given the weight of the private interests at stake, the social cost of even occasional error is sizable.

Raising the standard of proof would have both practical and symbolic consequences. . . . The court has long considered the heightened standard of proof used in criminal prosecutions to be a "prime instrument for reducing the risk of convictions resting on factual error". . . . An elevated standard of proof in a parental rights termination proceeding would alleviate "the possible risk that a fact finder might decide to [deprive] an individual based solely on a few isolated instances of unusual conduct [or] . . . idiosyncratic behavior". . . . "Increasing the burden of proof is one way to impress the fact finder with the importance of the decision and thereby perhaps to reduce the chances that inappropriate" terminations will be ordered. . . .

Two state interests are at stake in parental rights termination proceedings—a *parens patriae* interest in preserving and promoting the welfare of the child, and a fiscal and administrative interest in reducing the cost and burden of such proceedings. A standard of proof more strict that preponderance of the evidence is consistent with both interests. . . .

The logical conclusion of this balancing process is that the "fair preponderance of the evidence" standard prescribed by Fam. Ct. Act 622 violates the Due Process Clause of the Fourteenth Amendment. . . .

A majority of the States have concluded that a "clear and convincing evidence" standard of proof strikes a fair balance between the rights of the natural parents and the State's legitimate concerns. . . . We hold that such a standard adequately conveys to the fact finder the level of subjective certainty about his factual conclusions necessary to satisfy due process. We further hold that determination of the precise burden equal to or greater than that standard is a matter of state law properly left to state legislatures and state courts. . . .

We, of course, express no view on the merits of petitioners' claims. At a hearing conducted under a constitutionally proper standard, they may or may not prevail. Without deciding the outcome under any of the standards we have approved, we vacate the judgment of the Appellate Division and remand the case for further proceedings not inconsistent with this opinion.

Worker Discretion and Exposure to Liability

As the above implies, the ambitious but ambiguously stated goals of child abuse and neglect law pose practical dilemmas for child welfare professionals. On the one hand, they enjoy a certain degree of discretion in applying the law to specific cases and are expected to exercise their best judgment. On the other hand, these decisions have exposed many workers to civil liability or criminal prosecution. The exercise of discretion carries with it the responsibility to decide correctly, and experience has shown this is not always the case. This is not to suggest that social workers are always at fault. The law is frequently ambiguous and they do their best under unclear legal mandates and overwhelming practical conditions. Their exposure to liability serves more to underscore the fact that they can be victimized by trying to apply the law. For example, Besharov (1983) identifies four areas where social workers are often accused of exercising poor judgment: (1) inadequately protecting a child, (2) violating parental rights, (3) inappropriate foster care services, and (4) inadequate follow-up of children in foster care placements.

Legal ambiguities aside, however, the social worker must act. Through their agency, (s)he is assigned the task of operationalizing legislative goals (from child protection to the development of treatment plans), so it is not surprising that they stumble as they attempt to accomplish these aims. The situation is especially troublesome because the ambiguity can either prod the worker into responsible decision-making or, just as easily, lull him into inattentiveness to legal requirements. And even when the worker is responsible the worst can happen (i.e. a child can be injured or die), because, even under the best circumstances, some obstacles emerge. These include (1) the fact that the worker's decision often must be based on incomplete and misleading information, (2) limited staff time for investigation, (3) the inability to absolutely predict the "correct" decision, and (4) home situations deteriorate without warning and there is no way to predict when it will happen (Besharov, 1983).

The situation for social workers is, at best, difficult. Under the present law, they risk acting hastily (incurring the wrath of parents and exposing themselves to civil liability), or not acting quickly enough (risking possible criminal liability). The current result is at once unfair and unavoidable. As a practical matter, then, the social worker must be sufficiently knowledgeable about the law to apply it to both hard *and* easy cases. The latter are typically apparent, but the former seldom arrive waving flags. Ultimately, the worker has to make certain judgments on the law and its application, and must do so in the light of the prohibitions against child abuse and the larger legal principles that govern the entire decision-making process (Cunningham, 1984; Besharov, 1985; Hurley, 1985; Snyder, 1985; Smith & Meyer, 1984; Weisberg & Wald, 1984).

The Conflict between Legal Requirements and Service Delivery

Perhaps more than any other area, the child welfare field illustrates the tension inherent in structuring service delivery to comply with legal mandates. The legal context, as described above, has pressed workers to attend to both legal constraints and service delivery needs. The situation pulls the professional in two directions simultaneously, thus resulting in complaints (especially from child protective service workers) that the system forces them to make sense of apparently incompatible goals and expectations. The worker is placed at odds with the very structure (s)he must rely on to treat clients.

The mandated requirements in abuse and neglect provide an example. State and federal legislation typically require the worker to develop a case record (via fact finding, investigation, and interviewing) that will support an allegation of abuse and neglect. In the absence of such a record, no adequate adjudication can be made and a child is potentially put at risk. And the prerequisites for such records are unambiguous; they constitute the evidence to sustain an allegation. If the worker's responsibility was limited exclusively to such investigation and fact finding, there would be no problem. But the authority to intervene carries with it the collateral responsibility to treat, to devise a service plan to adequately meet the child's needs during the crisis. And even the most talented professional can frequently feel frustrated by the "rights" versus "treatment" conflict. The situation is further compounded by the fact that this conflict can generally take the form of social worker–lawyer disputes: each arguing for the superiority of their professional perspective.

What is the remedy? Unfortunately, the immediate future holds no promise for change. The state exhibits no reluctance to intervene to protect children, and perhaps this is a positive development. In so doing, however, the state, through the law, will continue to demand that the system simultaneously protect legal rights and foster treatment. The situation appears to have been conceived as socio-legal, and the structure has been designed accordingly. Equally true is the fact that the system offers little guidance for the worker who must reconcile these interdisciplinary tensions. (S)he will continue to struggle through this schizophrenic existence, to assume the at once weighty and ill-defined responsibility to act on behalf of the system's ultimate client—the child.

EDUCATION: "MAINSTREAMING" THE HANDICAPPED CHILD

Public Law 94-142 (The Education for All Handicapped Children Act), inaugurated the notion that all children, even the handicapped, are entitled to a free, appropriate education. Historically, parents shouldered the burden of educating their exceptional children, but this 1975 law shifted the burden back to the state.

The unambiguous intentions underlying Pub.L. 94-142 notwithstanding, several questions persist. What is an appropriate public education for the handicapped? Who should pay for this education? The questions are persistent because they revolve around costs, so it is likely they will continue to surface in future discussions about the Act. For example, there are three prominent cost–benefit issues addressed in this section, which follow from these questions: (1) "related services" (What are they?), (2) appropriate placements (What happens if none are available?), and (3) potential parent–school conflicts (How are they solved?).

"Related Services" Under the Act

Recently, two U.S. Supreme Court decisions addressed the related-services topic. The law on the subject is still in an embryonic stage— no surprise, given the Act's expansive definition of such services:

> [Related services are defined as] transportation, and such developmental, corrective, and other *supportive services (including* speech pathology and audiology, psychological services, physical and occupational therapy, recreation, and *medical* and counseling *services, except that such medical services shall be for diagnostic and evaluation purpose only) as may be required to assist a handicapped child to benefit from special education,* and includes the early identification and assessment of handicapping conditions in children [emphasis in original] (20 U.S.C. 1401 *et seq*).

Ultimately, this issue is important not only to determine whether social work services fall within the "related services" categories but also because it will have clear implications for identifying what constitutes an "appropriate education." [Griffith, 1985; Palomer, 1985; Bartlett & Wegner, 1985; Meyers & Jensen, 1984]

In *Irving Independent School District v. Tatro*, for example, the court concluded that clean intermittent catherization (CIC) services were related services under the Act. The court also provided additional practical guidance by articulating a two-step process for determining whether CIC was one of the intended services. First, is the service "required to assist a handicapped child to benefit from special education?" Second, must the service be excluded from coverage as a "medical service serving other than diagnostic and evaluation?" The court also identified some boundaries within which different services could be assessed to determine whether they are within the Act's scope:

> To keep in perspective the obligation to provide services that relate to both the health and educational needs of handicapped students, we note several limitations that should minimize the burden the petitioner fears. First, to be entitled to related services, a child must be handicapped so as to require special education. . . . In the absence of a handicap that requires special education, the need for what otherwise might qualify as a related service does not create an obligation under the Act. . . .
>
> Second, only those services necessary to aid a handicapped child to benefit from special education must be provided, regardless of how easily a school nurse or layperson could furnish them. For example, if a particular medication or treatment may appropriately be administered to a handicapped child other than during the school day, a school is not required to provide nursing services to administer it.
>
> Third, the regulations state that school nursing services must be provided only if they can be performed by a nurse or other qualified person, not if they must be performed by a physician. . . .

In a related 1984 case, *Robinson v. Independent School District No. 89 of Oklahoma*, the court continued the line of reasoning it initiated in *Tatro*. In *Robinson*, the court upheld a federal court's decision that daily occupational and physical therapy for a multiply handicapped student were covered under the Act.

State Responsibilities for Placement

What must states do, under the Act, when appropriate placements are unavailable? This question will provoke as much debate as the one above. As Gilbert (1982) notes:

> The answer to this question turns, in part, on the distinction between cases such as *Harris v. Cambell,* on the one hand, and *Howard S. v. Friendswood Independent School District,* and *North v. District of Columbia Board of Education,* on the other. In *Harris* the court dismissed an action in which the plaintiff sought an injunction to require the defendant, a school administrator, to place him in an appropriate school. The plaintiff was ordered to first exhaust administrative remedies. The court found that the defendants had acted in good faith in that the plaintiff had been placed in one appropriate school from which he had been

expelled, a second placement had been located, but there were no openings at the time, and the defendants had developed a homebound program pending the time when plaintiff could be appropriately placed.

In *Howard S.*, the defendants, who were high school administrators, had been provided with a history of plaintiff's emotional and learning problems from his earlier school years. Nonetheless, his difficulties were treated entirely as disciplinary problems without even referral to the special education director, even after plaintiff's parents complained. The school then dropped plaintiff from its rolls while he was hospitalized. Efforts to resolve the situation were met with apparent indifference. Under the circumstances, the court ordered immediate placement at the Brown Schools at the public expense.

In *North*, the defendants had taken no steps to place the plaintiff until ordered to do so by a hearing officer. After the first placement failed, the defendants did not place the plaintiff because the board of education and the Department of Human Resources disclaimed responsibility. The court ordered immediate placement in Dominion Psychiatric Treatment Center at defendant's expense.

From one point of view, the cutting edge of these cases is *the degree of good faith exhibited by the schools. However, the most important aspect of these cases is that none of the judges permitted inappropriate placement to last indefinitely* [emphasis supplied]. . . .

Resolving Parent–School Conflict

Finally, what happens when parent and school disagree? The Act's response to this question is built around a due process hearing presided over by an impartial hearing officer. The hearings are quasi-adversarial, so they allow representation by counsel, presentation of evidence, and cross-examination of witnesses, among other things. The hearings may also be open to the public. Although the Act provides for formal hearings, the parties may elect to mediate their dispute (Gallant, 1982).

Although the hearing process is in place, this topic too is largely unsettled. That the hearing must be held is clear. But related issues, such as who appoints the officer, are less clear (Lapham, 1980). Perhaps the major obstacle, however, is the "tone" of the hearing. That is, should it be adversarial (to argue about legal rights and obligations)? or should it emphasize collaborative problem-solving (both sides sharing issues and goals regarding the child)? In short, should the hearing be organized around consensus or conflict? The law, by design or unwittingly, allows for both (Zucker, 1985).

DEVELOPMENTAL DISABILITIES: ASSERTING AND PROTECTING THE RIGHTS OF THE MENTALLY DISABLED

Historically, the mentally disabled have enjoyed neither respect nor legal rights (Barton & Sanborn, 1978). The spectre of the mentally ill among society was sufficiently repugnant to encourage their abuse and neglect (Grob, 1973) or their banishment from the community. Absent familial support, the mentally disabled endured mistreatment and societal rejection. The establishment of mental hospitals promised to rescue them and provide safety and shelter. But eventually even these institutions began to display attitudes toward their charges that mirrored the general society. Consequently, these initially benign institutions are now suspect: We wonder about their competency and distrust both their motivations and their methods of treatment. Typically, the response to suspected inhumane practices has been cast in legal terms, some of which we will explore below. The implications for social work are built around a recognition of this group's emerging legal status, their right to dignity, and their continuing struggle for quality services.

Social Work and the Developmentally Disabled

Though currently aware of their role as advocates for human dignity for the mentally disabled, the profession, historically, has demonstrated little concern for this population. As Horejsi (1983) states:

> The social work profession as a whole has demonstrated little concern with the field of mental retardation and developmental disabilities, allowing itself to be represented by a relatively small number of standard-bearers. . . . An examination of the literature indicates that contributions by social workers in terms of both practice and research have been made in the following areas: (1) the provision of individual and group counseling to retarded persons, and, more recently, to their parents and siblings in an effort to treat the entire family system, (2) the provision of social evaluations as part of the interdisciplinary diagnostic process, (3) the development of alternative living arrangements, especially various types of foster homes, (4) the development of protective services and the provision of social brokerage and case advocacy services designed to assist families and retarded persons in obtaining the services they need, (5) intake, pre-release, discharge planning, and case management and movement within a service network, and (6) community organization, social planning, and administrative activities. [p. 16]

Fortunately, both social work and the general community have managed to change their perceptions. The "past 20 years have brought a dramatic turnabout in thinking, policy, and programs, and a shift from the automatic segregation of individuals identified as mentally retarded and/or developmentally disabled to a concerted effort to bring them into the mainstream of the community" (Gelman, 1982). And with this turnabout has come a heightened legal scrutiny of the treatment and needs of these populations (Savitsky & Karras, 1984).

The Changing Legal Context for Treatment of the Developmentally Disabled

The heightened legal scrutiny instigated by changing societal views of mental institutions and their charges has spurred significant legislative activity. Ranging from the Maternal and Child Health and Mental Retardation Planning Amendments of 1963 (Pub.L. 88-156), to the Developmental Disabilities Assistance and Bill of Rights Act of 1975 (Pub.L. 94-103), to the Education for All Handicapped Children Act of 1975 (Pub.L. 94-142), to the Mental Health Systems Act of 1980 (Pub.L. 96-398), these legislative initiatives underscored the target group's vulnerability and their need for quality services. They also prompted—intentionally or not—a renewed social work focus on service innovations and client advocacy for the mentally disabled.

This flurry of activity also resulted in a broadened definition of the mentally disabled, which poses several challenges for social work practitioners. As Gelman (1983a) observes:

> The definition of developmental disabilities since 1970 has expanded from mental retardation, cerebral palsy and epilepsy, to include in 1975 autism and dyslexia, and, finally, in 1978, the following: a developmental disability is a severe, chronic disability attributed to a mental and/or physical impairment, manifested before the person reaches age 22, which is likely to continue indefinitely. It also results in substantial functional limitations in three or more of the following areas of major life activity [(self care, learning, mobility, self-direction, economic sufficiency, receptive and expressive language, capacity for independent living) and] reflects the person's need for a combination of individually planned and coordinated care, treatment or other services that are of extended duration.
>
> The inclusiveness of this definition has important implications for social workers. The need for a range of available and accessible services will bring in increasing numbers those identified as having substantial handicaps. These agencies oftentimes are not accustomed to handling a great many of the developmentally disabled, but . . . agencies, however, must now be prepared.

The courts have also contributed to this legal environment, primarily through its pronouncements on the conditions for and rights to treatment in the "least restrictive manner". Through these decisions, which range from *Wyatt v. Stickney*, 325 F.Supp. 781 (M.D. Ala. (1971)), to *Pennhurst State School v. Halderman*, 451 U.S. 1 (1981), and *Youngberg v. Romeo*, 103 S.Ct. 2452 (1982), the courts have tried to articulate a standard by which the developmentally disabled could realize their right to treatment in the least restrictive settings.

Implications for Social Work Roles

Historical and legal developments have converged to thrust the social work practitioner into the debate over the "right to treatment in a least restrictive setting". Although the profession comes late to these concerns, it has become significantly intertwined with service delivery and law reform issues (Moss, 1984). Social work's contribution to this socio-legal area, as Keenan and Parker (1982) suggest, must grow along two lines: the identification of additional service delivery opportunities and increased concern with quality services and policy advocacy.

CRIMINAL JUSTICE, CORRECTIONS, AND SOCIAL WORK

The social work profession's current link with the criminal justice system, particularly corrections, marks a "re-entry" into an historically important but neglected area. Fox (1983) states that the social work role was expressed in relation to two competing professional developments. On the one hand, corrections was "an anathema to the field of social work," because of the early social worker's preoccupation with problems of the poor, families, and children. Professional social work, consequently, backed away from the corrections field. The phenomenon can be traced to the nascent profession's focus on:

1. the large caseloads
2. the doctrine of self-determination that prevented them from working in an authoritative setting
3. the definition of "authority" as a withholding of services, rather than as an authoritative person or agency, and
4. the belief that social work techniques should remain the same, regardless of the clientele and the circumstances of the host agency, which is an oversimplification in the correctional setting" (Fox, 1983, *xii*).

On the other hand, however, by the 1940s we witness some interest in the area. This development can be traced to both a repudiation of the profession's earlier assumptions about "traditional" social work and a recognition that social work could embrace this non-traditional role without forfeiting its "professionalism". This "going back and forth" between a view of correctional social work as irreconcilable with social work values and as an under-explored celebration of these values has characterized the profession's perception of practice roles with the incarcerated (Fox, 1983).

The profession's "re-entry" into the area is now expressed in several forms, including social work with delinquents, with probation and parole, and with correctional (minimum, medium, and maximum security prisons) institutions (Roberts, 1983). The renewed interest is very timely, given the strain juvenile and adult criminal justice systems are experiencing due to: "(1) the steady upward trend in the rate of most major offense categories, (2) the backlog, inconsistency, and often ineffectual processing and sentencing of convicted felons, (3) the lack of adequate professional personnel, overcrowding, and antiquated conditions at the institutional level, (4) the excessive caseloads of probation and parole agent, and (5) the lack of comprehensive diversion, restitution, and victim assistance programs". (Roberts, 1983, xix) The potential impact, in the light of increased need and professional abilities, cannot be overlooked.

There are numerous topics from which to choose, but our examination in this section will be limited to a brief discussion of the substantive rights for incarcerated adults, the pattern for juvenile procedures, and the essential differences between adult and criminal processes.

Stages in the Criminal Justice Process

The criminal justice process begins with (1) an act that violates the criminal code or (2) conduct that constitutes a delinquent act.

Both processes incorporate a very unusual tension. On one level we note the amount of discretion officials may exercise prior to prosecution. For example, once the police become aware of an adult's crime, they can (1) issue a warning or reprimand, (2) issue a summons (particularly where the offense does not require arrest), or (3) diversion (where the offender is referred out of the system for treatment) (Abadinsky, 1979). Similarly, not all cases referred to juvenile court

Table 13.1 The Adult Criminal Justice Process [a]

Event	Comment
Pre-Trial Stage	
1. Arrest.	The arrest involves taking someone into police custody. It is the initial deprivation-of-liberty step.
2. Appearance before a magistrate or judge.	This initial appearance is to inform the accused of the charges, to make a determination regarding bail, and to outline the subsequent events in the process.
3. Preliminary hearing.	The preliminary hearing determines whether there is probable cause to believe that the accused committed the crimes with which he/she is charged.
4. Indictment.	The indictment is a formal charge. It may be issued by a Grand Jury or (if there is no Grand Jury required) it can be contained in a legal document known as an "information."
5. Arraignment.	The arraignment is a pre-trial court proceeding in which the accused is formally charged with the crime. The accused also enters a plea at this point.
Trial Stage	
6. Selection of a jury.	Though not all trials are by jury, those that are involve jury selection—also known as "voir dire."
7. Opening statements of counsel.	Both counsel—for the defendant and for the government—summarize the facts they will try to prove at trial.
8. Government presents its case.	The government begins. It introduces its evidence and questions the witnesses for its side (direct examination) and the witnesses for the defendant (cross-examination).
9. Defendant presents its case.	The defendant also introduces evidence and questions witnesses on direct examination and cross-examination.
10. Counsel's arguments to jury.	
11. Charge to the jury.	The jury is given its charge, or instruction on the applicable law, by the judge.

Table 13.1 (continued)

Event		Comment
12.	Verdict of the jury.	
13.	Judgment of the court.	The court announces its judgment or final statement on the trial.

Appeal Stage

14.	Counsel appealing decision files notice of appeal.	The notice states counsel's intention to appeal the trial decision to a higher tribunal.
15.	Appellant and appellee file briefs.	The party bringing the appeal (appellant) and the party against whom it is brought (appellee) file written arguments (briefs) that specify their views about whether the trial court decided correctly.
16.	Argument by counsel.	
17.	Decision of appellate court.	The decision may be appealed to a higher court until the case reaches the state's (or the federal) highest court.

[a]The above stages are illustrative of the pattern of events that unfold in the criminal justice process. Though not all criminal litigation will follow this pattern, it expresses the key elements of the process.

result in the filing of a petition. Instead, (1) the youth may be warned, (2) the basis for the complaint may be too trivial, or (3) the child may be placed on probation. The important thing to note is that the police or the judge may, at the point of entry into the system, exercise some discretion (Atkins & Pogrebin, 1982).

In contrast, there are the relatively fixed events following prosecution. The process for both adult and juvenile offenders is built around an array of procedural safeguards designed to ensure fair treatment at the hands of the government. The tension—or perhaps more accurately, the strain—created by this going back and forth between discretion and due process permeates the entire system: from first contact, to arrest, to prosecution, to incarceration.

Establishing Substantive Rights for Incarcerated Adults

The Right to Medical Treatment. The right to treatment has several dimensions. Though expressed in several forms, they all are linked to the following United States Supreme Court decision, *Estelle v. Gamble*, 429 U.S. 97 (1976), which addresses the right to medical care.

ESTELLE v. GAMBLE
429 U.S. 97 (1976)

Mr. Justice Marshall delivered the opinion of the Court.

Respondent J. S. Gamble, an inmate of the Texas Department of Corrections, was injured on November 9, 1973, while performing a prison work assignment. On February 11, 1974, he instituted this civil rights action under 42 U.S.C. 1983, complaining of the treatment he received after the injury. Named as defendants were the petitioners, W. J. Estelle, Jr., Director of the Department of Corrections, H. H. Husbands, warden of the prison, and Dr. Ralph Gray, medical director of the Department and chief medical officer of the prison hospital. The District Court . . . dismissed the complaint for failure to state a claim upon which relief could be granted. The Court of Appeals reversed and remanded with instructions to reinstate the complaint. . . . We granted certiorari. . . .

. . . According to the complaint, Gamble was injured on November 9, 1973 when a bale of cotton fell on him while he was unloading a truck. He continued to work but after a few hours he became stiff and was granted a pass to the unit hospital. At the hospital a medical assistant, "Captain" Blunt, checked him for a hernia and sent him back to his cell. Within two hours the pain became so intense that Gamble returned to the hospital where he was given pain pills by an inmate nurse and then was examined by a doctor. The following day, Gamble saw a Dr. Astone who diagnosed the injury as a lower back strain, prescribed Zactirin (a pain reliever) and Robaxin (a muscle relaxant), and placed respondent on "cell-pass, cell-feed" status for two days, allowing him to remain in his cell at all times except for showers. On November 12, Gamble again saw Dr. Astone who continued the medication and cell-pass, cell-feed for another seven days. He also ordered that respondent be moved from an upper to a lower bunk for one week, but the prison authorities did not comply with that directive. The following week, Gamble returned to Dr. Astone. The doctor continued the muscle relaxant but prescribed a new pain reliever, Febridyne, and placed respondent on cell-pass for seven days, permitting him to remain in his cell except for meals and showers. On November 26, respondent again saw Dr. Astone, who put respondent back on the original pain reliever for five days and continued the cell-pass for another week.

On December 3, despite Gamble's statement that his back hurt as much as it had the first day, Dr. Astone took him off cell-pass, thereby certifying him to be capable of light work. At the same time, Dr. Astone prescribed Febridyne for seven days. Gamble then went to a Major Muddox and told him that he was in too much pain to work. Muddox had respondent moved to "administrative segregation." On December 5, Gamble was taken before the prison disciplinary committee, apparently because of his refusal to work. When the committee heard his complaint of back pain and high blood pressure, it directed that he be seen by another doctor.

On December 6, respondent saw petitioner Gray, who performed a urinalysis, blood test, and blood pressure measurement. Dr. Gray prescribed the drug Ser-Ap-Es for high blood pressure and more Febridyne for the back pain. The following week respondent again saw Dr. Gray, who continued the Ser-Ap-Es for an additional 30 days. The prescription was not filled for four days, however, because the staff lost it. Respondent went to the unit hospital twice more in December; both times he was seen by Captain Blunt, who prescribed Tiognolos (described as a muscle relaxant). For all of December, respondent remained in administrative segregation.

In early January, Gamble was told on two occasions that he would be sent to the "farm" if he did not return to work. He refused, nonetheless, claiming to be in too much pain. On January 7, 1974, he requested to go on sick call for his back pain and migraine headaches. After an initial refusal, he saw Captain Blunt who prescribed sodium salicylate (a pain reliever) for seven days and Ser-Ap-Es for 30 days. Respondent returned to Captain Blunt on January 17 and January 25, and received renewals of the pain reliever prescription both times. Throughout the month, respondent was kept in administrative segregation.

On January 31, Gamble was brought before the prison disciplinary committee for his refusal to work in early January. He told the committee that he could not work because of his severe back pain and his high blood pressure. Captain Blunt testified that Gamble was in "first class" medical condition. The committee, with no further medical examination or testimony, placed respondent in solitary confinement.

Four days later, on February 4, at 8 a.m., respondent asked to see a doctor for chest pains and "blank outs." It was not until 7:30 that night that a medical assistant examined him and ordered him hospitalized. The following day a Dr. Heaton performed an electrocardiogram; one day later respondent was placed on Quinidine for treatment of irregular cardiac rhythm and moved to administrative segregation. On February 7, respondent again experienced pain in his chest, left arm, and back and asked to see a doctor. The guards refused. He again asked the next day. The guards again refused. Finally, on February 9, he was allowed to see Dr. Heaton, who ordered the Quinidine continued for three more days. On February 11, he swore out his complaint.

The gravemen of respondent's 1983 complaint is that petitioners have subjected him to cruel and unusual punishment in violation of the Eighth Amendment, made applicable to the States by the Fourteenth. . . . We therefore base our evaluation of respondent's complaint on those Amendments and our decisions interpreting them.

The history of the constitutional prohibition of "cruel and unusual punishment" has been recounted at length in prior opinions of the Court and need not be repeated here. . . . It suffices to note that the primary concern of the drafters was to proscribe "torture[s]" and other "barbar[ous]" methods of punishment. . . .

Our more recent cases . . . have held that the Amendment proscribes more than physically barbarous punishments. . . . The Amendment embodies "broad and idealistic concepts of dignity, civilized standards, humanity, and decency . . .," against which we must evaluate penal measures. . . . Thus, we have held repugnant . . . punishments, which are incompatible with "the evolving standards of decency that mark the progress of a maturing society," . . . or which "involve the unnecessary and wanton infliction of pain,". . .

These elementary principles establish the government's obligation to provide medical care for those whom it is punishing by incarceration. An inmate must rely on prison authorities to treat his medical needs; if the authorities fail to do so, those needs will not be met. In the worst case, such a failure may actually produce physical "torture or a lingering death,". . . . In less serious cases, denial of medical care may result in pain and suffering, which no one suggests would serve any penological purpose. . . .

We therefore conclude that deliberate indifference to serious medical needs of prisoners constitutes the "unnecessary and wanton infliction of pain," . . . proscribed by the Eighth Amendment. This is true whether the indifference is manifested by prison doctors . . . or by prison guards in intentionally denying or delaying access to medical care or intentionally interfering with the treatment once prescribed. Regardless of how evidenced, deliberate indifference to a prisoner's serious illness or injury states a cause of action under 1983.

This conclusion does not mean, however, that every claim by a prisoner that he has not received adequate medical treatment states a violation of the Eighth Amendment. An accident, although it may produce added anguish, is not on that basis alone to be characterized as wanton infliction of unnecessary pain. . . .

Similarly, in the medical context, an inadvertant failure to provide adequate medical care cannot be said to constitute "an unnecessary and wanton infliction of pain" or to be "repugnant to the conscience of mankind." Thus, a complaint that a physician has been negligent in diagnosing or treating a medical condition does not state a valid claim of medical mistreatment under the Eighth Amendment. Medical malpractice does not become a constitutional violation merely because the victim is a prisoner. In order to state a cognizable claim, a prisoner must allege acts or omissions sufficiently harmful to evidence deliberate indifference that can offend "evolving standards of decency" in violation of the Eighth Amendment. . . .

The above opinion explicitly deals with the prisoner's right to medical care, but it also relies on a standard used in subsequent rulings on other related issues, including the right to psychiatric care, proper medical diets, prison assignment and regulations, handicapped persons, dental care, medical exams, prison emergencies, and drug dependency treatment. Collectively, the cases comprise a multi-dimensional right to treatment, as Manville (1984) describes below in detail.

Psychiatric Care*

Denial of adequate psychiatric care may violate the Eighth Amendment. Courts have condemned various aspects of psychiatric care and treatment of mentally ill prisoners, including lack of qualified staff, absence of a separate facility for psychiatric care, and the housing of the mentally ill in disciplinary segregation units. Some courts have stated that psychiatric treatment may be "limited to that which may be provided upon a reasonable cost and time basis," and one court held that a prisoner's complaint of "depression" was not a serious medical need requiring treatment.

The Supreme Court has held that under the Due Process Clause [prisoners] are entitled to notice and a hearing before being transferred to a mental hospital; the Court held that the stigma attached to psychiatric commitment and the possibility of involuntary subjection to psychiatric treatment constituted a deprivation of liberty requiring due process. . . . Similarly, if [a prisoner is] involuntarily committed to a hospital for the criminally insane because [he is] unable to stand trial, officials have a duty to inform the committing court when [the prisoner] no longer require[s] treatment. Under the Eighth Amendment or the Due Process Clause, courts have also struck down the use of various types of psychiatric treatment for disciplinary purposes and the psychiatric confinement or isolation of prisoners under degrading or excessively restrictive conditions. The use of seclusion and physical restraints even for psychiatric purposes has also been restricted by the courts.

---

*From Daniel E. Manville, Prisoner Self-Help Litigation Manual. pp. 112–116. © 1983 Oceana Publications, New York. Reprinted by permission of Oceana Publications.

Medical Diets

Several courts have held that prisons must provide medically required special diets to prisoners.

Prison Assignments and Regulations

A prisoner may not be given a work assignment inconsistent with his/her medical condition. However, no constitutional claim is stated where prison medical personnel have authorized the assignment. Prison regulations may be enjoined in particular cases if they have adverse medical consequences.

Handicapped Prisoners

The obligations of prison officials to accommodate the special problems of handicapped prisoners have not been fully explored by the courts. Prisoners may sue under the federal Rehabilitation Act of 1973, which bars programs receiving federal funds from discriminating against persons on the basis of their handicaps. Prisons may be obligated to seek appropriate treatment or placement in a more acceptable institution for severely handicapped prisoners.

Dental Care

Several courts have held that dental care must be provided to prisoners, although some have limited the services that must be provided.

Medical Examinations

Some courts have held that medical examinations on intake, at least for the purpose of identifying persons with communicable diseases, are required. However, prisons are generally not required to provide routine physical examinations.

Prison Emergencies

Routine medical services may be curtailed during emergencies such as lockdowns. However, essential medical care must be provided.

Drug Dependency Treatment

Prisons and jails are required to provide some form of treatment for drug withdrawal, but recent cases hold that they need not provide methadone maintenance even for persons who were in methadone programs outside prison. One court has held that alcoholism treatment programs are matters of rehabilitation rather than medical care and need not be provided.

The Right to Rehabilitation

The right to rehabilitation has been defined in terms of non-medical services, such as education and counseling, and as such, is distinguished from medical services, which are required under the Eighth Amendment. The courts have backed away from finding this right explicitly, so claims for it will probably be addressed on a case-by-case basis (Van den Haag, 1985; Brenner & Galanti, 1985).

Juvenile Court Procedure

The administration of juvenile courts may vary among states, but each will follow the general pattern described below.

Arrest. This initial step brings the alleged minor to court. The child is not always detained, and the police may simply issue a warning or contact the parents or otherwise divert the youth from the system. Detention (taking into custody), on the other hand, results only under certain conditions. For example, a minor may be detained: (1) if (s)he is found responsible e.g., for specific delinquent acts; for running away from a correctional facility or from some other non-correctional facility in which (s)he has been lawfully placed; (2) if determined to be ill or requires removal from an imminently dangerous situation or environment; or (3) if it is determined that (s)he lacks supervision.

Juvenile Court Intake. This procedure offers another opportunity for diversion. The purpose, at this point, is to identify matters beyond the court's jurisdiction, to eliminate cases that don't belong within the system or cases otherwise not sufficiently serious to be adjudicated, to arrange for some degree of informal supervision of the child, or to identify instances where the evidence is insufficient.

Complaint (Petition). The complaint states the charges and asks the court to adjudicate them.

Detention Hearing. This hearing must be held within a specified time after the juvenile's detention. The purpose is to discover whether there is a sufficient legal basis for detention.

Adjudication Hearing. This hearing is similar to a trial. It determines whether the minor committed the offenses with which (s)he is charged.

Dispositional Hearing. This stage deals with post-adjudication matters — What to do with the (now) adjudicated delinquent? Relying on social investigations and service plans, frequently supplied by social workers, the court determines the next steps in the minor's future. The choices include: (1) a fine, (2) probation, (3) dismissal, or (4) placement in an appropriate setting. (This decision is subject to subsequent review.)

Differential Criminal Law Responses to Juveniles versus Adults

Discrepant Assumptions. Historically, adults and juveniles have been treated differently by our criminal justice system. Though the underlying rationale for the practice was not always apparent, the conventional wisdom was that age differences dictated unique approaches and responses. Contemporary assumptions about juvenile versus adult offenders have not strayed far from these historical predispositions, as Hazard (1976) notes below.

> The departures in juvenile law from the assumptions in criminal law begin with an uncertainty about whether young persons should be held fully responsible for their conduct when they violate the criminal law. The particular underlying notions are rarely articulated: Is it meant that young people lack the capacity of adults (of what age?) to control their behavior? That they should not be burdened with the same weight of guilt as adults? That they should not be made to suffer punishment of the same severity as adults? When these questions are asked about adults, the answers at best have been contradictory or unintelligible. Such questions seem never to have been systematically raised about young offenders. In practice, they are answered by action rather than by analysis. Young offenders above a specified age are treated like adults and proceeded against in criminal court; offenders below that age are proceeded against in juvenile court, where their acts are attributed to them but categorically mitigated in some unstated way. The underlying question of responsibility remains unexplicated, either to the court or to the child.
>
> The second modification of assumptions concerns punishment. Ostensibly, the juvenile court does not punish but only "treats" or "corrects." To the extent that this displacement occurs or is believed to occur, it means that the punishments which legal process can impose are ineffective or inappropriate when applied to the young offender. This is a major difference in position. . . .
>
> The third [modification of assumptions] . . . is the way the court looks at the offenders' state of mind, their emotional and social development, their fixedness of purpose in life, and their prospects for somehow growing out of their inclination to commit crime and get caught at it. The outlook in

juvenile law tends to be more sympathetic, more optimistic, more tenta-tive, and less judgmental than in the criminal law. . . . These sentiments are shared not only by the court and its personnel but by the legislature and the general public. . . . The result is an ambivalence toward the juvenile offender that is less often displayed toward his adult counterpart.

Different Procedural Safeguards

The differences identified above are also expressed in the procedures for prosecuting the juvenile offender (Blasko, 1985; Lee 1984, 1985; Mahmey, 1985; Quaintance, 1986; Worrell, 1985). Perhaps the major contribution on this score has been *In Re Gault*, 387 U.S. 1 (1967), which significantly narrowed the differences between the adult and juvenile proceedings. *Gault* specified the rights that must be afforded at the adjudicatory stage of the juvenile proceeding. These included (1) notice of charges, (2) right to legal representation, (3) right to confrontation, and (4) protection against self-incrimination. Addi-tionally, the "beyond a reasonable doubt" standard was made appli-cable to juvenile cases, where the juvenile is in jeopardy of confine-ment for criminal violations, by *In Re Winship*, 397 U.S. 1 (1967). These differences, according to Mnookin (1978), can be traced to con-ceptions about age and competence and about the parental–child relationship. He offers the following selected variables on which differential treatment is most apparent.

Arrest.[*] Generally, the same substantive standards apply to juveniles and adults concerning the legality of an arrest. In some states, however, a youth may be arrested for delinquency, where the underlying "crime" is a misdemeanor that would not for an adult justify an arrest. Moreover, some offenses . . . may be "delinquent" for a minor, although the same action would not be criminal for an adult.

Pretrial Detention. Must the youth be released pending trial if an accused adult would be let out on bail or on personal recognizance? There is case law suggesting that adult standards need not govern the pretrial detention of a youth accused of delinquency.

Searches. If a search is illegal, the exclusionary rules that apply in adult criminal proceedings also apply in juvenile court delinquency pro-ceedings. . . . On the other hand, if a youth has acquiesced or consented to

---

*From Robert H. Mnookin, Child, Family and State: Problems and Materials on Children and the Law, pp. 812–815. Little, Brown and Co. © 1978 Little, Brown and Co., Boston. Reprinted by permission of Little, Brown and Co.

a search, presumably the "voluntariness" of that consent issue may take the youth's age into account.

The Voluntariness of Juvenile Confessions. . . . In two cases decided before *Gault*, the Supreme Court had held that the confession of a juvenile was not "voluntary," and that it therefore violated the juvenile's due process rights under the Fourteenth Amendment for it to be considered in evidence. In each case, the Court made plain that the age of the accused was a relevant factor in applying the voluntariness test. . . . Confessions to probation officers before the adjudicatory hearing can pose special problems, because the youth may know that the probation officer may be responsible for later making a recommendation concerning disposition if a youth is found to be a delinquent. *Miranda*. In *Miranda v. Arizona*, 384 U.S. 436 (1966), the Supreme Court held that a person must be informed that: (1) he had a right to remain silent; (2) that anything he said could be used against him; (3) that he had the right to consult with an attorney and to have an attorney with him during interrogation; and (4) that an attorney would be appointed for him if he could not afford one. The *Miranda* requirements have been applied to juveniles held in custody. . . . When applied to juveniles, however, special problems arise.

Parental Role. *Miranda* has been interpreted to mean if either a child or the child's parents ask for a lawyer, questioning by officials must stop. What if the youth asks for his parents? Must questioning stop? [Yes! See *People v. Burton*, 6 Cal.3d 375, 491 P.2d 793 (1971).] . . .

Miranda and the Possibility of Transfer to Adult Court. Must a child be specifically advised that a confession may be used against him in an adult criminal proceeding if the juvenile court waives jurisdiction? Compare *Mitchell v. State*, 464 S.W.2d 307 (Tenn. Crim. App. 1971) . . . with *Harling v. United States*, 295 F.2d 161 (D.C. Cir. 1961).

Waiver of a Juvenile's Rights. Should a youth be able to waive his constitutional rights? For adults, *Miranda* made clear that an accused may waive his rights so long as such "waiver is made voluntarily, knowingly, and intelligently." 384 U.S. at 444. Should the same standard apply to juveniles? [*State in Interest of S.H.*, 61 N.J. 108, 293 A.2d 181 (1972) implies it does.]

The *Gault* decision did not erase entirely the differences between adult and juvenile processes. For example, in *McKeiver v. Pennsylvania*, 403 U.S. 528 (1971), the U.S. Supreme Court held that a jury trial was not constitutionally required for delinquency proceeding. "Through *McKeiver*," according to McCarthy (1984), "it became clear that the court was not equating delinquency proceedings with criminal prosecutions. Rather, it was applying a test under the Fourteenth Amendment's due process clause which took into account the distinctive nature of the juvenile court. Not all rights observed in a

criminal court are applicable to juvenile cases. . . . While the Supreme Court has decided several other cases since *McKeiver*, the
precise context of the court's analysis is not clear. It may be that the
court is employing a due process analysis through which the integrity
of the fact-finding process can be preserved proportionately with the
extent of the deprivation of liberty. If so, many of the values represented in criminal procedures . . . which do not affect the reliability of
the fact-finding process may be inapplicable."

LIABILITY OF NONPROFIT AGENCIES

Social work is conducted primarily in public and private agencies.
(Sole practitioners are the exception to this rule.) Practice in these
settings is generally structured by agency guidelines that address all
aspects of service delivery and professional–client relations. The
authority for these guidelines vary: public agencies turn to their
enabling legislation (see Chapter 6), while private agencies are governed primarily by state laws for non-profit corporations. The focus in
this section will be on the private sector; specifically, on selected legal
principles that govern the duties and liabilities for board directors and
officers of voluntary agencies.

Nonprofit corporations, such as private social service agencies, and
colleges and schools, are created in compliance with statutory requirements. The legislation specifies the procedures by which an
entity can become incorporated as nonprofit and the duties, powers,
and obligations of such organizations. For example, the law spells out
who can be designated, how to incorporate, the general powers and
obligations of the Board of Directors, standards for their duties as
trustees, etc. Consequently, entities that obtain nonprofit status are
entitled to selected privileges, such as tax exemption and postage
reductions, and are able to sue and be sued, acquire and sell property, and perform other activities not prohibited by state law.

The Reasonably Prudent Person Standard

Nonprofit organizations, through their Board, are required to operate
and make decisions in a "reasonably prudent" manner. Directors are
expected to fulfill their responsibilities the way a reasonably prudent
person would fulfill them. The conduct required by the standard may

vary with the facts for each situation, but the standard, per se, remains constant.

This standard is important because its violation can expose the agency and the individual Board member to legal liability. It also implicitly imposes a "fiduciary" duty—a legal obligation imposed on a person (in fact or as a corporate entity) who has a responsibility to act on someone else's behalf. Fiduciary duties require the trustee to make decisions as though (s)he was actually effected, to treat the assigned interests as though they were his/her own. Pennsylvania law, for example, states that "Officers and directors shall be deemed to stand in a fiduciary relation to the corporation, and shall discharge the duties of their respective positions in good faith and with that diligence, care and skill, which ordinary prudent men would exercise under similar circumstances in their personal business" (Purdon's Penn. Stat. Ann., Title 15, 7506). For private social service agencies, these duties are realized through prudent management and supervision of agency assets. Typically, violations of fiduciary obligations stem from (1) failure to manage or supervise prudently and (2) conflicts between the Board members' personal and fiduciary interests (this situation is often referred to as "self-dealing"). Extreme examples of these violations are the easy cases (patently bad management practices or decisions, fraud, embezzlement, etc.). The problem is with the ones that are less clear, and these will turn on the facts and the court's interpretation of the law. Board members, therefore, should learn about state laws regulating such decisions and strive to stay within these legal limits.

Acting in Good Faith

Board members must not only act prudently, they must be able to show they have acted in "good faith". The two requirements naturally converge in making decisions, but each deals with a slightly different facet of Board membership. Good faith, in this context, refers to conscientious efforts to simply do what is best for the agency. It requires the Board member to exercise his/her best judgment at all times. Ironically, decisions thus rendered may actually turn out to be incorrect, but even bad judgment (mistakes, in lay terms) can survive legal scrutiny if the judgment was informed by so-called good faith efforts to advance the agency's best interests. Needless to say, the determination of good faith will be a question of fact for the court to decide (not surprisingly, "good faith" is a subjective determination), but the following suggestions, supplied by the National Center for Voluntary Action (1978), illustrate ways to demonstrate good faith:

1. Attend all board and committee meetings. If unable to attend, be able to show a valid reason for absence.
2. Have a thorough knowledge of the duties and provisions within the bylaws and charter.
3. Heed corporate affairs and keep informed of the general activities and operation of programs.
4. Ensure minimum statutory or technical requirements are met: filing annual reports, withholding employee taxes, etc.
5. Record personal conduct and register dissents in the minutes or by letter.
6. Avoid any semblance of self-dealing or enrichment. Discourage any business transactions between directors and the corporation, unless conducted entirely openly and with stringent safeguards.
7. Make no pecuniary profit except that expressly provided in compensation or reimbursement within the bylaws.

In *Stern v. Lucy Webb Hayes National Training School for Deconesses and Missionaries*, 381 F. Supp. 1003 (1974), for example, the court discussed the way these principles surface in nonprofit, charitable organizations. Although the case deals specifically with nonprofit hospitals, the judicial analysis, supplied below, sheds light on the general state of the law. (For more specific guidance, the reader is encouraged to research his/her relevant state laws.) The case concerned allegations of mismanagement, nonmanagement and self-dealing by several board members of Silbey Memorial Hospital. The plaintiffs (representing a class of patients similarly situated) alleged that the board had failed to supervise the decisions made by several board members who, by virtue of the board's historical lax approach to its duties and the certain interlocking memberships with financial institutions and savings and loan associations that handled Silbey Hospital's accounts, had come to dominate board decisions. The principal contentions are that the defendant trustees conspired to enrich themselves and certain financial institutions with which they were affiliated, and that they breached their fiduciary duties in the management of Silbey Hospital funds.

Breach of Duty. Plaintiffs' second contention is that, even if the facts do not establish a conspiracy, they do reveal serious breaches of duty on the part of the defendant trustees and the knowing acceptance of benefits from those breaches by the defendant banks and savings associations.

The Trustees

Basically, the trustees are charged with mismanagement, nonmanagement and self-dealing. The applicable law is unsettled. The charitable corporation is a relatively new legal entity which does not fit neatly into the established common law categories of corporation and trust. As the discussion below indicates, however, the modern trend is to apply corporate rather than trust principles in determining the liability of the directors of charitable corporations, because their functions are virtually indistinguishable from those of their "pure" corporate counterparts.

Mismanagement

Both trustees and corporate directors are liable for losses occasioned by their negligent mismanagement of investments. However, the degree of care required appears to differ in many jurisdictions. A trustee is uniformly held to a high standard of care and will be held liable for simple negligence, while a director must often have committed "gross negligence" or otherwise be guilty of more than mere mistakes of judgment.

This distinction may amount to little more than a recognition of the fact that corporate directors have many areas of responsibility, while the traditional trustee is often charged only with the management of the trust funds and can therefore be expected to devote more time and expertise to that task.

Nonmanagement

Plaintiffs allege that the individual defendants failed to supervise the management of Hospital investments or even to attend meetings of the committees charged with such supervision. Trustees are particularly vulnerable to such a charge, because they not only have an affirmative duty to "maximize the trust income by prudent investment," . . . but they may not delegate that duty, even to a committee of their fellow trustees. . . . A corporate director, on the other hand, may delegate his investment responsibility to fellow directors, corporate officers, or even outsiders, but he must continue to exercise general supervision over the activities of his delegates. . . . Once again, the rule for charitable corporations is closer to the traditional corporate rule: directors should at least be permitted to delegate investment decisions to a committee of board members, so long as *all* directors assume the responsibility for supervising such committees by periodically scrutinizing their work.

Total abdication of the supervisory role, however, is improper even under traditional corporate principles. A director who fails to acquire the information necessary to supervise investment policy or consistently fails even to attend the meetings at which such policies are considered has violated his fiduciary duty to the corporation.

Self-dealing

Under District of Columbia Law, neither trustees nor corporate directors are absolutely barred from placing funds under their control into a bank having an interlocking directorship with their own institution. . . . A deliberate conspiracy among trustees or Board members to enrich the interlocking bank at the expense of the trust or corporation would, for example, constitute . . . a breach [of the duty of loyalty] and render the conspirators liable for any losses. . . . In the absence of clear evidence or wrongdoing, however, the courts appear to have used different standards to determine whether or not relief is appropriate, depending again on the legal relationship involved. Trustees may be found guilty of a breach of trust even for mere negligence in the maintenance of accounts in banks with which they are associated, . . . while corporate directors are generally only required to show "entire fairness" to the corporation and "full disclosure" of the potential conflict of interest to the Board.

Most courts apply the less stringent corporate rule to charitable corporations in this area as well. . . . It is, however, occasionally added that a director should not only disclose his interlocking responsibilities but also refrain from voting on or otherwise influencing a corporate decision to transact business with a company in which he has a significant interest or control.

Although defendants have argued against the imposition of even these limitations on self-dealing by the Silbey trustees, the Hospital Board recently adopted a new bylaw, based upon guidelines issued by the American Hospital Association, which essentially imposes the modified corporate rule described above.

Having surveyed the authorities . . . the Court holds that a director or so-called trustee of a charitable hospital organized under the Non-Profit Corporation Act of the District of Columbia . . . is in default of his fiduciary duty to manage the fiscal and investment affairs of the hospital if it has been shown by a preponderance of the evidence that:

1. while assigned to a particular committee of the Board having general financial or investment responsibility under the bylaws of the corporation, he has failed to use due diligence in supervising the actions of those officers, employees or outside experts to whom the responsibility for making day-to-day financial or investment decisions has been delegated; or

2. he knowingly permitted the hospital to enter into a business transaction with himself or with any corporation, partnership or association in which he then had a substantial interest or held a position as trustee, director, general manager or principal officer without having previously informed the persons charged with approving that transaction of his interest or position and of any significant reasons, unknown to or not fully appreciated by such persons, why the transaction might not be in the best interests of the hospital; or

3. except as required by the preceding paragraph, he actively participated in or voted in favor of a decision by the Board or any committee or subcommittee thereof to transact business with himself or with any corporation, partnership or association in which he then had a substantial interest or held a position as trustee, director, general manager or principal officer; or

4. he otherwise failed to perform his duties honestly, in good faith, and with a reasonable amount of diligence and care.

Minimizing Exposure to Liability

Knowledge of and action consistent with the above principles ("prudent person", "fiduciary", "good faith") is a good starting point for the Board member who wants to limit his/her exposure to legal liability. This is not to put the Board member on the defensive; rather, the suggestion is that all members should invest the time to become familiar with the legal context for their entirely noble activities. Nonprofit social service agencies depend on the expertise and enthusiasm of their members, and their continued support is essential. How can the support be insured? Iannotti (1978) supplies one proposal for preventive measures: understand the agency charter and bylaws; attend meetings; avoid even the appearance of self-dealing; appoint an independent audit committee; retain professional counsel; and insure members. In addition, the following excerpt prepared for the Planning and Management Assistance Project, *The Board of Directors of Nonprofit Organizations* (1977), offers some very sound practical considerations.

I. WHY HAVE A BOARD OF DIRECTORS ANYWAY?

Every nonprofit organization needs a board of directors, for two main reasons: (a) to register as a tax-exempt corporation and (b) to manage itself effectively.

When incorporating, any requirements specific to your state can be determined by checking with the state Secretary of State, a lawyer familiar with applications for tax-exempt status . . . or an organization that provides management support for nonprofit organizations. In general, state law requires that a tax-exempt organization be incorporated and that the corporation be managed by a board of directors or trustees. In . . . many . . . states, at least three directors are required before an organization can be recognized as a nonprofit tax-exempt corporation.

In practice, nonprofit organizations often move ahead even after incorporation, under the leadership of one or more persons who are not themselves members of the board. These leaders are normally those who have had the insight and initiative to begin the organization, and they are often responsible for its incorporation. This practice creates the illusion that these administrators are solely responsible for the organization. Whatever the illusion, legal responsibility for the organization rests with the board of directors.

. . . board members may not even be aware of their legal responsibility. Nevertheless, as directors . . . they will be responsible for the governance of the organization and for its adherence to state and federal laws. They will be expected to discharge their duties . . . "in good faith and with a degree of diligence, care, and skill, which ordinarily prudent men would exercise under similar circumstances in like positions. . . . It is the board . . . that local, state, and national government will turn to ultimately if the organization's administrators do not meet regulations or reporting requirements."

The second major reason for a board of directors is managerial: a board can be a powerful tool for achieving effective management. . . . Moreover, there are basic organizational functions which, in most nonprofit organizations, a properly designed and managed board is far more likely to perform with maximum effectiveness. . . .

In the light of the above considerations, it is clear that the contemporary board member must be both practical and well-meaning. That is, (s)he can no longer rely on good intentions to govern an agency's operations. The law has infused the board member role with an increased complexity, and this has shaped the way boards carry out their programmatic and legal responsibilities. The new role that has thus emerged is complicated, but Gelman's (1983B) proposal to mod-

ify the traditional relationship between board members and social
service agencies supplies an important framework for responding to
the challenge.

In view of the emerging trend toward greater liability for board members
this author would like to suggest a modification in the way that directors
relate to social agencies. The modification would require board members
to play more active roles within the agency, in line with the reason for
their selection or designation as board members. Board members are
usually selected on the basis of their specialized knowledge or expertise,
their standing in the community, or because they represent a specific
constituency. While more active involvement may create some problems
with staff, it may also serve to make activities related to accountability
more palatable for professional staff.

Traditionally, problems have developed when board members enter
areas normally assigned or assumed by professional staff. This problem of
role invasion becomes critical when the members possess relevant professional expertise, which exceeds that of the administrator and staff of the
agency. As agencies are forced to become increasingly more responsible,
they will find it necessary to seek out board members who have specialized knowledge and expertise in order to handle increasing demands for
funding and program evaluation. A board with commitment and expertise
coupled with a technically competent administrator and staff can result in
better service and greater accountability. [87–88]

Source: American Bar Association. Law and the Courts, pp. 20–21. © 1974 American Bar
Association, Chicago, IL. Reprinted with permission of the Public Education Division, American Bar Association.

REFERENCES

Atkins, B., & Pogrebin, M. (1982). *The Invisible Justice System:* Discretion and the Law. Cincinnati, OH: Anderson Publishing Co.

Auerbach, J. S. (1976). *Unequal Justice: Lawyers and Social Change in Modern America*. New York: Oxford University Press.

Auerbach, J. S. (1983). *Justice Without Law?* New York: Oxford University Press.

Bartlett, K. T., & Wegner, J. W. (1985). Children With Special Needs: A Symposium. *Law and Contemporary Problems, 48* (1) 1–219; (2) 1–294.

Barton, P., & Byrne, B. (1975). Social Work Services in a Legal Aid Setting. *Social Casework, 56* (4) 226–234.

Barton, W. E., & Sanborn, C. J. (1978). *Law and Mental Health Professions.* New York: International Universities Press.

Baum, L. (1980). The Influence of Legislatures and Appellate Courts Over the Policy Implementation Process. *Policy Studies Journal, 8* (4) 560–574.

Benditt, T. M. (1982). *Rights.* Totowa, NJ: Rowman and Littlefield.

Bernard, S. E., Folger, J. P., Weingarten, H. R., & Zumeta, Z. R. (1984). The Neutral Mediator: Value Dilemmas in Divorce Mediation, in John A. Lemmon (Ed.), *Mediation Quarterly*, (4) 61–74.

Bernstein, B. (1980). Lawyers and Social Workers as an Interdisciplinary Team, *Social Casework, 61* (7) 416–422.

Bernstein, H. C. (1984). Psychotherapist—Patient Privilege Under Federal Rule of Evidence 501. *Journal of Criminal Law and Criminology, 75* (2) 388–412.

Besharov, D. (1983). Parents' Right to Counsel in Proceedings to Terminate Parental Rights: Factors To Consider. *Child Welfare, 61* (4) 247–51.

Besharov, D. J. (1983). Protecting Abused and Neglected Children: Can Law Help Social Work? *Family Law Reporter, 9* (41) 402–403.

Besharov, Douglas S. (1985). The Vulnerable Social Worker. Liability for Serving Children and Families. Silver Spring, MD: National Association of Social Workers.

Bitner, E. (1985). Family Law—Child Abuse—Hearing Conducted Under Pennsylvania; Child Protective Services Law Afforded Necessary Procedural Safeguards to Alleged Abuses. Cruz v. Commonwealth, 572 A.2d 725 (Pa.) *Dickinson Law Review, 89* (3) 797–808.

Black, D. (1972). The Boundaries of Legal Sociology. *Yale Law Journal, 81* (6) 1086–1101.

Black's Law Dictionary (1968). St. Paul, MN: West Publishing Co.

Blasko, M. L. (1985). Saving the Child: Rejuvenating a Dying Right to Rehabilitation. *New England Journal on Civil and Criminal Confinement, 11* (1) 123–159.

Bodenheimer, E. (1974). *Jurisprudence: The Philosophy and Method of the Law*. Cambridge, MA: Harvard University Press.

Bodenheimer, E., Oakley, J. B. & Love, J. C. (1980). *An Introduction to the American Legal System*. St. Paul, MN: West Publishing Co.

Bohannan, P. (1967). *Law and Warfare*. New York: Natural History Press.

Bohannan, P. (1980). Law and Legal Institutions. In W. Evan (Ed.), *Sociology of Law*. New York: Free Press. pp. 3–11.

Bradway, J. (1929). *Law and Social Work*. Chicago: University of Chicago Press.

Brager, G. (1968). Advocacy and Political Behavior. *Social Work, 13* (2) 5–15.

Brennan, W. J. (1986). In Defense of Dissents. *Pennsylvania Gazette, 84* (4) 20–23.

Brenner, S. W., and Galanti, D. M. (1985). Prisoners' Rights to Psychiatric Care. *Idaho Law Review, 21* (1) 1–34.

Carlin, J. E., Howard, J., & Messinger, S. L. (1966). Civil Justice and the Poor: Issues for Sociological Research. *Law and Society Review, 1* (1) 9–90.

Caulfield, B. A. (1985). *Child Abuse and the Law: A Legal Primer for Social Workers*. Chicago, IL: National Committee for Prevention of Child Abuse, 43–56.

Cavanaugh, R. & Sarat, A. (1980). Thinking About Courts: Toward and Beyond a Jurisprudence of Judicial Competence. *Law and Society Review, 14* (2) pp. 371–420.

Chambers, D. E. (1985). Policy Weaknesses and Political Opportunities. *Social Service Review, 59* (2) 1–17.

Cohen, M. L. & Berring, R. C. (1983). *How to Find the Law*. St. Paul, MN: West Publishing Co.

Compton, B. R. & Galaway, B. (1979). *Social Work Processes*. Homewood, IL: Dorsey Press.

Congressional Quarterly, Inc. (1982). *Regulation: Process and Politics*. Washington, DC: Congressional Quarterly, Inc.

Constantino, C. (1981). Intervention with Battered Women: The Lawyer–Social Worker Team. *Social Work, 26* (6) 456–461.

Cowan, T. A. (1958). Group Interests. *Virginia Law Review, 44* (2) 331–346.

Craige, H. & Saur, W. (1981). The Contribution of Social Workers to Legal Services Programs. *Clearinghouse Review,* (8) 1267–1274.

Craige, H., Saur, W. & Arcuri, J. B. (1982). The Practice of Social Work in Legal Services Programs. *Journal of Sociology and Social Welfare, 9* (2) 307–317.

Cunningham, C. D. (1984). Vanishing Exception to the Psychotherapist — Patient Privilege: The Child Abuse Reporting Act. *Pacific Law Journal, 16* (7) 335–352.

Davies, J. (1975). *Legislative Law and Process*. St. Paul, MN: West Publishing Co.

Davis, A. (1975). *The Social Settlements and the Progressive Movement, 1890–1914*. Philadelphia, PA: Temple University Press.

Davis, K. C. (1971). *Discretionary Justice: A Preliminary Inquiry*. Urbana, IL: University of Illinois Press.

DeWolfe, R. (1985). Closing the Federal Door to Prison Litigation: Recent Developments in Prison Law. *Clearinghouse Review, 18* (9) 1084–1089.

Dickson, D. (1976). Legal Skills for Social Workers. In B. Ross & S. Khinduka (Eds.), *Social Work Practice*. Washington, DC: National Association of Social Workers. pp. 170–177.

Dodd, L. L. & Schott, R. L. (1979). *Congress and the Administrative State*. New York: John Wiley and Sons.

Dreyfuss, J. & Lawrence, C. III (1979). *The Bakke Case: The Politics of Inequality*. New York: Harcourt, Brace, Jovanovich.

Dworkin, R. (1979). How to Read the Civil Rights Act. *New York Review of Books, 26* (37).

Dywad, G. (1970). Prevention as a Goal for Social Work: Is Social Work Ready to Meet the Challenges of Mental Retardation. In Meyer Schreiber (Ed.), *Social Work and Mental Retardation*. Scranton, PA: John Day Co.

Echenbarger, W. (1982). The Life and Death of Senate Bill 742. *Today Magazine*. Philadelphia, PA: *Philadelphia Inquirer*. *306* (31) 16–19, 23–27.

Epstein, I. (1981). Advocates on Advocacy, An Exploratory Study. *Social Work Research and Abstracts*, *17* (2) 5–12.

Evan, W. M. (1980). *The Sociology of Law*. New York: Free Press.

Everstine, L. (1980). Privacy and Confidentiality in Psychotherapy. *American Psychologist*. *35* (Summer) 828–40.

Foster, H. (1964). Social Work, the Law and Social Action. *Social Casework, 45* (7) 383–392.

Fox, V. (1983). Foreword to Albert R. Roberts (Ed.) *Social Work in Juvenile and Criminal Justice Settings*. Springfield, IL: Charles C Thomas. pp. *ix–xv*.

Freedman, J. O. (1981). *Crisis and Legitimacy*. Philadelphia, PA: University of Pennsylvania Press.

Gallant, C. (1982). *Mediating Special Education Disputes*. Silver Springs, MD: National Association of Social Workers.

Gaskins, R. (1981). Discretion in the Legal and Social Services Systems. *Social Casework, 62* (7) 387–397.

Gelman, S. (1981). Who Should Administer Social Services? *Social Work, 26* (4) 327–332.

Gelman, S. R. (1983A). The Developmentally Disabled: A Social Work Challenge. In Lynn Winkler and Maryanne P. Keenan (Eds.), *Developmental Disabilities*. Silver Springs, MD: National Association of Social Workers. pp. 12–14.

Gelman, S.(1983B). The Board of Directors and Agency Accountability. *Social Casework, 64* (2) 83–91.

George, J. C. (1985). *Hedland* Paranoia. *Journal of Clinical Psychology, 41* (2) 291–294.

Gevers, J. K. M. (1983). Issues in the Accessibility and Confidentiality of Patient Records. *Social Science and Medicine. 17* (16) 1181–1190.

Gilbert, J. (1982). Future Legal Implications of Recent Court Decisions For Social Workers. In R. T. Constable & J. P. Flynn (Eds.), *School Social Work*. Homewood, IL: Dorsey Press.

Greenberg, J. (1976). *Judicial Process and Social Change: Constitutional Litigation*. St. Paul, MN: West Publishing Co.

Griffith, E. I. (1985). Special Education: Revisited. *New York State Bar Journal, 57* (7) 38–40.

Grob, G. N. (1973). *Mental Institutions in America*. New York: Free Press.

Handler, J. (1979). *Protecting the Social Services Client: Legal and Structural Controls on Official Discretion*. New York: Academic Press.

Handler, J. F. (1978). *Social Movements and the Legal System: A Theory of Law Reforms and Social Change*. New York: Academic Press.

Handler, J. F. & Trubek, L. (1985). Introduction to the Conference: Poor Clients Without Lawyers: What Can Be Done? *The Clearinghouse Review. 19* (4) 371–374.

Hannah, C. T., Christian, W. P. & Clark, H. B. (1981). *Preservation of Client Rights*. New York: Free Press.

Hardin, M. (1983). *Foster Children in the Courts*. Boston, MA: Butterworth Legal Publishers.

Hazard, G. (1976). The Jurisprudence of Juvenile Deviance. In M. Rosenheim (Ed.) *Pursuing Justice for the Child*. Chicago, IL: University of Chicago Press, pp. 3–19.

Hershkowitz, S. B. (1985). Due Process and The Termination of Parental Rights. *Family Law Quarterly, 19* (1) 245–296.

Hetzel, O. J. (1980). *Legislative Law and Process*. Charlottesville, VA: The Michie Company.

Hoebel, E. (1954). *The Law of Primitive Man:* A Study in Comparative Legal Dynamics. Cambridge, MA: Harvard University Press.

Hoffman, K. S. (1983). Women Offenders and Social Work Practice, in Albert R. Roberts (Ed.), *Social Work in Juvenile and Criminal Justice Settings*. Springfield, IL: Charles C Thomas Publisher, 329–348.

Holmes, O. W. (1968). *The Common Law*. London: Macmillan.

Holtzoff, A. (1966). The Vitality of the Common Law in Our Time. *Catholic University Law Review, 16* (23).

Horejsi, C. (1983). Developmental Disabilities: Opportunities for Social Workers, in L. Winkler & M. P. Keenan (Eds.), *Developmental Disabilities*. Silver Springs, MD: National Association of Social Workers. pp. 15–20.

Horowitz, D. L. (1977). *The Courts and Social Policy*. Washington, DC: The Brookings Institution.

Horowitz, H. & Karst, K. L. (1969). *Law, Lawyers and Social Change*. Charlottesville, VA: The Michie Co.

Hoshino, G. (1974) The Pursuit of Justice in the Administrative State. *Public Welfare, 32* (3) 62–67.

Houseman, A. W. (1985). Community Group Action: Legal Services, Poor People and Community Groups. *The Clearinghouse Review, 19* (4) 392–402.

Hunter, M. S., and Grinnell, Jr., R. M. (1983). Social Workers Perceptions of Privacy: A Research Note. *Social Work, 28* (1) 68–69.

Hurley, M. H. (1985). Duties in Conflict: Must Psychotherapists Report Child Abuse Inflicted by Clients and Confided in Therapy? *San Diego Law Review, 22* (2/3) 645–668.

Hurst, J. (1982). *Dealing with Statutes*. New York: Columbia University Press.

Iannotti, L. W. (1978). Legal Responsibilities of Trustees. *Philanthropy Monthly* (June) 6.

Jacobstein, J. M., & Mersky, R. M. (1981). *Legal Research Illustrated*. (2nd Edition) Mineola, NY: Foundation Press.

Janes, N. K. (1985). Mediation Programs for the Poor: The Role of Legal Services. *The Clearinghouse Review, 19* (4) 430–431.

Jankovic, J., & Green, R. (1981). Teaching Legal Principles to Social Workers. *Journal of Education for Social Work, 17* (3) 22–30.

Jenkins, I. (1980). *Social Order and the Limits of Law*. Princeton, NJ: Princeton University Press.

Joe, R. & Rogers, C. (1985). *By the Few for the Few: The Reagan Welfare Legacy*. Lexington, MA: Lexington Books.

Jones, H., Kernochan, J. & Murphy, A. (1980). *Legal Method: Cases and Materials*. Mineola: Foundation Press.

Jones, C. O. (1977). *An Introduction to the Study of Public Policy*. Belmont, CA: Duxbury Press.

Katkin, D. (1974). Law and Social Work: A Proposal for Interdisciplinary Education. *Journal of Legal Education, 26* (3) 294–317.

Keenan, M. P. & Parker, D. R. (1982). Deinstitutionalization: A Policy Analysis. In L. Winkler & M. P. Keenan (Eds.), *Developmental Disabilities*. Silver Springs, MD: National Association of Social Workers. pp. 224–234.

Kidder, R. (1983). *Connecting Law and Society*. Philadelphia, PA: Temple University Press.

Kutchins, H. & Kutchins, S. (1980). Advocacy and Social Work, in G. Weber & G. McCall (Eds.), *Social Scientists as Advocates*. Beverly Hills, CA: Sage Publishing Co.

Lapham, E. V. (1980). State Regulations Implementing P.L.94–142: Implications of Three Issues with Delivery of Social Services in Schools. In *Conference Proceedings in School Social Work and the Law*. Washington, DC: National Association of Social Workers. pp. 96–121.

Lawrence, M. (1984). Rape Victim—Crisis Counselor Communications: An Argument for An Absolute Privilege. *University of California, Davis Review, 17* (4) 1213–1245.

Lee, D. A. (1985). The Constitutionality of Juvenile Preventive Detention: Schall v. Martin—Who is Preventive Detention Protecting: *New England Law Review, 20* (2) 341–374.

Levi, E. (1949). *An Introduction to Legal Reasoning*. Chicago, IL: University of Chicago Press.

Levine, E. L. & Wexler, E. M. (1981). *P.L. 94-142: An Act of Congress*. New York: Macmillan Publishing Co.

Levine, M. & Howe, B. (1985). Penetration of Social Science into Legal Culture. *Law and Policy Quarterly, 7* (2) 173–198.

Liksky, M. & Wetherly, R. (1978). *Street Level Bureaucrats*. Cambridge, MA: Joint M.I.T.–Harvard Center for Urban Studies.

Llewelyn, K. (1930). Case Law. *Encyclopedia of the Social Sciences, 3* (249).

Llewellen, K. (1950). Canon's of Construction. *Vanderbilt Law Review, Vol. 3* (pp. 395–396).

Lubove, R. (1965). *The Professional Altruist*. Cambridge, MA: Harvard University Press.

Lukton, R. C. (1978). Social Services, Social Policy and the Law. *Social Casework, 59* (11) 523–529.

Lutkus, A. M., & Curtis, P. A. (1985). Client Confidentiality in Police Social Work Settings. *Social Work, 30* (3) 355–360.

McCarthy, F. B. (1984). *Pennsylvania Juvenile Delinquency Practice and Procedure*. Norcross, GA: Harrison Co.

Mahoney, A. R. (1985). Time and Process in Juvenile Court. *Justice System Journal, 10* (Spring) 37–55.

Malinowski, B. (1926, 1961). *Crime and Custom in Savage Society*. London: Routledge.

Manville, D. E. (1984). *Prisoners' Self-Help Litigation Manual* (2nd ed.). J. Boston (Ed.). New York: Oceana Publications.

Markowitz, J. R. & Engram, P. S. (1984). Mediation in Labor Disputes and Divorces: A Comparative Analysis, in John A. Lemmon (Ed.), *Mediation Quarterly*, (2) 67–78.

Mashaw, J. C. (1983). "Rights" in the Federal Administrative State. *Yale Law Review, 92* (4) 1129–1173.

Meeker, J. W., Dombrink, J. & Schuman, E. (1985). Legal Needs of the Poor: Problems, Priorities, and Attitudes. *Law and Policy Quarterly, 7* (2), 225–244.

Menkel-Meadow, C. (1985). Nonprofessional Advocacy: The "Paralegalization" of Legal Services for the Poor. *The Clearinghouse Review, 19* (4) 403–411.

Mermin, S. (1982). *Law and the Legal System: An Introduction*. Boston, MA: Little, Brown & Co.

Meyers, J. E. B., and Jenson, W. R. (1984). The Meaning of "Appropriate Educational Programming Under the Education for All Handicapped Children Act. *Southern Illinois University Law Journal, 1984* (3) 401–444.

Miller, J. (1980). Teaching Law and Legal Skills to Social Workers. *Journal of Education for Social Work, 16* (3), 87–95.

Mishkin, P. & Morris, C. (1965). *On Law in Courts*. Mineola, NY: Foundation Press.

Mnookin, R. H. (1978). *Child, Family and State*. Boston, MA: Little, Brown and Co.

Morales, A. (1981). Social Work with Third-World People. *Social Work, 26* (1), 45–51.

Moss, K. (1984). Institutional Reform Through Litigation. *Social Service Review, 58* (3) 421–433.

Mullen, E. (1978). The Construction of Personal Models for Effective Practice: A Method for Utilizing Research Findings to Guide Social Intervention. *Journal of Social Service Research, 2* (1) 45–64.

National Center for Voluntary Action. (1978). Liabilities and Responsibilities of Board Members of Non-Profit Corporations. *Volunteering* (July) 2.

Needleman, C. (1983). Conflicting Philosophies of Juvenile Justice, in Albert R. Roberts (Ed.), *Social Work in Juvenile and Criminal Justice Settings*. Springfield, IL: Charles C. Thomas Publisher, 155–164.

Nicholson, E. B. (1985). Final Federal "Baby Doe" Rule Released. *Mental and Physical Disability Reporter, 9* (3) 228–229.

Nonet, P. & Selznik, P. (1978). *Law and Society in Transition*. New York: Harper and Row.

Nunez, R. (1972). The Nature of Legislative Intent and the Use of Legislative Documents as Extrinsic Aids to Statutory Interpretation: A Re-Examination. *California Western Law Review, 9* (1) 128–133.

Oyen, E. & Beckford, J. A. (1982). Confidentiality: Theory and Practice. *Current Sociology, 30* (2) 1–82.

Palomer, J. D. (1985). School Health Services for Handicapped Children: The Door Opens No Further: Irving Independent School District v. Tatro, 104 S.CT. 3371. *Nebraska Law Review, 64* (3) 509–536.

Parsons, T. (1962). Law and Social Control. In W. M. Evan (Ed.), *Law and Sociology*. pp. 60–68, New York: Free Press.

Patterson, S. C., & Jewell, M. E. (1977). *The Legislative Process in the United States*. New York: Random House. pp. 286–290.

Patti, R. J. & Dear, R. (1981). Legislative Advocacy: Seven Effective Tactics. In Maryann Mahaffey and John W. Hanks (Eds.), *Practical Politics*. Silver Springs, MD: National Association of Social Workers. pp. 99–117.

Pearce, D. (1985). Welfare is Not for Women: Towards a Model of Advocacy to Meet the Needs of Women in Poverty. *The Clearinghouse Review, 19* (4) 412–418.

Planning and Management Assistance Project. (1977). *The Board of Dir ctors of Nonprofit Organizations.* Washington, D.C.: Center for Community Change.

Pound, R. (1908). Common Law and Legislation. *Harvard Law Review,* (21) 383–386.

Pound, R. (1943). A Survey of Social Interests. *Harvard Law Review, 57* (1) 1–39.

Quaintance, R. (1986). Waivers of Counsel in Juvenile Courts: Do Procedures Guard Against Invalid Waivers? *William Mitchell Law Review, 12* (1) 93–117.

Reamer, F. (1983). Social Services in a Conservative Era. *Social Casework, 64* (8) 451–458.

Redman, E. (1973). *Dance of Legislation.* New York: Simon and Schuster.

Reisner, R. (1985). *Law and the Mental Health System.* St. Paul, MN: West Publishing Co.

Ripley, R. B. (1983). *Congress: Process and Policy.* New York: W. W. Norton and Company.

Roberts, A. (1983). *Social Work and Juvenile and Criminal Justice Settings.* Springfield, IL: Charles C Thomas.

Robinson, G. O., & Gellhorn, E. (1972). *The Administrative Process.* St. Paul, MN: West Publishing Co.

Rose, C. M. (1978). *Some Emerging Issues in Legal Liability of Children's Agencies.* New York: Child Welfare League of America, Inc.

Rothman, D. J. (1982). Courts and Social Reform: A Post-Progressive Outlook. In J. K. Weinberg (Ed.), "Court-Ordered Change in Social Institutions," *Law and Human Behavior, 6* (2) 113–120.

Sabatier, P. & Mazmanian, D. (1980). The Implementation of Public Policy: A Conceptual Framework of Analysis. *Policy Studies Journal, 8* (4) 538–560.

Saposnek, D. T. (1984). Strategies in Child Custody Mediation: A Family Systems Approach, in John A. Lemmon (Ed.), *Mediation Quarterly,* (2) 29–54.

Savitsky, J. C. & Karras, D. A. (1984). In R. H. Woody and Associates (Eds.), *The Law and the Practice of Human Services.* San Francisco, CA: Jossey–Bass. pp. 289–390.

Savrin, P. W. (1985). The Social Worker—Client Privilege Statutes: Underlying Justifications and Practical Operations. *Probate Law Journal, 6* (3) 243–276.

Schlesinger, A. (1957). *Crisis of the Old Order: The Age of Roosevelt.* Boston, MA: Houghton–Mifflin.

Schottland, C. (1968). Social Work and the Law—Some Curriculum Approaches. *Buffalo Law Review, 17* (1) 719–731.

Schrier, C. J. (1980). Guidelines for Record-Keeping Under Privacy and Open-Access Laws. *Social Work, 26* (6) 452–457.

Schroeder, L. (1982). *The Legal Environment of Social Work.* Englewood Cliffs, NJ: Prentice Hall.

Schwartz, S. (1985). Nonprofit Organizations: A Symposium. *University of San Francisco Law Review, 19* (3/4) 299–412.

Schwartz, W. (1974). Private Troubles and Public Issues: One Social Work Job or Two? In R. Klein and R. Ryan (Eds.), *The Practice of Social Work.* Belmont, CA: Wadsworth Publishing.

Selznick, P. (1961). Sociology and Natural Law. *Natural Law Forum, 6* (1) 84–108.

Shanker, R. (1983). Occupational Disease, Workers Compensation and the Social Work Advocate. *Social Work, 28* (1) 24–30.

Simon, W. H. (1986). Legal Informality and Redistributive Politics. *The Clearinghouse Review, 19* (4) 384–391.

Sloan, J. B. & Hall, B. (1984). Confidentiality of Psychotherapuetic Records. *Journal of Legal Medicine, 5* (3) 435–467.

Sloane, H. W. (1965). The Juvenile Court: An Uneasy Partnership of Law and Social Work. *Smith College Studies in Social Work, 35* (3) 213–231.

Smith, S. R. & Meyer, R. G. (1984). Child Abuse Reporting Laws and Psychotherapy: A Time for Reconsideration. *International Journal of Law and Psychiatry, 7* (3/4) 351–366.

Snyder, F. (1985). Legal Liability: The Social Worker and Juveniles. *Journal of Juvenile Law, 9* (1) 36–52.

Sosin, M. (1979). Social Work Advocacy and the Implementation of Legal Mandates. *Social Casework, *(5), 265–273.

Sosin, M. & Caulum, S. (1983). Advocacy: A Conceptualization for Social Work Practice. *Social Work, 28* (1) 12–18.

Starobin, S. (1984). The Social Worker—Client Privilege—Commonwealth v. Collett, 439 N.E. 2d 1223 (Mass.) *Western New England Law Review, 6* (4) 1103–1129.

Statsky, W. (1975, 1984). *Legislative Analysis and Drafting.* St. Paul, MN: West Publishing Co.

Statsky, W. (1982). *Legal Research and Analysis.* (2nd ed.). St. Paul, MN: West Publishing Co.

Statsky, W. (1984). *Case Analysis and Fundamentals of Legal Writing.* St. Paul, MN: West Publishing Co.

Stein, J., & Golick, T. (1974). Public Legal Programs: A Team Approach, in F. Perlmutter (Ed.), *A Design of Social Work Practice.* New York: Columbia University Press.

Stone, L. (1978). Due Process: A Boundary for Intervention. *Social Work, 23* (5), 402–405.

Tapp, J. L. & Levine, F. J. (1974). Legal Socialization: Strategies for an Ethical Legality. *Stanford Law Review, 27* (1) 1–72.

Turk, A. T. (1976). Law as a Weapon in Social Conflict. *Social Problems, 23* (Feb), 276–290.

Urban, S. (1985). Trapped Within the System: Abused Children and Child Protective Services. *Dickinson Law Review, 89* (3) 773–796.

Urofsky, M. I. (1971). *A Mind of One Piece: Brandeis and American Reform.* New York: Scribner & Sons.

Urofsky, M. I. (1981). *Louis D. Brandeis and the Progressive Tradition.* Boston, MA: Little, Brown & Co.

Vanyo, J. P. (1971). Dynamics of the Legal Process and Environmental Law. *California Trial Lawyers Journal, 10* (Fall) 44–50.

Wald, M. (1975). State Intervention on Behalf of 'Neglected' Children: A Search for Realistic Standard. *Stanford Law Review, 27* (4) 985–1040.

Weber, M. (1954). *On Law in Economy and Society.* M. Rheinstein (Ed.). New York: Simon and Schuster.

Weil, M. (1982). Research on Issues in Collaboration Between Social Workers and Lawyers. *Social Service Review, 56* (3) 393–405.

Weil, M., & Sanchez, E. (1983). Impart of the Tarasoff Decision on Clinical Social Work Practice. *Social Service Review, 57* (2) 112–124.

Weisberg, R. & Wald, M. (1984). Confidentiality Laws and State Efforts to Protect Abused or Neglected Children: The Need for Statutory Reform. *Family Law Quarterly, 18* (2) 143–212.

Wigmore, J. (1961). *Evidence* (McNaughton Rev.) 8.

William, K. E. (1984). Confidentiality of Sexual Assault Victim—Counselor Communication: A Proposed Model Statue. *Arizona Law Review, 26* (2) 461–488.

Wilson, S. J. (1978). *Confidentiality in Social Work*. New York: Free Press.

Wilson, S. J. (1980). *Recording: Guideline for Social Workers*. New York: Free Press.

Winslade, W. J., & Ross, J. W. (1985). Privacy, Confidentiality and Autonomy in Psychotherapy. *Nebraska Law Review, 64* (4) 570–636.

Woods, L. (1985). Mediation: A Backlash to Women's Progress on Family Law Issues. *The Clearinghouse Review, 19 (4)* 431–436.

Woody, R. H. (1984). Professional Responsibilities and Liabilities. In R. H. Woody and Associates (Eds.). *The Law and the Practice of Human Services*. San Francisco, CA: Jossey–Bass. pp. 373–402.

Worrell, C. (1985). Pretrial Detention of Juvenile: Denial of Equal Protection Masked by Parens Patrial Doctrine. *Yale Law Journal, 95* (November) 174–193.

Zimring, F. (1982). *The Changing Legal World of Adolescents*. New York: Free Press.

Zucker, D. B. (1985). Rights of the Handicapped: Education Procedural Requirements: Section 1415; Free Appropriate Public Education; And Remedies. *Annual Survey of American Law*, (3) 575–598.

Index

Index

Developmental disability *(cont.)*
  social work and, 238–239
Dickson, D., 204
Dicta, 16
Dixon v. Commonwealth, 110
Donaldson v. O'Connor, 115
Due process
  in child welfare, 223–225
  in education, 237
  of juveniles, 251–252
  in social work, 200
Duty to warn
  generally, 188–191

Echenbarger, W., 55
Education
  see Handicapped children
Estelle v. Gamble, 244
Eubanks v. Clark, 110
Evidence
  best evidence, 141
  circumstantial, 142
  clear and convincing, 141
  defined, 139
  direct, 142
  hearsay, 142–146
  material evidence, 141
  preponderance of, 141
  relevant evidence, 141
  standards of proof, 140–142
Expert witness
  defined, 147
  examples, 147–148

Federal courts, 14
Finken v. Roop, 110

Gellhorn, E., 91
Gelman, S., 239, 260
Gilbert, J., 236
Goldberg v. Kelly, 227
Grove City v. Bell, 79

Handicapped children
  education for, 234–236
  parent–school conflict, 237
  placement of, 236–237

Harris v. Lewistown Trust, 29
Hayden v. Sec. Nat'l Bank, 131
Hazard, J. G., 250
Hearings
  administrative, 94–96
  juvenile court, 249–250
Hearsay evidence
  defined, 142
  example, 143–144
  exceptions to, 144–146
Hedlund v. Sup. Ct. of Orange Cty., 189
Hetzel, O., 136
Hoebel, E. A., 4
Holtzoff, A., 20
Horejsi, C., 238
Hoshino, G., 199

Institutional interdependence
  balance of powers, 81–82
  example, 108–119
Irving v. Tatro, 235
In Re Custody of J. S. S., 149, 164
In Re Gault, 110, 251
In Re PAAR, 174
In Re Winship, 251

Jewell, M. E., 85
Jones, C., 27
Jones, H., 14
Judicial Function
  in common law, 20
  and legal reasoning, 23–28
  see also Case law development
Judicial interpretation
  of case law, 20–22
  of regulations, 104
Judicial opinions
  briefing or analysis of, 17–20
  structure of, 17
Judicial process
  see Case law development
Juvenile Court
  juvenile versus adult, 250–253
  procedures, 249–250